John Whiting

PLAYS TWO

MARCHING SONG
THE GATES OF SUMMER
NO WHY
A WALK IN THE DESERT
THE DEVILS
NOMAN
THE NOMADS

Edited by Ronald Hayman

OBERON BOOKS
LONDON

Marching Song first published by Heinemann Educational Books Ltd in 1957. *The Devils* first published by Heinemann Educational Books Ltd in 1961. *The Gates of Summer, No Why, Noman, A Walk in the Desert, The Nomads* first published by Heinemann Educational Books Ltd in 1969.

This collection first published in 2001 by Oberon Books Ltd. (incorporating Absolute Classics), 521 Caledonian Road, London N7 9RH. Tel: 020 7607 3637 / Fax: 020 7607 3629 e-mail: oberon.books@btinternet.com

A catalogue record for this book is available from the British Library.

ISBN: 1 84002 051 2

The photograph used on the covers of the three volumes of Whiting's work published by Oberon Books is by Houston Rogers, courtesy of the Theatre Museum, London.

Cover design and typography: Richard Doust.

Printed in Great Britain by Antony Rowe Ltd, Reading.

Contents

Chronology

1917   JW born in Salisbury on 15 November, the son of an army captain.

1922   The family moves to Northampton where, discharged from the army, JW's father starts a legal career.

1930   JW plunged into "the particularly hellish life which is the English public school" in Taunton.

1934   He leaves school to start training as an actor at RADA.

1937   Various acting jobs in repertory and under the direction of Robert Atkins in the Open Air Theatre at Regent's Park.

   In the company at Bideford, he meets Jackie Mawson (Asthorne Mawson).

1938   Repertory at Croydon.

1939   Registers as a conscientious objector, but, after changing his mind, joins the anti-aircraft section of the Royal Artillery.

1940   Marries Jackie Mawson after being promoted to the rank of corporal.

1942   Commissioned as second lieutenant.

1944   Begins his novel *Not a Foot of Land* while still in the army.

   Discharged for health reasons.

1944-5   Completes the novel.

   Repertory in Peterborough and Harrogate, where he begins to think seriously about a career in writing – not necessarily for the theatre.

1946   His father dies five months after Jonathan, the first of JW's four children, is born.

JW appears at the Lyric, Hammersmith, in Sean O'Casey's *Oak Leaves and Lavender*.

Writes *No More A-Roving* and *Conditions of Agreement*. He also begins some stories and plays for broadcasting, including the radio play *Paul Southman: An Appreciation for Broadcasting*.

Starts *Saint's Day*.

1947   Repertory in York.

Writes the radio play *Eye Witness* and begins *A Penny for a Song*.

1948   Finishes *Saint's Day* and starts *Marching Song*.

1949   The BBC broadcasts *Eye Witness*, another radio play, *The Stairway*, and two stories, 'Valediction' and 'Child's Play'.

1950   Repertory at Scarborough.

Finishes *A Penny for a Song*.

The BBC broadcasts the play *Love's Old Sweet Song*.

1951   In March *A Penny for a Song* opens at the Haymarket, directed by Peter Brook.

In October *Saint's Day* is produced at the Arts Theatre and wins first prize in the play competition organised for the Festival of Britain.

He joins John Gielgud's company to play Shakespeare at the Phoenix, where JW's parts include the Gaoler in *The Winter's Tale*.

1952   Finishes *Marching Song*.

Plays the Sexton in *Much Ado about Nothing* at the Phoenix.

In Gielgud's production of *Richard II* with Paul Scofield at the Lyric, Hammersmith, JW plays the Abbot of Westminster.

Through his agent, A.D. Peters, he gets work writing screenplays.

Reading Aldous Huxley's new book, *The Devils of Loudun*, he gets interested in its potential as a film.

The 22-year-old Peter Hall directs an undergraduate production of *Saint's Day* at Cambridge.

1953 Starts *The Gates of Summer*.

Peter Hall directs an undergraduate production of *A Penny for a Song*.

1954 *Marching Song* produced in the West End, directed by Frith Banbury.

1956 In September *The Gates of Summer* starts a pre-London tour, directed by Peter Hall, but fails to reach London, partly because the leading actress, Dorothy Tutin, is taken ill.

1957 Peter Hall, now artistic director of the Arts Theatre, commissions a one-act play. JW writes *No Why* and starts *The Nomads*.

1960 Peter Hall, now artistic director of the Memorial Theatre, Stratford-on-Avon, commissions JW to write a large-scale play for the company's first London season. It becomes the Royal Shakespeare Company before the season starts.

1961 In February *The Devils* opens, directed by Peter Wood at the Aldwych. It is the Royal Shakespeare Company's first production in London.

In June JW accepts the position of dramatic critic on the monthly *London Magazine*.

1962   In August a revised version of *A Penny for a Song* is presented by the RSC at the Aldwych, directed by Colin Graham.

In November JW is taken to hospital, where cancer is diagnosed.

1963   He works on adapting Ibsen's *The Lady from the Sea* for the screen.

He dies on 16 June at the age of forty-five.

MARCHING SONG

Introduction to

MARCHING SONG

S tarted in 1948, finished in 1951 and premiered in 1954, *Marching Song* is more ambitious and direct than any previous British play in tackling problems left by the war that had ended in 1945. One of the thorniest is whether the victors had succeeded in imposing democracy on the defeated Fascists.

Like the words *Fascism* and *Nazism,* the names *Germany* and *Berlin* are never mentioned, but the action is set in a house on the heights above the capital of a defeated country which is finally governing itself after the occupying forces have withdrawn. Cadmus, the Adenauer-like Chancellor, is cynical about the political and moral values being promoted by the victors. His opposition party, he says, "is liberal minded, and they have all the savagery possessed by good men. They say it is love, but they bare their teeth when pronouncing the word." Needing a scapegoat – a leader who can be held responsible for their country's defeat – they are demanding that General Rupert Forster, who has been in prison for seven years, should be put on trial. But Cadmus, not relishing the acrimony that would be generated by accusations and counter-accusations, asks him to commit suicide.

Like Melrose, Killeen and Chater in *Saint's Day,* and like Edward in *A Penny for a Song,* Rupert is a soldier. A soldier is a killer by profession, and Whiting's soldiers recognise this. Unlike the soldiers in *Saint's Day,* who go on killing gratuitously, Edward repents and embarks on a one-man crusade to stop the fighting. Rupert had been ambivalent about the act of killing, but had not been conscious of his misgivings. Like Paul Southman, he had risen out of the ranks, had become less human in the process and, much too late, had undergone a conversion when he recognised the losses involved in what he had gained. When his tanks were delayed by a crowd of children, he shot one of them and ordered his tank commanders to advance over the living obstacles, regardless of the cost in young lives. But his unconscious made him hesitate for too long on the wrong side of a river.

Released from prison, he has to choose between taking the poison Cadmus has provided and living in retirement – with or without Catherine, the former mistress who still believes she loves him. But she is a romantic who has been living in the past while he was in prison. Intent on living in the present, he cannot accept the love she is offering.

She sees that the only chance of influencing his decision is through a young girl who happens to be in the house. What Dido has in common with him is honesty and freedom from commitment. She is not a romantic, and she lives in the present: she likes singing, dancing and lying in the sun. Alone with her, Rupert can talk freely, and he says his ambition had been "to reach a point of achievement never before known by man". Arrogance (or *hubris*) had been characteristic of tragic heroes from Oedipus to Othello, but the play sways the audience to agree with Dido. After she has listened to his story about the tanks and the children, her verdict is: "You seem to me a very good man."

Reviewing the original production of *Marching Song,* the *Sunday Times* critic, Harold Hobson acknowledged "that the play extends the boundaries of English drama". But he undercut this enormous tribute with a facetious imitation of Whiting's prose style and a weary suggestion that the play had no bearing on what was happening in England. "He has a troubled and uneasy poetry whose shadowy tides never wash against the shores of our own land of cricket bats and football pools, of bells in the old school chapel and the Welfare State." Though he was more perceptive and less hostile than most of his colleagues, Hobson was dismally fainthearted. If he wanted to tell us that Whiting had extended the boundaries of English drama, should he have tried to convey the impression that this was something of no great importance?

Characters

HARRY LANCASTER

DIDO MORGEN

FATHER ANSELM

MATTHEW SANGOSSE

CATHERINE DE TROYES

RUPERT FORSTER

JOHN CADMUS

BRUNO HURST

Marching Song was first performed at the St Martin's Theatre, London, on 8 April 1954, with the following cast:

HARRY, Hartley Power

DIDO, Penelope Munday

CATHERINE, Diana Wynyard

RUPERT, Robert Flemyng

CADMUS, Ernest Thesiger

Director, Frith Banbury

ACT ONE

The scene is a room in CATHERINE DE TROYES' house set on the heights above a capital city in Europe. The time is the present: it is late evening moving to night. The house, of which the room is representative, was designed by a great German architect of the 1930s. Built into the hillside which ranges high above the city lying to the south, it transcends the mere purpose of a dwelling-place. The room is a shell caught within a web of glass and steel. It is dominated by the sky. Entrances to the room: a wide circular stairway leading down to the main door of the house. A second entrance: a gallery leading to an apartment of rooms above which stand alone. This is the highest point of the house. A third entrance: from a balcony of considerable size – a main feature of the room and of the house – projecting like a finger towards the city (or an arrow, perhaps, set within the bow of the room). The house is built of stone, glass and steel. Within the room there is an impression of air and space – an impression of delicacy, almost fragility, yet the place is a fortress in strength and position. A warmth is given to the room by the use of wood and fabrics in the decoration and furnishing. In the spare decoration of the room there is a plinth surmounted by an antique bronze helmet. It is the late evening of a spring day. The great expanse of sky above the room retains a savage brilliance, but within the room shadows have begun to form. The lights have not yet been put up. HARRY LANCASTER stands in the centre of the room. He is in the act of getting out of a heavy sheepskin coat which is half off his shoulders.

HARRY: You! (*He is shouting to a man who is standing on the balcony with his back to the room.*) I'm speaking to you! (*The man does not turn.*) All right, then. To hell with you! (*The man is motionless, silent.*) To hell, sweetheart, with you. (*HARRY throws the coat over a chair and speaks to another person.*) I said just now that my youth must be considered past – done with. Know why? Because – (*He turns to find himself alone in the room. After a moment he goes to the circular stairway and calls down.*) Come on up! Don't be scared. Come on up! (*He backs from the stairway keeping in sight and speaking to the ascending person.*) My youth – done with. For why? Because I want you for my workmate, believe me. And believe me truly, last Fall I'd have wanted you for my playmate. Last Fall – six months ago – I was young and loving. Now, I can only say – welcome.

(*DIDO MORGEN, a young girl, has come up the stairway and now stands within the room.*)

Welcome! Look – but look kindly – on these grey hairs. Trust this ancient head. Will you?

DIDO: Yes.

HARRY: That's the girl.

DIDO: Who's in this place?

HARRY: Relax. They're friends here.

(*DIDO silently points to the man on the balcony.*)

You're right. A stranger. Tourist, maybe. (*He shouts again to the man.*) Have a drink! (*The man is silent.*) Not an American, anyway.

DIDO: You are.

HARRY: I was made unhappy there so I came over to Europe. I'm unhappy here too – so I guess it's the condition of the man. Let's not blame places, shall we?

DIDO: A long way to come just to stay unhappy.

HARRY: And let's not talk around the point. My misery is my dearest possession – for God's sake leave me that. You're not one of those women who think men should be made happy, are you?

DIDO: No. But if you don't want to be made happy, why did you pick me up and bring me here?

HARRY: I want to give you a job. Why do you clip your hair?

DIDO: Keep it clean. Cleanliness before wantonness, you know. What sort of job?

HARRY: How long have you lived down in the city?

DIDO: All my life. Nearly twenty years.

HARRY: The day you were born there was music and laughter – and maybe they let off fireworks.

DIDO: It was a very obscure birth.

HARRY: But twenty years ago there was music and laughter every day. I know. I was there.

DIDO: Laughing with the best of them.

(*They laugh. From the well of the circular stairway FATHER ANSELM calls.*)

ANSELM: (*Off.*) May we come up?

DIDO: Who's that?

HARRY: It's all right. Mustn't be scared. Look, I'll show you. (*He leads her to the stairway, and together they look down.*) See! Nothing to frighten you, is there? (*He calls.*) Come on up, boys. (*HARRY and DIDO move from the stairs.*) Be nice to them.

DIDO: Who are they?

HARRY: Ssh!

(*ANSELM, an elderly priest, and MATTHEW SANGOSSE come up the stairway and into the room. They wear coats and carry hats.*)

Hullo, Father. Hullo, Doc.

ANSELM: Are we disturbing you, Harry?

HARRY: I'm doing nothing. (*To DIDO.*) This is Father Anselm, and this is the Doctor.

MATTHEW: My name is Sangosse.

HARRY: Have you got another name?

DIDO: Morgen.

HARRY: This is Dido Morgen. Where've you boys been?

ANSELM: For a walk.

MATTHEW: It's a strange feeling walking down there now that all the foreign soldiers have gone. You can miss something you dislike, I suppose.

HARRY: Do you know, it hadn't struck me they'd gone. But then you're a native. I'm not. Anyway, you had a good walk.

MATTHEW: We went as far as the monument and back.

HARRY: That must've taken you quite a time.

MATTHEW: Two hours.

ANSELM: Catherine sent us.

HARRY: Sent you? I've only just got back. Been out all day in the truck. So I don't know about things. Tell me, boys, what goes on?

ANSELM: Goes on, Harry?

HARRY: Yes. You were sent out for a walk. Sent out. And look – (*He points to the man on the balcony.*)

MATTHEW: Who is it?

HARRY: You don't know either.

MATTHEW: (*To the man.*) Excuse me, what are you doing out there?

(*The man does not answer.*)

HARRY: Was he there when you went out?

MATTHEW: No.

HARRY: Hell! Where's Kate? What is all this? Go find her. Tell her somebody's trying to break up the happy home.

ANSELM: Coming, Matthew?

HARRY: That's my boys.

(*ANSELM and MATTHEW go out.*)

Question is: good or bad?

DIDO: News?

HARRY: I don't want my quiet life disturbed. I'm happy. Looked after.

DIDO: Are there servants here?

HARRY: Plenty. Kate keeps them under cover. Like kids of an earlier generation – but better! – they're neither seen nor heard.

DIDO: But we kids of this generation – say me! – when do we eat?

HARRY: Hungry?

DIDO: Yes.

HARRY: Keep going. (*From his breast pocket he takes a bar of chocolate, which he throws to DIDO, who catches it.*)

DIDO: It's soft.

HARRY: From the warmth of my heart. You're too young to know – but that's the last part of you to die. The coldness creeps around your more private parts, but that public organ, your heart, just won't go out. (*He attempts to kiss DIDO but she pushes him away and laughs with her mouth full of chocolate.*) You'll make yourself sick.

DIDO: I don't care.

(*CATHERINE comes from the upper room. She wears a dressing robe.*)

HARRY: Don't care, eh?

DIDO: No. Don't care.

HARRY: Give him – (*The man.*) – a bit.

DIDO: No.

HARRY: Gimme a bit.

DIDO: No!

HARRY: Poor Harry! Gi'm li'l bit choc'late.

DIDO: No. No choc'late f'Harry. Eat't all m'self. (*She has stuffed the remaining chocolate into her mouth.*)
(*HARRY appeals to the man on the balcony.*)

HARRY: She's ate up – right up. Now, an't that nasty – plain nasty? No choc'late f'you'n'me s'none f'working men like you'n'me. Though what in hell your work is – standing there! – God knows.

CATHERINE: He's my new guardian angel, Harry. Don't abuse him. And how very interesting to hear that you look upon yourself as a working man.

HARRY: Why not? I've been out on the truck since early morning.

CATHERINE: (*To DIDO.*) He gives himself away every time. Have you found that?

HARRY: Sleeping! You should be ashamed.
(*CATHERINE has come down into the room, and again speaks to DIDO.*)

CATHERINE: He'll manage to put you in the wrong too, when you come to play your part. I take it you are one of his troupe, or whatever it is he makes his pictures with.
(*DIDO wipes her mouth with the back of her hand.*)

HARRY: This, incidentally – indeed, quite by the way – is Dido Morgen.

CATHERINE: I'm Catherine de Troyes. How do you do.

HARRY: Miss Morgen will be staying here. (*There is silence.*) For a few days. She's temporarily part of my troupe, as you'll have it. Just for a few days.

CATHERINE: (*To DIDO.*) Americans possess two endearing qualities. Their innocence, which delights me – and their feeling for hospitality which often inconveniences me. But of course you must stay, Miss Morgen. For tonight, at least. Did you come up those stairs on your way here?

(*DIDO nods her head.*)

Well, now go down them, and instead of turning through the main door – which will take you out into the world – turn the other way. There you'll find someone to attend you. Have you any night things with you?

HARRY: No, she hasn't.

CATHERINE: It can be arranged. (*There is silence. DIDO has not moved.*) Have you understood what I've said?

HARRY: Go on, honey. I'll be around to see you soon. We'll talk about the picture.

(*DIDO wanders to the stairway and begins to go down. Before she is out of sight or hearing CATHERINE speaks.*)

CATHERINE: Like a puppy. Where did you find it?

HARRY: In a bar.

CATHERINE: What do you want it for?

(*DIDO has gone.*)

HARRY: I've told you. For the picture. She's fine. Right out of that stinking city.

CATHERINE: Like the filthy old man we had up last month. What was he? Christ down on his luck, wasn't he? He came out of that stinking city. But he wasn't right after all.

HARRY: There was nothing back of his eyes. That's what I'm looking for to photograph. The something back of their eyes.

CATHERINE: And this girl has it?

HARRY: Maybe. I don't know yet.

CATHERINE: When will you know? When you've tried to sleep with her?

HARRY: That's not fair, Kate.

CATHERINE: What is fair, Harry? You, living here on my weakness and indulging your notions at my expense. Is that fair? I don't think it is.

HARRY: Go on – give. I'm expecting the worst.

CATHERINE: Here it comes. I'm afraid there'll be no more money for the film.

HARRY: No more money. What've I done?

CATHERINE: Nothing. That's the point. You should have made up your poor muddled mind before this, and finished the picture. Finished it while I was prepared to pay for your ridiculous antics.

HARRY: My ridiculous antics.

CATHERINE: I've gone beyond such amusements, Harry. I don't want – I shan't need you about any more.

HARRY: Suddenly seen sense, you have.

CATHERINE: You admit it? That however much money and time I give you, the film will never be made? You know, don't you, that all the business of getting the faces, finding the places – the right faces and the right places to photograph at the right time – it was nothing more than a putting-off because you've nothing to say any more. You see and you feel the misery – say down there in the city – but you can't do anything about it. You can't even represent it by your old love, the camera, on a screen. You're not big enough, Harry.

HARRY: Maybe not. But you knew what I wanted to do.

CATHERINE: Yes, I knew.

HARRY: That I wanted to go back of their faces.

CATHERINE: Yes.

HARRY: Back of their faces – those godawful masks – and get whatever it is.

CATHERINE: Yes, that.

HARRY: And keep it on film. That hope, that something –

CATHERINE: At the back of their eyes. But it's in everyone, Harry. You don't have to look for it. It's in me. But the failure to see is in you.

HARRY: Sure. So – no more money.

CATHERINE: No.

HARRY: No money – no picture. What about Poppa and the Doc?

CATHERINE: They must go too.

HARRY: No picture, no sweetness from the little white pills, no God any more. You've found something.

CATHERINE: Yes. You talk about it. You talk about love an awful lot, Harry. But do you understand what you say, I wonder?

HARRY: I talk to myself in a language I understand, if that's what you mean.

CATHERINE: I was a young woman when Rupert left to fight nine years ago, and through the two years' absence at war and the seven years of his imprisonment I've had to live on my kind of love. You don't understand, do you?

HARRY: I've never understood.

CATHERINE: You like me, Harry, because you're sorry for me. That's safe, isn't it? Because I'm one of your old tramps or funny little girls with my heart in the wrong place. Because I'm alone. But, Harry, you can stop being sorry for me. I'm not alone any longer.

HARRY: He's back.

CATHERINE: Yes. Rupert's back.

HARRY: Up there? (*He points to the upper room.*)

CATHERINE: He's sleeping. Very tired. Long journey.

HARRY: You've been up there with him.

CATHERINE: Yes. With him.

HARRY: You knew he was coming back today.

CATHERINE: This morning. They sent me a message.

HARRY: That's why you sent Poppa and Doc out for a walk.

CATHERINE: I wanted to meet him alone.

HARRY: You've muddled them. They don't know what goes on. I didn't either for that matter.

CATHERINE: I'll explain to them. Soon enough.

HARRY: And show them the door.

CATHERINE: Well, am I expected to have you three old things around my neck for the rest of my life?

HARRY: So Forster's back.

CATHERINE: Yes. And Harry – Harry, he's going to be free!

HARRY: Are they unlocking all the cages at the zoo today as well? Free. My, my! (*He points suddenly to the man on the balcony. It is darker and the man is barely visible.*)

CATHERINE: That man? He was sent with Rupert to guard him. There are two more below. They'll only be with us for a little while. Just so long as the country needs to get used to the idea of Rupert being free. All great men must be guarded in these days.

HARRY: Sure, sure.

CATHERINE: Well, got everything straight now?

HARRY: I guess so. Was there a need to be quite so harsh?
I suppose there was. I'd never get out of anywhere
nowadays without being pushed out. There's one thing I'd
like you to know – not important to you but important to
me. It's in you, Kate, that my lamented youth resides.
You're the person who represents all that I wanted to be
and believed I could be when we first knew each other in
the old days. I translated everything – ambition, talent, all
values – into your person. I suppose – in my own way,
a way you despise – I love you. Don't put up the lights for
a minute!

(*It is very dark within the room.*)

CATHERINE: Dry your tears. I'm not looking.

HARRY: It's just that I hate saying goodbye.

CATHERINE: The party's over, Harry.

(*ANSELM and MATTHEW have come into the room.*)

MATTHEW: Catherine?

CATHERINE: Yes, my dears. I'm here.

MATTHEW: May I put on the light?

CATHERINE: Not for a moment. We must allow Harry to
recover himself.

HARRY: Also, I'd imagine, we must give you time to think
of something you can say to these boys.

ANSELM: Are you upset about something, Harry?

HARRY: Poppa, we're all three of us going to be upset
together in a minute. Go ahead, Kate.

CATHERINE: You tell them, Harry.

HARRY: Well, I'm damned!

CATHERINE: Go on. Tell them.

HARRY: Poppa, Doc – we're fired. We're out, boys. On
our ears.

MATTHEW: Out?

HARRY: The life we've had here, bringing in our several
ways comfort to this lady, is finished. An incident
has occurred.

ANSELM: Have you quarrelled with Harry, Catherine?

HARRY: No, no. It's all quite friendly. Just this: we're being
told to leave, boys. Find other quarters. As simple as

that. Go fasten your suckers, you suckers, on somebody else. But don't forget we have done her some small service. That's why the light's out; to spare her blushes. (*CATHERINE does not speak. HARRY continues, very softly.*) If you listen very hard both of you, you'll hear the sounds of war. Coriolan – Coriolan. You'll hear the soft stumbling tread of returning men. Men out of order and out of heart. There's no trumpet left will call them to attention. There's no drum can fit the broken rhythm of their march. But they are come back – they have come home.

(*RUPERT FORSTER calls quietly from the gallery before the door of the upper room.*)

RUPERT: Catherine! (*The lights go up in the room.*
CATHERINE – she has her hand on the light switch – and the three men look up at RUPERT. He speaks to CATHERINE.)
You left me alone. You promised not to do that.

CATHERINE: I was coming back.

RUPERT: Shall I come down? I'm quite awake now. (*He comes down into the room.*) Good evening, gentlemen. I overheard – forgive me! – the lament spoken by one of you. Coriolan, may I remind you, was a tyrant. But yes, I've come back.

CATHERINE: Have you had a good rest?

RUPERT: How long have I been asleep?

CATHERINE: Only two hours or so.

RUPERT: It must have been the darkness that woke me. It can, you know.

CATHERINE: Are those the only clothes you have?

RUPERT: I borrowed them from my servant. I'm no longer allowed to wear uniform.

HARRY: Too bad!

(*CATHERINE speaks to MATTHEW and ANSELM.*)

CATHERINE: This is Rupert Forster, Father Anselm and Doctor Matthew Sangosse.

(*They shake hands as CATHERINE turns to HARRY, who speaks.*)

HARRY: Remember me, sir?

(*RUPERT stares at him without recognition.*)

CATHERINE: It's Harry Lancaster, darling.

HARRY: Well, if my face doesn't mean anything to him it's scarcely likely my name will.

RUPERT: You must forgive me. I've been away.

HARRY: I know.

RUPERT: Away for a long time. I can't recall –

HARRY: Ever having seen me before in your life. I know.

RUPERT: Won't you help me?

HARRY: It was a long time ago. And it doesn't matter.

CATHERINE: You met Harry when he was making a film here. Remember?

HARRY: Years ago.

RUPERT: God! Yes, of course. I'm so sorry. What are you doing here now?

HARRY: I was making another picture of your beautiful city. It was to be a sequel to the first picture you remember so well. It was to show how all the pretty little girls of the first picture have become cellar drabs. How the dirty finger of time has pushed in all their sweet little cheeks. It was to show how all the fine young men in their uniforms of the first picture have – well, it was to show that they aren't around any longer.

RUPERT: It sounds most entertaining.

HARRY: Yes, it's the sort of thing would make you laugh a lot.

RUPERT: And you were going to film it in the city.

HARRY: Yes. There – or in somebody's armpit.

CATHERINE: Harry, do you think you should so neglect your girl?

HARRY: My girl? You want us to get out at once?

CATHERINE: Of course not. Stay, at least, tonight.

HARRY: Many, many thanks. (*He has moved to the stairway. He looks down.*) I promised her lots.

CATHERINE: Fulfil your promises.

HARRY: For one thing I told her she was among friends.
(*HARRY goes down the stairs.*)

CATHERINE: I thought we'd have dinner later.

RUPERT: Yes, I'm a little –

CATHERINE: What?

RUPERT: I'm a little confused. What is it? Early evening?

CATHERINE: (*Laughing.*) Yes, darling. Later, then.

RUPERT: Remember I've been on a prison diet.

CATHERINE: What was it like?

RUPERT: Not bad. Everything had onions in it.

CATHERINE: Everything?

RUPERT: Even the shaving water.

(*ANSELM and MATTHEW have been speaking together. ANSELM now comes forward.*)

ANSELM: I'm speaking for myself and Matthew.

CATHERINE: What's that?

ANSELM: When do you want us to leave, Catherine?

MATTHEW: No arrangements have been made, of course.

CATHERINE: Have you anywhere to go?

ANSELM: We shall stay together. Matthew has a sister living in the country. He thinks it probable she'd welcome us.

MATTHEW: I'll telephone her tomorrow.

CATHERINE: Very well.

MATTHEW: For tonight we'll go to our rooms. Unless you need us for anything.

CATHERINE: No, I shan't need you.

ANSELM: Your prayers, later.

CATHERINE: Not tonight.

(*ANSELM and MATTHEW go out.*)

RUPERT: Why are they here?

CATHERINE: To look after me. To keep me well and safe until you came back.

RUPERT: But why those men? So shabby, so at odds with the world.

CATHERINE: Are they shabby? I suppose they are. I've never noticed. They needed somewhere to live after the war. And I needed friends.

RUPERT: Friends?

CATHERINE: No, that's not the word, is it? I needed someone to notice that I was here and that I was human. You've been away a long time, Rupert.

RUPERT: They're not what I'd have expected to find with you. And the American – I don't remember him at all.

I said I did, but it's not true. Faces and names, you know, they just disappear. Not one thing about him remains.

CATHERINE: He's changed since the old days. He was amusing then, I think. But he's been home and seems to have picked up the national failing: he sees everyone as a distorted reflection of himself. He feels he should straighten out the image. So he questions strangers on their misfortune. It doesn't amuse him to have a woman now unless she's down on her luck. There's a girl in this house at the moment. Brought her back this afternoon. She's to be in the film, he says. Ach! he's pathetic. He doesn't even take them into his bed any more – only into his great, big American heart. He came over six months ago, penniless, and asked me to put him up.

RUPERT: You took them all in because you were sorry for them.

CATHERINE: Not exactly. Darling, you make the place sound like a charity lodging house. They're none of them quite as bad as that, you know. Father and the Doctor do their jobs professionally, and Harry once made very good films.

RUPERT: So they've filled your life for the past seven years in place of the others I remember.

CATHERINE: The others?

RUPERT: The men who dressed your hair and painted your face, designed your clothes and fitted your shoes. Those are the people I remember with you.

CATHERINE: When they sent you away to prison and I was left alone I did a very natural thing – I got down on my knees. But the words that had been there since childhood weren't there any longer. I just couldn't say them. It was Father Anselm who in his own muddled way gave me back the words. We started from the beginning – it was 'say after me' all over again. As for the Doctor, he's easy to explain. I was not able to sleep – not for a long time – and he had magic in his boxes and bottles.

RUPERT: Now you've told them they must go. You feel you can do without them.

CATHERINE: Of course. You're back, Rupert. Why should I need anything more?

RUPERT: Catherine – (*In silence he measures, in a number of paces, a certain distance across the room.*) – that, square, was the exact measurement of my room at the camp. I was sent to that place direct from the freedom of a battlefield. I occupied it for seven years. That little space could have been my childhood nursery, my cadet's room at the military academy, my old battlefields, this room in this house with you – indeed, it could have been any of my particular heavens or hells. Imagination could have made it so. And I could have been any man I wished to be. A free man, if I liked. I chose that the room should be a brick and steel cell in a prison camp in the mountains and that I should be its occupant. A man called Forster.

CATHERINE: You're accusing me. I don't understand why.

RUPERT: I'm not accusing you. You told me of your life during my absence. I'm telling you of my life at that time. Nothing more. There's no accusation.

CATHERINE: I've got into the habit of imagining things.

RUPERT: Yes.

CATHERINE: You're trying to tell me something.

RUPERT: How I lived at the camp. My room was entered twice a day by my servant – the first time to clean the room, the second time to attend me, the prisoner. I left the room once a day for exercise – alone. I was permitted to walk to the boundary of the compound and return at once. I was allowed to look at the sky. The camp commandant visited me once a week, but as a gesture of faith didn't enter the room. That procedure was followed exactly for the first two years. Now, tell me from that description, Catherine, is that the man you remember?

CATHERINE: Of course not. Never imprisoned – never! No, I think of you as –

RUPERT: Let me go on. In the third year the conditions in the camp altered. I was given more food and a change of bedding. The comforts multiplied. One day I was sent a message saying that if I wanted a woman, a young girl could be obtained from the village below the camp. The message came by a junior officer, who assured me that the child would be bathed and deloused before being sent to my room. I refused the offer.

CATHERINE: Because you loved me.

RUPERT: It had nothing to do with love.

CATHERINE: Because you remembered me.

RUPERT: You don't understand, Catherine. I didn't think of you in that place. I didn't think of you at all. If I'd done so, it would have become a place of freedom. In fact, it was a prison.

CATHERINE: Some men would have tried to get out if only by imagination – by memory –

RUPERT: Some men dream away their lives without having to be put behind bars. I'm not one of them.

CATHERINE: You talk like this because we made love only a little while ago. You were always cruel afterwards.

RUPERT: That demand hasn't changed, certainly. I refused the girl at the camp – but not you.

CATHERINE: There is a difference. Take a risk and think back for a moment. You'll remember, I love you.

RUPERT: You love the man your loneliness has created, perhaps.

CATHERINE: Then tell me: what are you now?

RUPERT: A defeated soldier who is allowed to live only to further his disgrace.

CATHERINE: All right! I'll accept that.

(*Then, from all the speakers of a public address system which covers the city, a man's voice speaks.*)

ANNOUNCER: The time is twenty hours. The time is twenty hours. It is now – officially – night.

(*A bell is struck.*)

RUPERT: What is it?

CATHERINE: It comes from the public address system all over the city.

RUPERT: What are they – amplifiers?

CATHERINE: Yes. Rupert, kill your pride – kill it!

RUPERT: Who put up those things?

CATHERINE: John Cadmus. To speak to the people. There are speakers in every street – even all over the hillside in the trees. They make announcements.

RUPERT: Has John Cadmus been here?

CATHERINE: Yes. Very often.

RUPERT: Why?

CATHERINE: I asked him to come the first time. It was a few days after your arrest when he was recalled as Chancellor at the time of the defeat. I asked him to use his authority to have you released. He said it was impossible. The second time he came here without invitation. We sat in this room and talked. I can't remember what about – not about you. After that he came here at irregular intervals but very frequently.

RUPERT: What you're saying, in effect, is that you formed some kind of friendship with him after that first meeting.

CATHERINE: He was kind and often amusing. Sometimes he gave me small gifts. For instance, the last time he brought a string quartet which played Beethoven for three hours. I went to sleep in front of them.

RUPERT: Why didn't you ask him about me? He got a weekly report on my behaviour.

CATHERINE: I didn't want a weekly report on you – to hear of you growing older and sadder and more and more hopeless.

RUPERT: Why not? If it was true.

CATHERINE: I want to know you as you were! If they've changed you I don't know what I shall do. O God! I remember you, Rupert. But do you remember me – do you remember me?

(*HARRY has come a little way up the stairs.*)

HARRY: Forgive.

CATHERINE: What is it?

HARRY: There's been a message.

CATHERINE: Well?

HARRY: Over the telephone.

CATHERINE: Yes?

HARRY: The Chancellor is on his way here to see General
　　Forster. His arrival is imminent. Poppa's waiting to
　　receive him at the door.

CATHERINE: All right, Harry. Thank you. What does he
　　want, Rupert?

HARRY: Affairs of State, maybe. Ssh!

CATHERINE: Go away, Harry.
　　(*He remains.*)
　　Tonight. Why must he come tonight? (*She begins to move
　　to the upper room.*)

RUPERT: Where are you going?

CATHERINE: I must dress. Were you expecting
　　him tonight?

RUPERT: No. Were you?

HARRY: There's one you're going to have to tell yourself,
　　Katie. Tell him he's like the rest of us boys – just not
　　welcome here any more. All right! I didn't speak – I'm
　　not here.
　　(*CATHERINE goes into the upper room.*)
　　This can hardly be the return you imagined in your
　　youth, General.

RUPERT: What's that?

HARRY: I say, when you were a young man you must've
　　thought the return from war to your native city would be
　　very different.

RUPERT: In what way?

HARRY: Oh, come now. Where is the triumphal drive
　　through the streets, the heroic music, the garland of war?
　　Where is the howling mob upping its sweaty nightcaps?
　　Where are the young virgins casting themselves in front
　　of your jeep?

RUPERT: You're a romantic, Mr Lancaster. I suppose all
　　entertainers are that.

HARRY: I wonder what it is the world finds so unfunny
　　about you? In my part of professional entertainer you
　　interest me. Suppose I put you in a cage like a wild
　　beast, would they pay their pennies to come and look at
　　you? I doubt that. I doubt it very much.

RUPERT: Please leave me alone.

HARRY: Tell me, sir, is your release unconditional? If so, who is our constant companion?

RUPERT: I'm told he's to protect me from annoyance.

HARRY: Then he's not doing his job, is he? Why don't you call him to order?

RUPERT: I've no authority to do that.

HARRY: Authority. That's an interesting word. Are you sure you don't mean power?

RUPERT: No, Mr Lancaster, I mean authority. I have power. Power to throw you down those stairs, for instance. That remains.

HARRY: Would you resort to violence, General?

RUPERT: You're a small man.

HARRY: Has that anything to do with it?

RUPERT: The use of power? Of course, you fool!

DIDO: (*From below the stairs.*) Harry!

RUPERT: You're being called.

HARRY: All right, honey: I'm talking to what looks like a man. They tell me he's something more, but he looks like a man. I guess the failure to see is in me. Eh, Kate? (*CATHERINE has come from the upper room. She is dressed. She does not answer HARRY.*)

CATHERINE: Is this an amusing dress, Rupert?

HARRY: Even if you think it is, General, you're not supposed to laugh. I once made that mistake. (*HARRY goes down the stairs.*)

CATHERINE: There's one good thing about this visit of John Cadmus. We shall know your exact position. What have they told you?

RUPERT: Nothing. What have they told you?

CATHERINE: There was a message this morning giving me the time of your arrival.

RUPERT: Is that all?

CATHERINE: What do you mean?

RUPERT: I thought you must know something more.

CATHERINE: It was enough. To know you were coming back was enough. (*ANSELM appears on the stairway.*) Yes?

ANSELM: The Chancellor is here.

CATHERINE: All right. Bring him up.

(*ANSELM goes down the stairway.*)

When did you see him last?

RUPERT: Seven years ago. On my way to the camp. Catherine, we really know nothing of what's happening.

CATHERINE: He'll tell us. We'll just let him talk himself out of the house. We'll be alone together soon, and then we can find our way. We've wandered off the road for a while, that's all. It's only to be expected.

(*JOHN CADMUS, assisted by ANSELM, comes up the stairs. He is a man of great age, physically and spiritually wasted by many years spent in the exercise of power.*)

CADMUS: After such a climb as that I always expect to find myself in heaven. (*To CATHERINE.*) Angel! (*He kisses her.*) Somewhere to sit.

(*CATHERINE takes him to a chair, and he sits.*)

Hullo, Forster.

CATHERINE: Would you like something to drink?

CADMUS: Yes, I would. I'd like my usual warm milk.

CATHERINE: (*To ANSELM.*) Get it.

(*ANSELM goes down the stairs.*)

CADMUS: As a temporal power, Catherine, you speak with unusual authority to the spiritual. You must attend one of the tea parties I give for my princes of the church.

CATHERINE: They'd eat out of my hand.

CADMUS: As long as there was something in it. Otherwise they'd bite. A good journey, Forster?

RUPERT: Yes, sir.

CADMUS: Did we provide transport suitable to your position?

RUPERT: Three cars, six guards and an aide.

CADMUS: Excellent. And they brought you safely to this place.

RUPERT: They did. The guards are still here. I say, the guards have stayed on. I was told they are for my protection.

CADMUS: Forster, we all go in mortal danger. Can we even trust the guards? The whisper of ambition is in

their hearts without a doubt. Who is to guard the guards?
That's an old question which has never been answered.

RUPERT: What am I to understand by it?

CATHERINE: Wait. He never asks questions he can't answer.

CADMUS: Ah! It's possible to breathe up here. Down in
the city the smell of corruption becomes insufferable.
The stench of the spilt guts of the world is always in the
nose. D'you know, Forster, twice in a lifetime I've been
brought from retreat to stand over the murdered body of
our country. They turn to me. The misfortune of being
the father image. I'm known as Daddy Cadmus now. Did
I say I'd like some hot milk?

CATHERINE: It's coming.

CADMUS: You'd imagine the aftermath of war to be
depressing, wouldn't you? Not a bit of it. Defeat has
resulted in a splendid get-together. At least, socially.
The difficulty is to keep them apart. The birth-rate is
astounding. Politically we are split exactly down the
middle and, however I play the submissive female part,
we remain distressingly infertile. A few weeks ago it
was thought the body politic might produce a tiny
policy, but it was only wind. Seven years married too.
But my problems of administration don't interest you.

RUPERT: They might, but I'm out of touch.

CADMUS: Has my gadget spoken to you yet? The
amplifiers, I mean.

RUPERT: They announced the time.

CADMUS: They can do better than that. When I'm faced
with excitement in the city – they riot, you know – those
things pour out music and it works like a charm. The
angry fellows have their grievances washed away by the
memory of what has been or the thought of what might
be. The way to prevent revolt is to stop men living in
the present time. Given a sad song they drift off with
their wives and sweethearts and resolve their misery in
quite the oldest way. That, of course, gives rise to
another problem already mentioned. But the human milk
supply luckily remains constant.

(*ANSELM comes up the stairway. He carries a tray on which there is a flask of milk, a drinking glass and a bowl of sugar.*)
From the cow, I hope.

ANSELM: Quite fresh, sir.

CADMUS: Pour it out. Three spoons of sugar.
(*ANSELM serves the milk.*)
I find a grave distaste for all food now. For instance, this innocent-looking liquid on which I'm compelled to live is actually the glandular secretion of a dying animal. But then, if we were to look too closely at any of our main supports, we'd – (*He stops speaking for a moment and tastes the milk.*) What would happen, Forster? You've had plenty of time to think about such things. Let's have your opinion.

RUPERT: I'm afraid I can't share your obvious horror of material existence.

CADMUS: You can't? That's a pity.

RUPERT: Why a pity?

CADMUS: I'll tell you. (*To ANSELM.*) Thank you.
(*ANSELM goes down the stairs.*)
Catherine, would you like to leave us?

CATHERINE: No.

CADMUS: Very well. First of all, Forster, I can take no credit for fetching you out of prison today. If I had my way you'd remain shut up for the rest of your life.

RUPERT: That's very interesting. Who am I to thank for this – freedom.

CADMUS: Freedom? You're back here for a purpose. It's three shots-a-penny at you now, Forster. But I'm confusing you. You may or may not know that modern government is based not on theory or even practical policy but on emotion. This country has been compelled to accept that system of government from the conquerors. It is known as democratic. It means that I have an opposition party. This, of course, is a great novelty. My opposition party is liberal-minded, and they have all the savagery possessed by good men. They say it is love but they bare their teeth when pronouncing the word. It is these men who have brought you back.

RUPERT: Why?

CADMUS: We're now an autonomous state again. The occupying forces were withdrawn some weeks ago. For seven years we've been able to refer our major problems to foreigners. Now, once again, as in the war, we're on our own. We have to make up our minds about bigger things than the city drainage. One of these bigger things, my opposition tells me, is to find out who was responsible for this country losing the war. There has to be a man, Forster. Something they can stretch out and touch, which breathes and reasons and answers questions. They can't put Bad Luck in the dock, Forster, but they can put you there.

RUPERT: I'm to stand some kind of trial?

CADMUS: That's the intention. It's to be a big show. It'll take place in the Parliament House. Your accuser is the State and its People. The charge will be treason arising from cowardice in the face of the enemy. Your behaviour during that last battle in the East appears to give certain grounds for such an accusation.

RUPERT: Do you expect me to defend myself – to you, here and now?

CADMUS: No.

RUPERT: You said – I think – that you would not have brought me back.

CADMUS: I did say that. But these men who've asked for your return have the country behind them. So, you see, I can't refuse to have you brought to trial. It would look, you must admit, as if I defended your behaviour. And I can't do that. It seems on the face of it a reasonable request.

RUPERT: My section of the Eastern front was comparatively small. Too small, I should've thought to have merited consideration as a factor of absolute defeat.

CADMUS: That has nothing to do with it. You're a man. More, you're Rupert Forster. These good men must give the country something worth having. Something the butcher, the baker and the candlestick-maker – in their guilty sickness – can recognise as the cause of defeat and disgrace. Those ordinary people want to go out into the world and say, I wasn't responsible for the war starting or for the war ending in defeat: it was that man Forster. He was tried, you know, and found guilty. That's why the people of this country will back the group of men who oppose me. You are about to be taken into the great mouth of that modern monster, the Demagogue.

RUPERT: The result of the trial is a foregone conclusion, then.

CADMUS: Not at all. If it takes place, I shall do everything to ensure that it's fairly conducted.

RUPERT: What do you mean, if it takes place?

CADMUS: Catherine, a social fact of some importance to you. I can allow no one to leave this house for thirty-six hours or so. No one, that is, except myself. And I must go straightaway. (*He rises.*) I had luncheon with the actor, Constant, today. I asked him how he would go about telling a man that it was necessary, indeed imperative, that he should kill himself.

RUPERT: What did he say?

CADMUS: He said drama was, of course, inherent in such a situation for the essence of drama is the dilemma of the central heroic figure. He was very interesting about that.

RUPERT: Did he advise you further?

CADMUS: Yes.

RUPERT: May we not be told?

CADMUS: Certainly. Constant went on to say that if he was to play such a scene in the theatre, the prosaic details would be sufficient.

RUPERT: Will you not tell me those details?

CADMUS: I was about to do so. The time: within thirty-six hours. That is, by dawn of the day after tomorrow.

RUPERT: The place?

CADMUS: Within this house, secretly. The means – (*He has taken a jewelled box from his pocket.*) I have removed the dismal original package. Look upon this box as a gift, Forster. The substance within, I'm told, is also used for extracting gold from its ore. A factor which, applied philosophically, may be of comfort to you.

(*RUPERT takes the box.*)

CATHERINE: You don't take it seriously. You're smiling.

RUPERT: Am I? Why didn't you get her out of the room, Cadmus?

CADMUS: He takes it seriously, Catherine, and you must bring yourself to believe it is right.

CATHERINE: Right!

CADMUS: The thing to do. You must bring yourself to believe it is necessary.

CATHERINE: But why, John, why?

CADMUS: Because I cannot allow this trial to take place. I love this country, Catherine, and I believe that given a few years I can make it again seem worthy of a place in Europe. But not if I have this trial forced on me. The mud that is thrown won't only hit Forster. It will stick to every man, woman and child of this nation. That is why I will not allow the trial to take place. That is why Forster must kill himself.

CATHERINE: You've no authority to give such an order.

CADMUS: It wasn't an order. It was a request. I thought that was understood.

RUPERT: Perfectly.

CATHERINE: A request. Is that all? Can we do anything else for you?

CADMUS: Nothing. Will someone help me down? I've a horror of falling nowadays.

CATHERINE: You're not to touch him, Rupert! You've done the wrong thing, John. He's safe with me.

CADMUS: Any complete protection – even one of love, Catherine – is also an effective prison. Yes, he's safe with you. (*He takes RUPERT's arm and they go down the stairs. CATHERINE remains alone until RUPERT returns.*)

CATHERINE: Can you ask for a man's life as simply as you'd ask for his advice?

RUPERT: Yes, you can. I've done it. With many lives.

CATHERINE: You were their commander.

RUPERT: Yet the final decision remained with each man. We never really command. We only – like Cadmus – request.

CATHERINE: And you were obeyed. Why is John so sure that you'll obey him?

RUPERT: (*He is standing beside the bronze helmet.*) I found this helmet beneath the tracks of my carrier in battle. I picked it up and a skull rattled inside. After hundreds of years he'd come to the surface, and we were still fighting over the same ground. Nothing had been gained since the day he'd fallen. I was attempting with my armoured vehicle only to do what he'd tried to do with his armoured head and his antique sword. His end on that field was death, mine was disgrace. But I was left as surely and eternally in that clay-cold earth as was this comrade-in-arms of mine. Our intentions must now be effected by another man in another time: it no longer rests in us. They've taken away the means of achievement, my soldiers. I can't stretch out to the future because I've nothing to use. Cadmus knows that. When I was young I could see far into the future and that makes a man alive. When he cannot see – as at this moment – then a man may as well grant such a request. Cadmus knows I'll do what he asks because there is no future action for me. He knows there is nothing here – nothing anywhere to detain me.

CATHERINE: I am here.

RUPERT: I'm no longer in love with you, Catherine. Such things need to be said. When they are true and the time has come, such things need to be said.

CATHERINE: You have a great regard for the truth. I knew the truth all through today – but I pretended that you still loved me. Couldn't you have done that? Truth of your kind is for the very young – not for me.

RUPERT: Did you want me to lie?

CATHERINE: It would've been for such a short time. John said within thirty-six hours.

RUPERT: I gave you the truth in the past.

CATHERINE: Now you give it to John Cadmus.

RUPERT: I loved you, Catherine.

CATHERINE: In the past. What do you want?

(*She speaks to DIDO, who has come a little way up the stairs.*)

DIDO: Can I come up here? My honour is imperilled.

CATHERINE: What does that mean? Harry?

DIDO: Yes. He talked about God, social injustice – he cried a little there – war and love of mankind. What he meant, of course, was love of his own kind. I want to go home.

CATHERINE: And they won't let you out.

DIDO: The men at the door said I stay. So here I am.

RUPERT: I'm sorry. It's my fault.

DIDO: You're General Forster, aren't you? My experiences with soldiers have so far been unfortunate. (*She holds out the palm of her hand.*) That scar was a mortar shell fragment in the street fighting when I was a baby. (*She touches her face.*) This, a broken bottle in bar-room fighting when I was somewhat older.

RUPERT: I hope our acquaintance – however short – will be more peaceful.

DIDO: I thought you were dead, but Harry said you were up here. You know, he doesn't like you.

RUPERT: I know. What's your name?

DIDO: It doesn't matter.

CATHERINE: Yes, it does. She's called Dido.

DIDO: Please don't laugh. Blame my father. He was an archaeologist. Always grubbing in the past. Disgusting occupation. I say, am I bothering you?

CATHERINE: No.

DIDO: Well, with those men on the door it looks as if I'll be here for a time.

CURTAIN

ACT TWO

The scene is the same. The time: the following night. The room is in darkness. A small film projector has been set up, and is in action with a film showing on the screen. Before the screen in the darkness sit RUPERT, CATHERINE, DIDO, ANSELM and MATTHEW. HARRY is standing by the projector as operator. The film is in its final sequence. It ends.

HARRY: Will somebody put up the lights?
> (*MATTHEW puts on the lights of the room. RUPERT and DIDO are shown to be sitting together – DIDO on the floor with her head resting against RUPERT's knees.*
> *CATHERINE, turned away from the screen, is observing them as she must have been in the darkness.*)

That's all, everybody.

ANSELM: Thank you, Harry. It was most enjoyable.

HARRY: It's alright, Poppa. Anything I can do to make our enforced stay in this house tolerable – just call on me.

ANSELM: I thought the girl was rather like you, Miss Morgen.

HARRY: You're being spoken to, honey.

RUPERT: She's asleep.

HARRY: Well, I'm damned!
> (*ANSELM laughs.*)

CATHERINE: Wake her, Rupert.
> (*RUPERT ruffles DIDO's hair.*)

RUPERT: Wake up.

DIDO: What?

RUPERT: Wake up! The show's over. Do you want to be locked in?

DIDO: God! Sorry, everybody. Sorry, Harry.

HARRY: It's all right.

DIDO: Did I miss much of it?

HARRY: I don't know. Did you?

DIDO: From what I saw of it I'd say it was funny and old. The women! Did they ever look like that? Did they ever behave like that?

HARRY: They did. Just twenty years ago.

DIDO: The young ones look sort of muddy – and don't they grin a lot? Was there so much to laugh about in those days? (*She suddenly looks round at the others.*) I suppose all of you were young at that time.

HARRY: Yes. Yes, we were. Around that time.

DIDO: So that's your masterpiece, Harry?

HARRY: It is. You must see it sometime.

CATHERINE: Shall we go down to supper? It's ready.

HARRY: Let's do that. There's always eating left for us. I must clear up this junk first.

CATHERINE: Come along, Father – and Matthew.

RUPERT: (*To HARRY.*) I'll help you with this.

HARRY: I can manage. All right, pack up the screen, please. (*CATHERINE, with MATTHEW and ANSELM, goes below. HARRY begins to dismantle the projector and RUPERT the screen. DIDO stands beside RUPERT.*)

I'll not bother to rewind.

RUPERT: What's that?

HARRY: The film. I'm not bothering – oh, forget it. From all the sense it made tonight I might just as well run it backwards next time. Not that there'll be a next time.

DIDO: How long since you last showed it?

HARRY: Long time. Maybe ten years. I don't know.

DIDO: Why did you show it tonight?

HARRY: I thought – wrongly, of course – that it might relax the tension for a couple of hours. I thought it'd give Kate something to look at beside you two. You'll forgive me asking this: what the hell are you up to?

RUPERT: Where do you want this? (*He refers to the cinema screen.*)

HARRY: I'll take it down with me. For God's sake, Forster, couldn't you have kept this sort of thing until we were all let out of this place? I know you've been shut up for seven years, but you could surely have waited a while longer. Until you could have got this – this girl out of here. Away from Kate.

RUPERT: Anything else I can do? With this stuff, I mean.

HARRY: Not a thing. Do you think since you came back last night you've been playing fair?

RUPERT: Fair?

HARRY: Look. I'll try to explain. Don't you think it would have been better to pretend for a while? Pretend with Kate that everything is just as it has been. Christ, man, you're breaking her heart! Is that simple enough for you?

RUPERT: There! Everything packed. You can go down.

HARRY: All right. But just tell me this: how much longer are we going to be shut up here?

RUPERT: Not much longer.

HARRY: What's the reason for it anyway? I suppose we're the only people to know you're back and they don't want the news to leak. What are they going to do – suddenly release you into an unsuspecting world as the latest saviour? If so, I take cover. Who's the enemy going to be this time? Or haven't you decided yet?

RUPERT: I have to act on my decisions, Lancaster. Unlike you I don't make up my mind and regard it as an end in itself.

HARRY: Me! I'm just an old dreamy-eyes. But I don't murder.

RUPERT: When you have you'll find it simpler to tell the innocent from the guilty.

HARRY: You'll go to hell, Forster.

RUPERT: That, too? You go to supper.

DIDO: Harry, I'm sorry – sincerely sorry – that I went to sleep during your picture.

HARRY: The difficulty with you, sweetheart – and with him – is that you're honest about yourself. I'm sorry, but I've lost the talent for doing that sort of thing.

RUPERT: Can you carry all that?

(*HARRY is laden with cinema equipment.*)

HARRY: Sure. I'll tell Kate you're on your way. (*He goes down the stairs.*)

RUPERT: It's sad.

DIDO: Harry?

RUPERT: He has an affectionate nature which overrules his moral judgement. Because of what he believes he must censure me for being what I am – and you for accepting me – but he comes near to liking us. That conflict can upset a man.

DIDO: Surely that was a damned bad film.

RUPERT: I thought so.

DIDO: He told me you commanded the soldiers in it.

RUPERT: I believe I did. It was in my comic-opera days. We'd no other use for the army then.

DIDO: You found a better use for it later.

RUPERT: It was put to its proper use.

DIDO: All right. I don't need convincing.

RUPERT: I'm sorry. Anyway, that's all over.

DIDO: So what are you going to do? Live in retirement? Say, a house in the country, your feet up of an evening, early to bed. You'll be healthy all right, but I've doubts as to your wealth and wisdom. What else? You'll be able to walk round your estate in the morning and again in the evening. If you get very bored perhaps you could shoot a small animal ever so often. Do I make the prospect sound attractive?

RUPERT: No.

DIDO: I wasn't trying to. As an alternative you might make it up with Catherine, stay on here, and – as Harry suggested – pretend.

RUPERT: I'm not good at that.

DIDO: No good at pretending! Then I'd say your future is about as bright as a blind man's holiday.

RUPERT: You're very encouraging. What about you?

DIDO: People like me don't think about the future. We don't matter, you see. If we survive – that's good. If we go out – well, there's not much harm done. Mind, if somebody tries to put us out before we think it's time we fight. What for? Just to stay alive to see one more day end, have one more hot bath, be made love to once more, hear one more tune we've heard before and got fond of. This is apt to make us a nuisance about the place, but you people are getting better at making bigger gadgets to end all that.

RUPERT: In a little while they'll let you out of here. What will you do?

DIDO: Go back where I came from. Pick up where I left off. You're the problem. You can't pick up where you left off. Have you got any friends who might start a nice new war for you to fight?

RUPERT: There seems to be difficulty in financing such a project at the moment.

DIDO: We might start a subscription fund.

RUPERT: Do you think Harry would give something?

DIDO: You know, he might – just to get you out of here. That man's got principles, but he can sometimes step over them. Ought we to go down?

RUPERT: Not yet.

DIDO: I don't want to go down. I'm out of my depth with Catherine. I suppose I should be out of my depth with you.

RUPERT: Aren't you?

DIDO: No. And it's obvious to everybody. But Catherine – she's in a hell of a position. Do you know, we've talked to each other all day. Couldn't you try talking to her for a while? It's not easy, I suppose, but surely there's something left between you. There must be. It'd be too horrible if there wasn't even kindness left. Won't you try?

RUPERT: Why do you think I've spent my time with you today?

DIDO: Well, Harry's not your sort – nor are the boys. Catherine – difficult. That leaves me. You had no choice.

RUPERT: I could've shut myself up – alone.

DIDO: Yes, you could have done that. Look! I know I'm young but may I give you a bit of advice?

RUPERT: If you want to.

DIDO: You're about to make some kind of confession to me. Well, don't do it. I don't want to hear.

RUPERT: Very well.

DIDO: I don't want to get mixed up. I don't want to have any influence on what you think or do or say. I'm free, and I want to stay like that. It's been very nice and interesting talking to you, but now I must be getting back.

RUPERT: To what? Somebody down in the city? Are you in love?

DIDO: That's the point. I'm not. I've told you, I'm free and I want to stay free.

RUPERT: What's the danger here?

DIDO: Oh, don't be such a bloody fool! You are.
(*RUPERT laughs.*)
It's not funny! Think of Catherine. For seven years she's been shut up in her love for you. Everything she has done – everything she has thought and believed has been decided by that love. Was it worth it? I don't think so. She may get free again in time – she's brave, you can see that – but life's too short, too damned short for these stretches of hard labour.

RUPERT: I'm convinced.

DIDO: You are? Good. Start work to get me out of here.
(*CATHERINE comes up the stairway.*)

CATHERINE: Aren't you coming down to have some food?

RUPERT: I'm not hungry.

CATHERINE: Can't you persuade him, Miss Morgen?
(*DIDO shakes her head.*)

RUPERT: Is the telephone down there?

CATHERINE: Yes.

RUPERT: I want to speak to Cadmus. There's no reason to keep this girl here another night. I'm going to ask Cadmus to let her go home. (*He goes down the stairs.*)

CATHERINE: Do you want to go?

DIDO: Yes, please.

CATHERINE: Where will you make for?

DIDO: Back to my room.

CATHERINE: What's it like?

DIDO: My room? Oh, it's fine. It belongs just to me. I don't have to share it as you share this place.

CATHERINE: Where is it?

DIDO: In a part you wouldn't know. The house looks over – or rather, leans over, the river. I couldn't be more strange to you if I came from the moon, could I?

CATHERINE: (*She smiles.*) No. My manner towards you last
night when you arrived with Harry wasn't welcoming.
I'm sorry.

DIDO: I understand.

CATHERINE: I suppose you do. Harry tell you about
Rupert and me?

DIDO: In a way.

CATHERINE: Rupert's had a very bad time and he's
desperately uncertain of the future. We mustn't blame
him for what he does. You won't do that, will you?

DIDO: No, I won't blame him.

CATHERINE: He likes you very much so won't you stay on?

DIDO: No.

CATHERINE: For tonight, at least.

DIDO: No. I want to go home.

CATHERINE: Is there something urgent calling you back?

DIDO: No. I just want to get out of here.

CATHERINE: Please stay. For my sake.

DIDO: For you?

CATHERINE: Yes.

DIDO: I'll stay for you.

CATHERINE: You funny girl. Do you make a habit of the
unexpected? Anyway, thank you. Would you like a change
of clothes? You've been in those since you arrived.

DIDO: I haven't got any others.

CATHERINE: Well, you didn't come prepared to stay.
What can we do? I know. My maid has some very pretty
things. Run along and see her. I'm sure she'll help us.

DIDO: I don't want to.

CATHERINE: Now don't be silly. She dresses very well.

DIDO: Where do I find her?

CATHERINE: She'll be in her room.

(*HARRY has come from below. He has a glass of wine in
his hand.*)

And whilst you're there get her to comb your hair.

HARRY: Excuse me, Miss, but you're beautiful. You should
be in pictures.

(*DIDO passes HARRY and goes down the stairs.*)

Is Forster calling off the watch-dogs?

CATHERINE: What do you mean?

HARRY: He's on the telephone down there. He asked me to
    get the number. Didn't want to give his sacred name.
    He's speaking to Cadmus about something.

CATHERINE: (*To HARRY.*) Why did you tell that girl
    about the break between Rupert and me?

HARRY: Dear Kate, I didn't tell her. Not in so many words.
    It's been pretty obvious to everybody that – well, that –

CATHERINE: That he's not come home to me. Yes,
    I suppose so.

HARRY: You're putting up a good fight, Kate. I'm proud
    of you.

CATHERINE: It's not that he doesn't want to love me any
    more. It's really that in losing everything he lost me.

HARRY: Yes, that's the way it is. Kate, answer me
    two questions.

CATHERINE: What are they?

HARRY: One – why did Cadmus come here last night?

CATHERINE: To welcome Rupert back.

HARRY: Two – what big fish are you expecting to catch
    with my little girlfriend as bait? You're not going to
    answer that, are you?

CATHERINE: No.

HARRY: Here's an alternative. What are you fighting
    to keep?

CATHERINE: Nothing for myself. That surprises you,
    doesn't it? You've always thought me possessive. It's not
    altogether true. I don't like waste. There are some things
    worth keeping because they're rare and fine. Not for
    yourself. I suppose it's like having children. They're
    never yours – as a possession – but they're worth having
    and sending out to be themselves. That's me at this
    moment. I'm not fighting to keep something, Harry, but
    I am fighting to save something.

HARRY: To save something from going to waste?

CATHERINE: Just that.

(*HARRY looks into his wine glass.*)

HARRY: Empty. Yet if I bring this and the bottle below into
    union it will breed kindness in me. So down I go.

CATHERINE: Don't get too kind, Harry.

HARRY: Oh, Poppa and Doc asked me to say that they've gone to bed.

(*HARRY and RUPERT meet on the stairs.*)

If you don't want to keep on meeting me like this, Forster, you'd better do something about getting us all out of here.

RUPERT: Are you coming down?

HARRY: I am.

(*HARRY goes down the stair. RUPERT comes up into the room.*)

CATHERINE: Did you speak to Cadmus?

RUPERT: He's not at the Chancellery, but he's expected back within an hour. I left a message.

CATHERINE: The girl's staying.

RUPERT: What?

CATHERINE: I asked her to stay. For a little longer. That's what you wanted, isn't it? Rupert, it's not a sign of weakness to have someone with you through these hours. Why be afraid of showing that you're human? It's a failing the rest of us admit. Why not you? There have been times in the past when I've been able to comfort you. I don't remember them as moments of weakness.

RUPERT: Catherine, I didn't want it to end like this with you. Believe that. But I had to tell you.

CATHERINE: I know that, now.

RUPERT: I hate lying. Anyway, I'm no good at it.

CATHERINE: I wanted you to love me – not merely be faithful to me. That was before. Now I only want you to live.

RUPERT: Why try to save me? I'm useless now. I've been tamed by long captivity.

CATHERINE: That's not true. You've just forgotten how to fight, I think. And you're mistaking the enemy.

RUPERT: I don't think so.

CATHERINE: The real enemy is the darkness you hope to bring on yourself tomorrow morning.

RUPERT: There's a word for it.

CATHERINE: I know. I know from the past seven years. There was the early morning when I didn't want to wake, the sound of my footsteps going about this house, the end of each year. At those times I longed to stop fighting. But I believed it would be wrong to give in. Sinful, if you like.

RUPERT: In my profession death can never be a moral problem. You were always brave, Catherine.

CATHERINE: You've never thought of your absence in that way, have you?

RUPERT: No. No, I've not.

CATHERINE: Don't let it influence you. Live for yourself. Face this trial. How can they condemn you?

RUPERT: Very easily. I failed in what I set out to do.

CATHERINE: They'll not sentence you.

RUPERT: Perhaps not. Then I'll have to live. Where's the girl?

CATHERINE: Have you told her? About John's visit last night and the trial.

RUPERT: Of course not. Why should she be involved?

CATHERINE: Yet you want her to stay. You watch her. You wait for her to speak. What do you hope to hear?

RUPERT: I don't know.

CATHERINE: Something that can never come from me. So I asked her to stay. She may casually – without any thought at all – help you.

RUPERT: I think it's unlikely.

CATHERINE: You have to trust someone at this time. I'll leave it to the girl.

(*DIDO has come up the stairs and into the room. She is now in a simple dress and her hair has recently been brushed and combed.*)

DIDO: Be careful. I'm here.

CATHERINE: So you are. (*To RUPERT.*) What did you arrange on the telephone?

RUPERT: That Cadmus should call me when he got back.

DIDO: Is that about me?

RUPERT: For permission to leave this place.

DIDO: I always came and went as I pleased before I met you people. Anyway, I thought you wanted me to stay.

CATHERINE: I do.

DIDO: Well, I'm still here, so what's the fuss about? Are
you going?

(*CATHERINE has moved to the stairs.*)

Do you want me to come with you?

CATHERINE: No. Stay. (*She goes down the stairs.*)

DIDO: Well, I'm back. Looking different, but don't let that
put you off. What were we talking about?

RUPERT: I can't remember. What have you done
to yourself?

DIDO: She thought I was looking grubby. I probably was.
No pride, that's what's wrong with me.

RUPERT: It's very late. Don't you want to go to bed?

DIDO: No. If I do, I'll have just got in when there'll be
a very small knock on the door, and then a very small
American voice will ask to come in. Whatever I say, in
it will come. It'll want to know if I'm all right and it'll
move about the room for a while – somehow getting
near to the bed. When I feel its breath I'll say, Go to
hell! and off it will go – hurt. At least, that's what
happened last night. I'll stay up. What's going to be left
to me? By Catherine. I overheard. 'I'll leave it to the
girl.' That's what she said.

RUPERT: You mustn't bother your head about it.

DIDO: It's not my head that's bothered – it's my heart. I like
her, you see. I'm sorry for her too.

RUPERT: Save your pity.

DIDO: What did you say?

RUPERT: I said, save your pity.

DIDO: For you?

RUPERT: I don't need it.

DIDO: Who is there left? Harry. He'd love it. But not
tonight. What's the matter?

RUPERT: A little while ago you said it would be horrible if
there was nothing left between Catherine and me. Well,
there is that. I don't care to hear her pitied.

DIDO: Sorry. Forgive me asking this, but I've a conventional
mind: why didn't you marry her?

53

RUPERT: Because of my job. I was always away. She's not the sort of person who could've lived the life.

DIDO: That's not the reason. That's an excuse. Tell me the reason, please.

RUPERT: Very well. It was unwise to commit myself to another. Not from a sense of independence. Nothing so simple. One of my predecessors in war, an Irishman, once said: 'All the business of war, and indeed all the business of life, is to endeavour to find out what you don't know by what you do.' And he went on: 'That's what I called "guessing what was at the other side of the hill".' That's how he put it, and that has been my job – to guess what was at the far side of the hill. Towards the end my sense for doing that was highly developed, but only because I kept myself free. Were I committed I saw the other side of the hill with eyes not entirely my own. Do you understand?

DIDO: Let me tell you something before you go on. I'm not frightened of you.

RUPERT: Why did you decide to stay?

DIDO: Because of Catherine. I don't have to help or comfort many of my friends, you know, because none of us have much to lose. But people like Catherine, who've had a lot and lost it – well, that's new to me. And she was so damned proud when she asked me to stay. People are too often humble. She was fighting like hell at that moment. Suddenly I felt – well, this is as good a point as any for me to stop running away. I'm on the edge of a trap, but it can't be helped.

RUPERT: A trap? Do you mean a conspiracy?

DIDO: No, I mean a trap. The thing you catch wild animals in. Look! Now, look here. You kept yourself free because of your job. Well, I kept myself free because I'm not strong enough, good enough or wise enough to have another living, loving person with me. But the trap's always there. You – I've only to discover something about you – you've only to tell me something and I'm caught.

RUPERT: Tell you what?

DIDO: How do I know until I hear it? What was it shut the trap on Catherine all these years?

RUPERT: You think I'm preparing the same for you?

DIDO: Nobody – not even the proudest person – knows when their cry for help goes out. It may not even be spoken by you. When I was a kid there was a boy and he went to the war. He came back from the fighting earlier than was expected. I went to meet him at the East Railway Station, and it was there the trap was sprung. He'd come back without his eyes. I cut myself loose from that one easily enough, but as I get older it's more difficult. Everywhere I go there are the unhappy and the aimless waiting for me to put out my hand and walk into that trap made of human arms. Ach! this loving business. (*HARRY has appeared on the stairs. He carries a glass of whisky which he is careful not to spill.*) What do you want?

HARRY: Just to know if you're all right.

DIDO: How do I look?

HARRY: Different. You tired?

DIDO: So I look tired.

HARRY: I didn't say so. You going to bed?

DIDO: Not yet.

HARRY: You're all right.

DIDO: Yes.

HARRY: Sorry about this, but I feel responsible – bringing you here.

DIDO: Don't get that on your conscience as well, Harry.

HARRY: You're alright, then.

DIDO: I'm all right.

(*In silence she stares at HARRY. He goes down the stairs.*) Why do I do it? He means it kindly. Always has. He picked me up last night in that bar because he thought I was down on my luck. But he was really looking for somebody to do him a good turn. And you, Rupert. Catherine kept herself and this place for you in all kindness. You refused it. What's the matter with us?

What are we afraid of losing? You know, we must think
very highly of ourselves to keep ourselves so free.

RUPERT: You're young. You won't be free for long. You'll
have to commit yourself and love because you're a woman.

DIDO: It's an easy excuse for weakness. You kept free for
years. What's the secret? Being a man?

RUPERT: That and having an objective.

DIDO: Something you fought for in that war of yours.

RUPERT: Yes.

DIDO: They said it was for your country and for people
like me.

RUPERT: It was for myself. Not for Cadmus or country or
you, but myself. To impose myself.

DIDO: They say that's wrong. They say we should live,
suffer and finally die for others.

RUPERT: Yes, that's what they say.

DIDO: You don't believe it's true. Well, what do
you believe?

RUPERT: The night before that last battle I still believed
that I could reach a point of achievement never before
known to a man. The way I chose was conquest by war.
Some men need an art to fulfil themselves. Saints need
a religion. I had to pursue a triumph of arms. The
greatest the world has ever known. By that I believed
I could become myself, the man I was intended to be.

DIDO: But whatever you believed, you were caught like
everybody. You were caught in that battle.

RUPERT: Not by man. No man could have trapped me at
that time.

DIDO: You were caught. I heard about it, don't forget. The
papers were full of it. The radio chattered day after day.

RUPERT: Did anyone defend me?

DIDO: Not that I remember. But I was young – seven years
ago I was about fourteen.

RUPERT: Just the age to have been there. It might have
been you.

DIDO: Seven years ago.

RUPERT: It was a fine morning. The action was a small one
along the main route of advance. It would never have

found its way into the history books. The town lay in the bend of a river. I intended to take the place by a *coup de main*. The main enemy forces had evacuated the town and were in prepared positions on the far side of the river. My intention was to go in at dawn and take the town at my leisure through the day, but at dusk, with the full weight of my force, to establish two bridgeheads over the river and attempt a crossing that night: on the supposition that the enemy would expect a break between the attack on the town and the river crossing. You understand? It was to be a very beautiful battle, having an elegance difficult to achieve with the use of armoured forces. I was satisfied with the preparations, and at dawn the attack went in. I led in my command tank. We were not delayed by infantry movements as the infantrymen were on the flanks moving with us and not intended to engage, but to save themselves for the river crossing at night. On reaching the town I halted my force preparatory to its dispersal for street by street occupation. My own tank was halted beside a small church. I got down and walked the length of the street ahead alone. The place was deserted and there was no indication of the roads being mined. It seemed safe to proceed. I went back to my tank and climbed in. I had picked up the microphone of my transmitting set – I was using open communication – and I was about to give the order to continue the advance when the church door opened. I was shocked by the noise in the silence, and I turned. A little boy had come from the church and was standing on the steps. He put his hand to his mouth – oh, as if to put in a sweet – but it was a whistle he held. He blew the whistle and at once the children were upon us. Hundreds of them. They came from the church, from the houses in the street and from far off down the street itself. They rolled like a wave towards us, screaming and shouting, some armed with sticks, some carrying flags. Reaching us they beat themselves against the sides of our tanks. I saw my commanders and their crews laughing at them, cheering them on, encouraging them in their attempts to scramble over the armour. We might have been liberators and not an attacking force. Was I the only man to see the danger? We were virtually immobilised, for they were everywhere, even beneath our tracks. The laughter of my men became louder. Our concentration was broken. The attack – timed by seconds to co-ordination – was flinging itself to pieces. My central armoured force was the governing factor of movement. Delay it and the two infantry groups became as ineffective as naked men. The boy who had come first from the church had clambered on to my tank. He was black-haired and black-eyed and he carried a wooden sword which he swung above his head. He shouted something which I didn't understand, and then spat at me. That was no provocation for what I did: I had already decided, I stretched out and drew his head to my shoulder like a lover, and shot him in the mouth. I took him by the hair of his shattered head and held him up for my men to see. They understood. The shooting began. They also used knives to cut them free from the armour. The note of the children's cry changed and was in mercy drowned as the motors started up and we moved forward.

DIDO: They say four hundred were found dead.

RUPERT: Four hundred. Do they say that? I'd no idea.

DIDO: What was the place?

RUPERT: It was a children's colony, I was told later. They were of all nationalities. Some of the enemy, some of our own, herded together by the shuttle of armies. You always get such things in modern war. Nobody's discovered what they were about that morning. Was it a reckless imitation of their fathers and older brothers? Were they put up to it by unscrupulous commanders? Or had those children reached a point from which there is no further retreat and a stand – against whatever odds – must at last be made?

DIDO: They say you're a coward, you know.

RUPERT: I know.

DIDO: It's not true. What is true, then?

(*CATHERINE and CADMUS come into the room by way of the stairs. CADMUS is in evening dress.*)

CADMUS: I got your message, Forster. Forgive the fancy
dress but I didn't wait to change.

RUPERT: I was prepared to speak to you on the telephone.

CADMUS: Impossible. I never hold two-way conversations
on that instrument. It allows for great ambiguity of
meaning. Who is this?

CATHERINE: Miss Morgen. A friend of Harry Lancaster.

CADMUS: How do you do. What have you been talking to
Forster about, Miss Morgen, until this late hour? Has he
been telling you stories of his battles? He's a great
fellow. We shan't see his like again. But we must thank
the Lord we're not a couple of his soldiers. They tell me
he has them drilled until the blood boils in their tails.

DIDO: Has he got any soldiers now?

CADMUS: Not at the moment. But he will have – he will
have. Glorious legions at his command fighting for
a nobler cause than we can give him.

DIDO: You mean when he's dead.

CADMUS: Yes, I did mean that. Who are you?

DIDO: Dido Morgen. Don't bother! I know who you are.

CADMUS: There is an old-fashioned idea that extreme
youth and, if I may say so, beauty –

DIDO: I'm not beautiful.

CADMUS: No, you're not. I'm so sorry. Never mind.
Perhaps you're clever instead. Are you?

DIDO: No.

CADMUS: Oh, dear! Neither beautiful nor clever. You're
kindhearted, that's what it is. That's the gift God gave
you. To understand your fellow beings.

DIDO: That's it.

CADMUS: Catherine – Forster, will one of you disengage
me from this conversation, please.

DIDO: I'll go.

CADMUS: No, don't go. Catherine, would you do a little
errand for me?

CATHERINE: What is it you want?

CADMUS: You haven't forgiven me, I see.

CATHERINE: What do you want me to do for you?

CADMUS: Go to the car, outside at the door, and ask the driver for my benzedrine tablets. I shall want to take one in about five minutes.

CATHERINE: Very well. In about five minutes.

CADMUS: It's very good of you.

(*CATHERINE goes down the stairs.*)

Even at my age we play the game. She sees through that device to get her away for a while, and from the first I know she'll see through it. Yet we observe the convention. You, Miss Morgen, wouldn't do that, would you?

DIDO: No.

CADMUS: Then you're made of the same stuff as revolutionaries. Unlike poor Catherine. So intensely vulnerable by her love of life. I detest vulnerable people, don't you?

DIDO: I like her very much.

CADMUS: Oh, you've mistaken me. I was speaking generally. I love Catherine. Surely everyone does. I mean, rather, that I find it difficult to like people for whom I feel pity.

DIDO: Yes, that's true. So do I.

CADMUS: Good! A point of agreement. I am pleased!

DIDO: Are you?

CADMUS: Do you like Forster?

DIDO: Kind of.

CADMUS: Then you can't be sorry for him.

DIDO: Should I be? Look! I don't know anything. All right? I'm the girl you see on the edge of the crowd at a street accident. It's got nothing to do with me. I just happened to be there. I don't want to be a witness. All right?

CADMUS: What did you want to speak to me about, Forster?

RUPERT: Miss Morgen. Is it necessary for her to be shut up here? She came with Lancaster and it seems senseless for her to be virtually imprisoned. She can have no influence on your plans.

CADMUS: No influence. She can have no influence, you say.

RUPERT: None. May she go home?

CADMUS: Certainly.

DIDO: Thank you very much.

CADMUS: At once, if she wishes.

DIDO: We just wanted your permission. Liberty consists of doing what you want to do when you want to do it. That's in the books. I don't want to go yet. But it's good to know I can leave when I wish.

CADMUS: My car will take you back. Don't you think it would be wise to go at once?

DIDO: No, I don't.

CADMUS: Go away! I want to speak to Forster alone.

DIDO: (*She laughs.*) No conventional excuses for me. Go away, he says.

CADMUS: And I mean it. Also keep Catherine below for a time. I'm sure you've something in common to talk about.

DIDO: Yes, we have. (*She goes down the stairs.*)

CADMUS: Who is she?

RUPERT: Lancaster picked her up yesterday and brought her here.

CADMUS: Yes, but who is she?

RUPERT: One of the people you govern.

CADMUS: Forgive my astonishment. Are there many like that, I wonder? Is it a volcano I'm sitting on and not, as I'd supposed, a dung-hill?

RUPERT: It might be wise to reconsider your position in such a light.

CADMUS: What does that mean? Can it mean your own position?

RUPERT: Certainly it can mean that.

CADMUS: That's very interesting. But there's not much time, Forster, for a detailed reconsideration. When I saw you last night you were content with my proposal. You're not content now?

RUPERT: No, sir.

CADMUS: Why not, damn you?

RUPERT: What are you going to do if I don't use this stuff? (*He has taken the jewelled box from his pocket.*)

CADMUS: What can I do?

RUPERT: There's always assassination.

CADMUS: Don't be so tiresome. From the facts I gave you last night you must know that's impossible. There's only one course I can take: to produce you for trial. I'm asking you to make yourself unavailable. Something's occurred which makes you unwilling to do that, if I understand you correctly, but I'm now only asking you to make up your mind, Forster.

RUPERT: Where do I go if I'm still alive and kicking after dawn this morning?

CADMUS: You'll be taken to the military prison in the city. The place the soldiers laughingly call Arcady. I shall make a statement that you are there and that you are to be tried. The process of law will be set in motion. As the trial proceeds you'll be forgotten, and all we shall be aware of will be the rotting corpse of the country covered by the ordure of our recent history.

RUPERT: You're appealing to me as a patriot. I find that odd.

CADMUS: I'm doing nothing of the kind. I'm asking you to make up your mind. Decide.

RUPERT: My last positive action – by my decision – was the murder of that child seven years ago. From that moment I not only relinquished command of my army, but also of myself. For the seven years in prison I lived by other men's decisions regarding my habits, my actions and my thoughts. I did what I was told. Nothing more. I was content it should be like that. Soldiers, you know, are forced to action by their decisions. There's no getting out of it for men in my job. No going back and saying I didn't mean it, when in my hand I'm holding the casualty list for thousands. You'll forgive my contempt for men who think they've fulfilled their obligations by expressing an opinion.

CADMUS: My God, Forster, you're talking like the romantic 'man of action' which all the intellectuals are in love with nowadays.

RUPERT: I'm talking as myself, not as any man's conception of me.

CADMUS: Go on.

RUPERT: I found freedom only in the years of fighting. I waited for that war, Cadmus. I wanted it with physical desire. It came, and I was released into action. In the years of preparation before the war – ach! My life was a formality. Because a man is seen in a crowd it must never be thought that he is of the crowd.

CADMUS: What you're telling me is that solitariness – aloneness, if you like – cannot be imposed. In your case imprisonment was never a punishment. Have I got that straight?

RUPERT: Do you believe absolute imprisonment to exist?

CADMUS: Yours seemed very efficient. At least, it was intended to be so.

RUPERT: Absolute. With no line of communication.

CADMUS: Put it that way if you like.

RUPERT: An army's line of communication is both its strength and its weakness. It stretches back sometimes broad and firm, sometimes fine and worn to base. It is not a steady supply. It pulses like a human vein according to need. Yet it must always be kept open. It must always be kept alive. In war I have struck so far forward that the line back has been stretched until it is invisible to all eyes but mine. For it is not always a thing you can mark on a map – you can't neatly signpost it for everyone to follow. You can only feel it in your belly like homesickness. It is what makes an isolated group fight its way out of an apparently impossible situation. Faith that there's a way back.

CADMUS: Yes. I understand you.

RUPERT: A man is an army, a striking offensive force. Each one of us has the line of communication stretching out. With some of us it is weak and with some of us it is strong according to our courage. The line goes back to other people, places and ideas. From you and Catherine back into the past: from myself and the girl out to the immediate happening. But we all call it by the same

name, don't we, Cadmus? Love. And as long as that line
remains open we have to live.

CADMUS: How did you manage to keep contact in prison?
There are classic examples, of course. Did you adopt
a mouse?

RUPERT: No, it was not a mouse. It was a human voice.
On the hills behind the camp there was a goat-herd.
At dusk he greeted the night and at dawn the day with
song. I've no idea what he sang – some prayer, I suppose.
I tried to take it down phonetically but I failed. It must
have been in some local dialect. I don't know. Early on I
tried to resist it. I felt it was an intrusion. However, I was
compelled to accept him. I came to be fond of him – like
a man with a plain wife – and I ended by understanding
that you can't shut out the human voice – especially
when it's expressing itself in an act of faith. The pulse
became stronger. I continued to live.

CADMUS: I thought I knew exactly who would be in
this house today: Catherine, the doctor, the priest and
that clown of an American. I was safe with them. Not
one of them would touch the sensibilities of a man
such as yourself. But this girl – I'd not counted on her
being here. She is now the sentimental singer of your
goat-song, I suppose.

RUPERT: Yes.

CADMUS: Very well. You'll be taken down within six
hours. I shall send for you.

RUPERT: What are my chances?

CADMUS: Reasonable. Of getting away with your life.
You won't save anything else.

RUPERT: I go within six hours, you say.

CADMUS: At daybreak.

(*HARRY comes up the stairs.*)

HARRY: Where are the girls, Forster?

RUPERT: Below.

HARRY: Well, what are they doing?

RUPERT: I've no idea.

CADMUS: You're drunk.

HARRY: No, sir. Not yet. But I'm on the way. And when I am I'll have me to talk to, see? That'll be fine because myself and me will have some very interesting things to say to each other. But until that happy time I want someone to hold my hand. You'd look silly doing that so it'd better be one of the girls. Where are they? (*He shouts.*) Dido!

CADMUS: I'm told she's a friend of yours, Mr Lancaster.

HARRY: Dido? Well, I don't know about being a friend, but she'll hold my hand when the horror's on me, and I can only see the past and never the future. She's that sort of girl. A kind kind of girl, you know.

CADMUS: And you need her at this moment?

HARRY: Sure do. (*He shouts.*) Dido!

CADMUS: Would she hold Forster's hand if he needed her?

HARRY: She's been doing that all day, so now I move up for a bit of comfort.

CADMUS: She must be a very extraordinary girl.

HARRY: She is. Dido!

CADMUS: Pay attention, Mr Lancaster. Why should Forster need the comfort this girl's given him today?

HARRY: Because he's a man, I guess. Beneath the splendour, you know – (*He is beside the bronze helmet: he taps it with his fist.*) – empty. Hollow. Nothing. Nothing but a man signalling to be let out of the trappings of war. Asking to be taken back into the herd.

CADMUS: Is that so, Forster?

RUPERT: Lancaster has a liberal mind. To him no man is entirely evil. Not even me. And so he is compelled to mistake my gestures of defiance for signals of distress.

CADMUS: But Mr Lancaster says this girl has been with you all day.

HARRY: Holding his hand.

CADMUS: Where is she leading you, Forster?

RUPERT: Didn't we agree on that just before Lancaster came up?

HARRY: Excuse me. Were you two talking important when I broke in?

CADMUS: We were speaking of Forster's future.

HARRY: Oh, that. Well, I'm sorry for Kate, and in a little while I suppose I'll have to be sorry for Dido.

CADMUS: Couldn't you find a little sorrow for me, Mr Lancaster?

HARRY: Why? Is he breaking your heart, too?

CADMUS: He certainly is.

HARRY: Don't let him do it. That kind break more than hearts. They're not often caught as you've caught this one, and you don't often see the naked face out of its idiot covering. Don't let it go free.

CADMUS: But we're not, Mr Lancaster. Let me tell you: Forster is back here to be put on trial.

HARRY: Ah!

CADMUS: That makes you happy, I see.

HARRY: So they've finally caught up with you, Forster. What a chance for us all – all us little people – to take a smack at you.

CADMUS: Yes, Mr Lancaster, it'll give you all a splendid opportunity, won't it?

HARRY: Do I believe this? Are we moving into an age of enlightenment?

CADMUS: We can only hope so, Mr Lancaster.

HARRY: How y'going t'take it, Forster? You'll have to find the words to defend yourself now, not the actions. No more legend, Forster, hidden in the midst of any army or up in a camp in the mountains – just a man like any other. You're going to have to stand up and answer for what you did.

CADMUS: Yes, indeed, he'll have to be very truthful in the cross-examinations.

HARRY: I can't wait. I can't wait for the day when the whole world'll know what you are. How there was nothing back of those bloody murders but your lusting ambition. We only needed the opportunity, Forster – we just needed this to bring you down to our own level. That's all.

CADMUS: And when you've proved him your equal – what then?

HARRY: He may go off and live the best way he can. We'd
   be playing his game if we killed him. Mr Cadmus, I'd
   like to shake you by the hand. You're doing a fine job.
   Thank you, sir.

CADMUS: Thank you, Mr Lancaster. Well, Forster, he's
   given you a hint of the feelings of the ordinary people.
   I hope you'll respect those feelings.
   (*CATHERINE and DIDO come up the stairs.*)
   May I appeal to your good sense once more? Let go,
   give up and do what I ask.

CATHERINE: He says you have them with you, John.

CADMUS: Who says I have what with me?

CATHERINE: Your driver: the benzedrine tablets.

CADMUS: Have I? Probably. Well, Forster?
   (*RUPERT does not answer.*)
   Miss Morgen, will you help me down those stairs to
   the car?

DIDO: Of course. Aren't you afraid I might push you?

CADMUS: Why should you?

DIDO: I might be tired of the Government.

CADMUS: Who isn't?
   (*CADMUS and DIDO go below.*)

HARRY: Kate, sweetheart, I seem to have run out of drink.
   I mean the immediate supply below.

CATHERINE: Haven't you had enough?

HARRY: No, Kate, I've not had enough.

CATHERINE: Then you'll have to go to the kitchen. Ask
   for some. Take it to your room.

HARRY: I'll do that. Kate, how did you feel about the picture?

CATHERINE: Picture?

HARRY: The picture I showed tonight. My picture.

CATHERINE: It was very good, I think. Of course, it's old.
   Out of date now.

HARRY: That's right. Not much use now. It lacks the drama
   of these times. I should've put in a trial scene, eh, Forster?
   My, the newsreel boys'll have a hell of a time with you the
   next few weeks. Those cameras don't miss a thing – they
   pick it all up, you know, every bit of it. Wish I was going
   to be behind one. (*He goes down the stairs.*)

CATHERINE: What did all that mean?

RUPERT: That Lancaster thinks it a good thing I should be put on trial.

CATHERINE: How does he know about it?

RUPERT: Cadmus told him. And raised the rabble in him. It was done to frighten me, to make me understand what I must face when the time comes. As it seems it has.

CATHERINE: You've decided. It's terrible, you know, to watch a man going coldly along the edge of decision. You were beyond my reach. I was afraid to cry out and make you look back. Couldn't trust myself. I had to leave it to the girl. She could speak in a matter-of-fact way which you'd understand.

(*DIDO has come up the stairs into the room.*)

DIDO: That man – that old Cadmus man – he says there's going to be some sort of trial. Are you going to let them do that to you?

CATHERINE: There's only one other way out. Because of you he's not going to take that way.

DIDO: Because of me. What've I done?

CATHERINE: Enough. Thank you.

DIDO: I don't want thanks. Thank you, you say and smile. So, all right. I've made you happy. Rupert's come to a decision because of something I've said or done. Fine for you – yes! – but for me – ? Try to catch some of my bloody misery when that old man said –

RUPERT: What did he say?

DIDO: He said, 'You shouldn't have held him back. He had a chance to finish clean. Now, because of you, he's going to finish dirty and old and lonely and angry. Because of you.' That's what he said.

CATHERINE: John Cadmus thinks that. We know better.

DIDO: I don't know anything. I don't want to know anything!

CATHERINE: Then why did you stay?

DIDO: Oh, leave me alone!

CATHERINE: Alone? Is that what you want? Yet you're not happy. You're not even free.

DIDO: It'll do for me. As I am.

CATHERINE: For how long? It is the middle of the night. No time for envy or pain. Quite soon now the day will come when you'll have to admit that the anger and despair you feel is not because of other people. It is for them. (*To RUPERT.*) I suppose they'll send for you.

RUPERT: Yes.

CATHERINE: Call me. I'll be in my room below. (*She has moved to the stairs.*)

DIDO: Catherine!

(*CATHERINE has gone from the room.*)

RUPERT: First of all I must tell you – that old Cadmus man is an honest man. He believed what he said.

DIDO: You've been brought back for this trial.

RUPERT: Yes. John Cadmus doesn't want it to be. He wants me to take Catherine's 'other way out'. He wants me to die clean. That's what he meant when he spoke to you.

DIDO: And he thinks I'm stopping you.

RUPERT: Yes, but don't worry. The decision is entirely mine.

DIDO: It is, isn't it, Rupert?

RUPERT: Do you want me to live, Dido?

DIDO: I want you to do what is right for a man like you. Life's not everything, I know, for men of your sort. But you must decide.

RUPERT: I've told Cadmus I'll stand the trial. They're coming at daybreak to take me to the military prison in the city.

DIDO: You'll be in Arcady. It's just across the river from my place.

RUPERT: The questioning will begin there. The investigation of the past.

DIDO: Will you tell them the truth?

RUPERT: Yes, but they won't be interested.

DIDO: And when it's all over?

RUPERT: They'll let me go.

DIDO: To be old and angry and lonely. No!

RUPERT: You mustn't concern yourself. Keep free.

DIDO: All right. I love you, if that's what you want to hear me say. I love you. You seem to me a very good man.

RUPERT: I'd like you to stay with me through the rest of the night. Only a few hours.

DIDO: You will say exactly what you mean, won't you?

RUPERT: I mean only that. Stay with me until first light. Until they come for me.

DIDO: Long time since I saw the dawn come up. I was walking back alone from a party. I'd danced all night and I was a bit drunk because I thought I was in love again. I was going home the long way – making it last out. Restless, you know, because his arms had been around me as we danced. And I'd got a tune in my head and it wouldn't get out. (*She sings*.)
'Don't shut your eyes to,
You must get wise to
The fact that we're in love.'
I was singing it as I walked in the comfortable darkness when the dawn came up and smacked me in the face so hard I nearly fell on my back. Another day. They always take me by surprise.

RUPERT: I've always prepared for the day. I could never let myself be taken by surprise. The dawn's a time of great danger, you know. I remember how cold it was, summer and winter, and how still. The men about me whispered and a cough sounded like a shot. I would stand staring into the darkness towards the enemy and he would be looking into my eyes. Then, at the appointed time, the darkness would dissolve. Towards the end of the campaign I almost came to believe that it was the intensity of my vision which dispelled the night and the strength of my faith which lifted the sun into the sky.

DIDO: I'm not surprised they shut you up when you talk like that. You're dangerous.

RUPERT: I'm sane, you know.

DIDO: Yes, and they know it. That's the danger. You're safe with me. Here, with me. The Doctor and the Father are in bed, Harry's getting drunk in the kitchen, and Catherine's at prayer. You and me – here. That's fine. My singing in the streets and you staring into the East –

that's the past. You going to Arcady and me going back to my room – well, that's in the future. But you and me, here. That's now.

RUPERT: Yes, we're safe.

DIDO: Of course we are. Safe.

RUPERT: How will you remember the time you've spent in this house? When you're free of it. Will you remember?

DIDO: I suppose so. Something'll bring it to mind. (*She is crying.*) Sorry. Doesn't mean a thing. For instance, always happens when somebody gives me a present. Stupid!

RUPERT: I've nothing to give.

DIDO: I don't want anything from you. Did your soldiers – those men who waited with you for those other daybreaks – did they expect you to reward them? That night seven years ago – after the fight with the children – were your men against you then?

RUPERT: They were with me.

DIDO: Well, then. So am I. What happened.

(*A pause.*)

I'm not just curious.

RUPERT: I didn't go on. I waited. On the wrong side of the river.

DIDO: Yes?

(*RUPERT does not speak.*)

Would like to roll up and sleep for a while? I'll watch. Oh, come on. I'm not such a fool. You've trusted people before me. Rest. I'll watch. Sleep.

RUPERT: Yes, you have to trust someone. That's the comradeship of soldiering. The knowledge that you're a man. And need to be watched over in the last hours of the night. Protected. From hurt. And death.

DIDO: Rest.

RUPERT: Watch.

CURTAIN

ACT THREE

The scene is the same. The time is later the same night moving to dawn. RUPERT and DIDO are within the room.

RUPERT: If you stand there I shan't be able to see the sun rise.

DIDO: Ah! that's cheating. I thought you were asleep. You haven't spoken for ages.

RUPERT: Do you like dancing?

DIDO: Oh, yes. Two things I like best of all are dancing and going to the Lido and lying in the sun. I'll do that all through this summer. I've been saving my pennies.

RUPERT: There was a lot of music for dancing in the old days, I remember.

DIDO: You remember. That's why you've been so quiet. Were those days good – so good?

RUPERT: No better than others.

DIDO: But you – did you have a good time, then?

RUPERT: I was a very serious young man deep in the study of war. But I loved Catherine very much and she liked the things you like and so, of course, I did them. I was stricken by the time they took from my studies, but yes, I enjoyed myself. I think I danced very well – especially waltzes. Do they waltz much now?

DIDO: Not very much. We dance to a lot of American music.

RUPERT: Catherine was beautiful when she danced. She's always been most beautiful when happy. You know, I wasn't in love with her when we first met. She was travelling in this country. She gave up everything she had at that time in her own country and settled down here. She seemed to find what she needed in me.

DIDO: It must've hurt you to tell her that it was over. Yesterday, I mean. Why did you do it?

RUPERT: I found her love for me remained, but it was the love of her young days.

DIDO: She thought you were going to be free.

RUPERT: Yes. She meant to take advantage of that and drag me back into the past. I was to live what should have been in the last few years if the war hadn't taken me away. But I want the present time as offered to me by John Cadmus. And I want it alone. I have to take it alone to make what I wish of it.

DIDO: What do you want to make of the present?

RUPERT: A triumph.

DIDO: Haven't you ever – in all your life – loved a small thing? Something I could share with you?

RUPERT: I've a great fondness for natural things. Flowers and things of young growth, of brief life. Through the war I collected wild plants. I kept little boxes for the purpose in my command wagon. The men knew this, and I think they laughed at me. But even though they laughed they'd bring me unknown flowers taken from the roadside and stand by whilst I identified them. My pride and happiness, Dido, has been that the soldiers loved me. Did someone call?

DIDO: Yes. Catherine.

(*CATHERINE comes up the stairway.*)

CATHERINE: Miss Morgen, will you come down? Harry's asking for you. There's been an accident.

DIDO: What's happened?

CATHERINE: Harry's burnt his hands very badly. So stupid. He put those rolls of film into the electric furnace in the kitchen. They flared up and caught his hands. I've got the doctor out of bed, and he's dressing the burns now, but Harry is asking for you. Will you go down? I'm afraid he's very drunk.

(*DIDO goes down the stairs.*)

RUPERT: Why did he do it? A quixotic gesture, surely. I mean, there must be more than one copy of a thing like a film.

CATHERINE: Apparently not. Everyone's forgotten it except Harry. That was the last copy. A personal possession.

RUPERT: It didn't remotely resemble life before the war. It was a fiction, a fairy-tale with everyone in love and happy ever after.

CATHERINE: Perhaps it's unfortunate that life's longer than six reels of celluloid.

RUPERT: It's as well he hasn't the talent to make this new film. It's entertaining to misrepresent happiness, but there's nothing funny in lying about misery.

CATHERINE: He's not lying. That's the way he sees it. Why should you say it's wrong for him to take the world he knows and try to make something beautiful and tragic? Why should you say that?

RUPERT: I don't. I say it's unwise and dangerous to distort the world around you to satisfy your longing.

CATHERINE: There's more danger, you know, in trying to destroy it to satisfy your ambition. You made me say that. I don't want to drag up the past any more. The damnable part of it is that men of your kind shatter the ordinary, everyday human pride of people like me.

RUPERT: By that you're at last seeing me as I am.

CATHERINE: I believe so. Let me look at you.

RUPERT: It will be easier for you – in the future – if you understand me. At this time.

CATHERINE: If I understand you, see you for what you are – I'll not be in love with you. Is that what you hope? There's your true weakness. Believing love can be recognised, evaluated, made to fit into the situation of the moment. It's not so. Not so at all. Even at the height of your power you could never control that. Never.

(*MATTHEW comes up the stairs.*)

MATTHEW: Catherine, I think you should know that the Chancellor's car has just driven up.

CATHERINE: Thank you, Matthew. (*To RUPERT.*) Did he say he was coming back?

RUPERT: No. I thought he'd just send the guard. I've nothing more to say to him.

CATHERINE: How's Harry, Matthew?

MATTHEW: Miss Morgen's with him. He's quieter now. His hands are badly burnt. I've done what I can in the way of dressing them, but until I can get out for more stuff he'll have to do. He's scorched one side of his face

74

which makes him look rather comic, but that's not serious. He'll be better when he's sober.

CATHERINE: Thank you for all you've done.

MATTHEW: It's many years since I've been got from my bed to attend a case. Makes me feel quite a youngster. (*CADMUS and BRUNO HURST come up the stairway. BRUNO is a young man of twenty-two years.*)

CADMUS: You look as if you might be attending someone in a professional capacity, Doctor.

MATTHEW: I have been. Harry Lancaster's burnt himself about the hands.

CADMUS: Combustion by righteous indignation, I suppose. Otherwise everyone is well. Forster?

RUPERT: Perfectly. Spare me your bedside manner.

CADMUS: I'm not trying to be kind.

RUPERT: Then shall we get this visit over?

CADMUS: Certainly. This is Captain Hurst who is now responsible for you. He is the guard commander and had better tell you of the arrangements himself. Shall we go down, Catherine? Forster is now a state secret and we mustn't listen. Come along.

CATHERINE: I shall see him before he goes?

CADMUS: Of course. This'll only take a moment. (*CATHERINE, CADMUS and MATTHEW go down the stairs.*)

RUPERT: Well, Captain Hurst?

BRUNO: Do you want to know the particulars of the escort, sir?

RUPERT: Is there anything out of the ordinary about them?

BRUNO: Nothing, sir.

RUPERT: Then I'll take them as read. Why aren't you in uniform?

BRUNO: My orders were to report in civilian clothes, sir.

RUPERT: You're very young to have reached your captaincy.

BRUNO: We are very young now, sir. Because of the reformation of the army.

RUPERT: Is this a routine detail or have you special qualifications?

BRUNO: I've been on guard duty at the Chancellery.

RUPERT: And Cadmus took you from there today.

BRUNO: Yes, sir.

RUPERT: I'll try to give you my co-operation.

BRUNO: Thank you, sir. I'm to start thirty minutes after daybreak.

RUPERT: The details are not important.

BRUNO: Will you please take leave of your friends before that time?

RUPERT: Yes, Captain Hurst, I will. Is there anything else?

BRUNO: No, sir.

RUPERT: Very well.

BRUNO: I've orders not to leave you, sir.

RUPERT: I see. Then sit down, Captain Hurst. How long is it to sunrise?

BRUNO: Twelve minutes.

RUPERT: It will be light now over the mountain camp.

BRUNO: Yes. I found night duty out there worse than anywhere.

RUPERT: You know the place?

BRUNO: I was stationed in the Eastern Provinces last year.

RUPERT: Ah! Then you, too, have heard the goat-singers.

BRUNO: Yes, sir. (*He laughs.*) Those songs.

RUPERT: You know what they are?

BRUNO: The goat songs? Of course.

RUPERT: Well?

BRUNO: They are obscene.

RUPERT: Obscene?

BRUNO: It's the goat-herd's expression of love – to his goats. The songs don't make sense.

RUPERT: Go on.

BRUNO: They're just filth. That's all. Did you hear them at the camp, sir?

RUPERT: What? Yes, I heard them there. (*He is silent.*)

BRUNO: Talk to me if it helps you.

RUPERT: What did you say?

BRUNO: I said, Please talk to me if you want to.

RUPERT: Thank you. Have you ever put your faith in love songs, Captain Hurst? Believing them to be something

more. How did it go? 'Don't shut your eyes to, you must
get wise to the fact' – And do you like dancing and
going to the Lido and lying in the sun? And being in
love? Do you like being in love?
(*BRUNO does not answer: he does not move.*)
Forgive me, I'm in a privileged position. Yet I was
a young soldier once, you know. Twenty years ago,
I might very well have been you.

BRUNO: I have been you, sir.

RUPERT: What?

BRUNO: I have been you. I've been Rupert Forster.

RUPERT: Tell me what you mean.

BRUNO: I fought that last battle of yours several times.
I fought it in the streets of this city. I was fifteen. I wanted
to be a soldier. My command truck was an old bicycle, my
troop of tanks were toys, my battle ground was the waste
around the railway yards. But my enemy, sir, was the
same. All the howling children of the neighbourhood.

RUPERT: I hope you conducted the affair with more
success than I did.

BRUNO: Every evening for weeks the shout would go up:
Let's play Forster's game! They'd all run away and hide.
Then, with six others, I'd pedal my way to the head of
the street, dismount, and walk the length of the street.
I'd hear them laughing in their hiding places – they
knew they wouldn't properly die. I'd go back to my
machine, mount it, and be about to give the signal when
they would be upon us. That was all very simple. You
had set me an example. I'd only to follow it.

RUPERT: Not absolutely, I hope.

BRUNO: There were broken heads, nothing more. Perhaps
a few pinched fingers. But after that I was lost. You had
disposed of the children. The forward movement was
poised. I wanted to go on, but I couldn't because it was
not your course. May I ask you something?

RUPERT: Yes.

BRUNO: Why did you wait for twelve hours before
continuing the advance? The attack over the river
which failed. Why did you wait?

RUPERT: Would you have gone on?

BRUNO: Yes. Every time I played the game and got to that
point it was agony to hold back. The forward impetus
was overwhelming.

RUPERT: I wasn't playing a game, Hurst.

BRUNO: Neither was I at the end. I was planning for the
future. I don't want to be caught in the way you were
caught. Think back. Why did you wait?

RUPERT: The armour moved on over the children and
through the town.

BRUNO: Yes?

RUPERT: There was no more opposition. I had occupied
the town by late afternoon.

BRUNO: You set up headquarters?

RUPERT: My staff had done so. In a deserted schoolroom.
It was a convenient place.

BRUNO: You waited.

RUPERT: Until night. It had begun to rain. A little. Nothing
much. They'd put my maps on a long trestle table. The
situation was there. Clearly marked.

BRUNO: You waited.

RUPERT: Reports began to come in. The room was very
noisy. The footsteps of men were deafening as they came
to me across the wooden floor. Someone put a meal in
front of me.

BRUNO: You say reports were coming in. What did
they show?

RUPERT: That everything was exactly as I'd planned.

BRUNO: Then why didn't you act?

RUPERT: I was trapped. Trapped by the memory of the
child. I couldn't free myself from that moment. The
moment when I stood alone, sad, lost, childless, with the
child in my arms. And looking down saw that it was
a human being. Warm, as the bitter smell of its body
struck up at me: dirty, fearful, brave and – living. It was
then the secret was forced on me. I'd shut it out until that
morning by making my own prison, Hurst, years before
they sent me to the camp in the mountains. A prison of

pride and ambition. – Then, when I caught the child to me, the secret was revealed. I suddenly understood what a man is. For I held it close.

BRUNO: If you felt this why did you shoot?

RUPERT: I had no choice. The way I'd chosen to live led to that encounter, which was in itself a challenge. Are you so great? Then fire! I fired, and the secret flew up leaving only blood on my sleeve. I became human. So I waited.

BRUNO: For twelve hours.

RUPERT: For twelve hours. It was my second-in-command who took the pencil from my hand and wrote the order for the attack across the river. It was too late.

BRUNO: You went over with them?

RUPERT: Yes. And lived.

BRUNO: Have you admitted this before?

RUPERT: Never.

BRUNO: You must consider yourself guilty.

RUPERT: I do.

BRUNO: Are you prepared to go on trial for this, to admit your error as you have to me, to be found guilty and to be sentenced? You'll serve the rest of your time at the camp in the mountains. And your comfort will be the goat-songs.

RUPERT: You're exceeding your authority!

BRUNO: You did more. You misused yours. You had as your responsibility a part in a great conquest and you lost faith. I shall fight over that ground again in future years and next time the attack will go on.

RUPERT: I'm content to leave it in your hands. I'll fight no more.

(*DIDO comes up the stairs.*)

DIDO: I'm sorry I had to leave you. He's disgustingly drunk, and he's burnt his hands very badly.

RUPERT: What have you done with him?

DIDO: He's sitting down there talking to himself. He doesn't need me. He doesn't need anybody. They've come for you, have they?

RUPERT: Yes. This is Captain Hurst of the escort.

BRUNO: How do you do.

DIDO: Hullo. Is the old man here, too?

RUPERT: He's down with Catherine.

DIDO: Going to make sure they get you away, aren't they?
How many soldiers?

BRUNO: Eight.

DIDO: Certainly making sure. Enough to carry you away if
necessary with full military honours.

BRUNO: We're an escort, ma'am, not a bearer-party.

DIDO: (*She laughs.*) Did you hear what he called me? He
called me 'ma'am'! (*To BRUNO.*) Are you doing the
right thing?

BRUNO: That doesn't concern me.

DIDO: Not concern you. You just do what you're told.

BRUNO: Yes.

DIDO: Leave the room! Well, go on.

BRUNO: Don't be a fool.

RUPERT: You mustn't make fun of him. He's an unenviable
job in front of him.

DIDO: Can't he wait downstairs. Oh, hell!
(*HARRY has come up the stairway. His hands are bandaged
and the burns on his face have been treated with a vivid dye.*)
Go 'way, Harry.

HARRY: Peace, honey. Forster, I want to say something
t'you. I want t'say something t'you. Listen – now listen.
It's this. You're wrong, see. The whole way you've gone
is'n insult to what y'could be. Don't ask me why it's
wrong. I d'know why. But I feel it – here! Is that
g'enough for you? I'm a man. All right, too, I'm a drunk.
I've no pretty pictures left in me no more, I was born in
a barn and my mammy knew my daddy just five minutes
one hot afternoon – but I'm a man, Forster. And the way
I've lived has been right, Forster, and the way you've
lived has been wrong. You know something? You're
wicked. That's it! You're just wicked. (*He sways at the head
of the stairs.*)

DIDO: For Godsake, Harry!

HARRY: That's all, sweetheart. I've said it. That's all.

DIDO: Well, if you've said it just go off to bed.

HARRY: You want me to go to bed. That's funny. It's no remedy now, Dideeodo. No remedy at all. Can't draw the blanket of love over our heads now. Why can't? Because it's too late. Look, it's morning. Time to get up!

DIDO: Oh, you're –

HARRY: Drunk, I know. These damned stairs! They look to go so far down – they look like they might go to hell.

DIDO: Try them.

HARRY: Hullo.

(*He speaks to CATHERINE, who has come up the stairs.*)

CATHERINE: There you are.

HARRY: Here I am. You want me?

CATHERINE: No, I don't want you. What are you doing up here?

HARRY: Just looked up to tell Forster something.

CATHERINE: The doctor said you were to lie down. Try to sleep.

HARRY: Sleep it off? My hands hurt like hell, Kate. My hands.

CATHERINE: Well, what do you expect? It was a very silly thing to do.

HARRY: It was the only thing to do, surely. I just wanted you to feel something for me. Just anything – pity, or whatever you've left over. (*He goes down the stairs.*)

CATHERINE: Captain Hurst, the Chancellor wants to speak to you.

BRUNO: I've orders not to leave General Forster.

CATHERINE: Who gave you those orders?

BRUNO: The Chancellor.

CATHERINE: Well, then –

BRUNO: Where is he?

CATHERINE: Immediately below.

(*BRUNO goes down the stairs.*)

Are you ready to go?

RUPERT: I'm ready when they are. They said daylight.

(*The first light has come to the eastern sky. DIDO has put on HARRY's sheepskin coat and gone on to the balcony. She stands beside a man who can now be seen beyond the window.*)

CATHERINE: Will you need anything? Anything I can get for you.

RUPERT: I've everything I want. Did Cadmus really ask to
see the boy, or did you invent that?

CATHERINE: No, he asked for him.

RUPERT: Why?

CATHERINE: I don't know. Now I'm trying to think of
something to say that will keep you with me for a little
longer. This seeing people off.

RUPERT: Walk away. Just let me go.

CATHERINE: I've always done that. First to war and then
to prison. All in all, I've been a good soldier's woman,
haven't I? And yet I wish I could have come a little
nearer to you in the past few hours. I've failed. It's not
a pleasant feeling. Have I been too concerned with
myself? I wouldn't like to leave you with the thought
that I've intruded my own unhappiness. Haven't you
anything to say to me?

RUPERT: I don't think so.

CATHERINE: My God, couldn't you make up something
for this moment? Dear, dear Rupert, there's nothing of
the harlot player about you, is there? If you've nothing
to say then you keep quiet. This is goodbye, Rupert –
goodbye. When the trial's over you'll not come back
here. I know that. We'll never see each other again.
Never. I'm sorry. I'm behaving like this because I don't
understand. I've tried. There are some things that are
right to me and there are some things that are wrong.
I can't tell you why they are right or wrong because
I don't know. I suppose like most women I feel – I don't
reason. And it is the feeling for rightness which made me
take you and will make me love you for ever. There.
Now I just want to say goodbye.

RUPERT: Goodbye, Catherine.

CATHERINE: Goodbye.

(*RUPERT has moved to CATHERINE. He puts his arms
about her for a moment. She whispers.*)

No, don't say you love me.

(*CATHERINE goes down the stairs. RUPERT stands
watching her. Then, he calls.*)

RUPERT: Time to go home, Dido.

(*DIDO comes into the room.*)

DIDO: I know. Funny – this morning didn't take me
by surprise.

RUPERT: You were watching for it.

DIDO: I suppose so. Would you like this coat? We could
steal it from Harry. He'd never know. It's warm. Keep
you warm in Arcady, it would.

RUPERT: No.

DIDO: Can I send you things? Will they let me do that?
Cigarettes and things.

RUPERT: I don't smoke.

DIDO: Of course you don't. Well, books and – oh, you
know – cakes. I cook sometimes.

RUPERT: They won't allow anything to be sent.

DIDO: Letters?

RUPERT: No. Save your pennies.

DIDO: All right. You want to finish here and now.

RUPERT: Here and now. I want to give you this, that's all.
(*He takes the jewelled box which was given to him
by CADMUS from a pocket and holds it out to DIDO.*)
Take it.

DIDO: Thank you:

RUPERT: There's nothing in it, I'm afraid. Just a box.
Do to keep your powder dry.

DIDO: Did it belong to Catherine?

RUPERT: No.

DIDO: Then I'll take it. Thank you very much.

RUPERT: I want you to go now. I want you to leave at
once. Don't wait about. On your way give a message to
Captain Hurst from me. You know, the young soldier.

DIDO: What is it?

RUPERT: Tell him he's mistaken if he thinks he has learnt
or will learn anything from my behaviour. I faced the
same problems over the same ground as that man – (*The
wearer of the helmet.*) – and young Hurst will face them in
the future. They are unchanging but the time and place
of decision is personal.

DIDO: I'll try to remember that. To tell him, I mean. Have you anything to tell me?

RUPERT: Only this. Don't stay caught in the memory of the past day. Escape. Get out.

DIDO: I will.

(*She holds out her hand. RUPERT takes it with his left hand. Leaving DIDO he goes to the upper room.*)

RUPERT: Goodbye, Dido.

DIDO: Goodbye.

(*RUPERT enters the upper room. An ANNOUNCER on the public address system of the city speaks.*)

ANNOUNCER: The time is zero four one five hours. The time is zero four one five hours. It is now – officially – day.

(*A bell is struck. The man on the balcony enters the room, crosses, and goes down the stairs. The ANNOUNCER speaks again.*)

Attention! Here is a statement. General Rupert Forster is dead. General Rupert Forster is dead. Further reports follow later.

(*A bell is struck. DIDO is staring towards the upper room. CATHERINE comes from below.*)

CATHERINE: Where?

(*DIDO points to the upper room.*)

Is it true?

DIDO: I don't know.

CATHERINE: Go up. Go up there.

(*DIDO moves slowly to the upper room. CATHERINE calls.*)

Rupert! Rupert!

(*DIDO, at the door of the room, looks back.*)

Go on. Please!

(*DIDO enters the room. CADMUS, alone, comes up the stairs. CATHERINE speaks to him.*)

You're lying! I don't trust you.

(*DIDO returns.*)

DIDO: It's true. There's a little stain at the corner of his mouth.

CADMUS: He'd only to break the glass before his face. He knew well enough.

CATHERINE: And you knew he'd do it.

CADMUS: Yes.

CATHERINE: Surely enough to tell them to say that over the speakers while he was still alive?

CADMUS: Yes. I gave instructions for the guard to be withdrawn and for that announcement to be made at daybreak. I gave those instructions some hours ago. (*DIDO has come down into the room and now goes down the stairs.*)
The news of his return was beginning to get out. The morning papers might have got it. I couldn't allow it to happen that way. I could never have controlled the demand for him. They won't want a dead man. Also that was the only method by which I could tell the opposition of their failure. To tell them I was forced to tell everyone – even you – in that way.

CATHERINE: You were so sure? You can't have been! It was a gamble.

CADMUS: It was a certainty. I knew the man and I knew the situation. That was all I needed.

CATHERINE: Did you know him so well? You must have known him better than I did for I believed he would live.

CADMUS: I knew him as a man to be very much like myself. But he'd something I've had to put away whilst I'm in office. Honour. So I knew what the end would be.

CATHERINE: Honour. That means nothing. A word.

CADMUS: You're thinking of these last hours as a struggle between you and myself for his life. It was nothing of the kind. He was quite free to choose.

CATHERINE: Why do you say that? You wanted him to do it for a purpose.

CADMUS: I don't deny it. But I'm an old man, Catherine, and apart from the smallest things I don't do much to please myself. All I said of the situation in the country at the moment is true.

CATHERINE: You murdered him.

CADMUS: No. We're all victims of injustice, Catherine, every moment of our lives. We can shut ourselves up in the day and lie awake at night dreaming of revenge. But revenge against whom? Against each other? Why? Forster had great cause to dream in that way. It was an injustice that we had to imprison him, and he had reason to sit in that camp in the hills thinking up ways of reckoning. But he didn't do that. All he wanted was to be taken back into the service of the world. The world wouldn't have him and so he turned away. In acceptance. There was no hatred in – him. He was a great soldier. Learn from him.

CATHERINE: Will you learn?

CADMUS: I can't allow myself to do so. At ten o'clock this morning I shall make a statement to the House and tell them the lies they want to hear. I shall belittle Forster's past achievements and say that he died under a burden of conscience. The sooner forgotten the better. That's the great thing. That he should be forgotten.

CATHERINE: Go, now. Go down and tell your lies.

CADMUS: Very well. Do I need to say how much your friendship has meant to me. In the past.

CATHERINE: Are you trying to tell me that you, too, have made a sacrifice?

CADMUS: I suppose I am.

(*BRUNO comes from below.*)

BRUNO: The guard is dismissed, sir.

CADMUS: Thank you, Captain Hurst.

BRUNO: You called me away from him, sir.

CADMUS: What's that?

BRUNO: You called me away. If you'd not done so this wouldn't have happened.

CADMUS: Wouldn't it?

BRUNO: I shall deny dereliction of duty.

CADMUS: It won't be necessary, Captain Hurst. What are you afraid of?

BRUNO: The incident was unavoidable, sir. I didn't want to leave him.

CADMUS: I called you away. The responsibility is mine.

BRUNO: Thank you, sir.

CADMUS: But sometime – when you've nothing better to do – reflect on the consequences to yourself if I'd refused to admit it. Catherine, you'd better have someone here for a day or two. Hurst can make all arrangements for this and that.

CATHERINE: Very well.

CADMUS: May I call on you once again?

CATHERINE: I think not.

(*CADMUS goes down the stairs.*)

BRUNO: The house is no longer under guard, ma'am. You're free to go where you wish.

CATHERINE: Where do you suggest?

BRUNO: There's no need to concern yourself any longer with General Forster. All arrangements will be made.

CATHERINE: Then I'll forget him at once, Captain Hurst. At once.

(*DIDO comes up the stairs. She has changed into her own clothes.*)

DIDO: The old Cadmus man has gone, and now I must be going. I suppose that's all right.

BRUNO: Everyone in the house is quite free now.

DIDO: Well, I've come up to say goodbye.

CATHERINE: Did Rupert tell you what he was going to do?

DIDO: No. He just said goodbye and walked up there.

CATHERINE: You don't seem touched by what's happened.

DIDO: There was nothing else for him to do, was there?

(*BRUNO turns to go from the room.*)

I've got a message for you.

BRUNO: For me?

DIDO: From Rupert. Let me get it right. You're not to think that you learnt anything from him. You'll face the same problems – same place, perhaps – but you've got to find your own way out. All right?

BRUNO: Yes. (*He goes down the stairs.*)

CATHERINE: Did Rupert give you a message for me?

DIDO: No. He said he loved you.

CATHERINE: I'd like you to stay here.

DIDO: I can't do that. The life I live isn't much, I know, but it's the way I want it.

CATHERINE: And you think I'd take that from you.

DIDO: Well, I'd not have it in this place. Why do you want me to stay now? Good turn?

CATHERINE: Oh, no – it's for my sake, not yours. I'd like to try to live again. Help me.

DIDO: Please let me go now.

CATHERINE: Wait! I'm not offering the things I'd have offered before. Money, clothes and amusement. I've learnt enough from you to know they won't keep you. I'm not offering you anything. Listen! You are the only person in nine years who has broken into my life against my wish. I've chosen others – people who wouldn't lead me away from Rupert. So, you see, they can't help me, but you can. Just for a little while, Dido.

DIDO: No! You'll eat me right up. Then you'll be fine, but where shall I be?

CATHERINE: You can have absolute freedom, I promise. Just live here.

DIDO: I like you, Catherine – always have. And you're good and strong, really. You can do it all without me.

CATHERINE: I'm not. Rupert's dead.

DIDO: Well, then, it's too bad. You'll just have to go downhill. Look, the sun's shining. It's going to be a fine day.

(*HARRY comes up the stairs.*)

Perhaps I'll walk out into the country and sleep through the day in the open. Who knows?

HARRY: You going? Hey! you can talk to me. I'm sober.

DIDO: I'd talk to you if there was anything to say, but there isn't. Goodbye. (*She goes down the stairs.*)

HARRY: I've been thinking, Kate. Let's sell up – sell out. You settled here because of him, that's all. Nothing to keep you now. Let's get away.

CATHERINE: No.

HARRY: All right. We stay. Kate, he wasn't any good. He wasn't worth waiting for. It wasn't what he was but what he did. You made a mistake anybody might've made and I'm sorry for you. Truly, I'm sorry for you. He walked

out on you, Kate. I'm staying with you. Surely that's in
my favour. And I'll get on with the picture. Honest.
(*ANSELM and MATTHEW come up the stairs. CATHERINE
has moved to stand looking through the windows over the city.*)
Hullo, boys. So here we are. Let's start the day. I'll do
that with a bath. God! I'm filthy. Kate, can I go and
freshen up?

CATHERINE: Do as you like. There's no need to ask me.
Please go on as you've done in the past. There's all the
time in the world now for us to be kind, for us to do
good. Let me look at you. Come here. How shall we
spend the time? All the time that's left. What shall we do
with it? This fortune to be rid of. Shall we be charitable?
Give me your part and I'll give you mine. But we have
equal portions which makes it absurd. We shall end up
where we began with no more and no less. There'll be no
loss, no gain, but it will pass the time – the time we have
to spend – it will pass the time, this give and take – it
will pass the time: Dear Christ, I'm cold!
(*HARRY takes up the sheepskin coat and puts it over
CATHERINE's shoulders. Then, with his arm about her, he
leads her back into the room. The morning light catches
CATHERINE's face: it shows her as an aged woman.*)

HARRY: Not to worry, Kate. We're here. We won't let
anybody hurt you – not any more we won't.
(*DIDO comes up the stairs.*)
What do you want? Well, what d'you want? You back for
something?

DIDO: (*Whispers.*) Go 'way, Harry.

HARRY: What're you back for?

DIDO: Changed my mind.

HARRY: So, all right, you've changed your mind. From
what to what?

DIDO: Go 'way, Harry, go 'way. (*She moves towards
CATHERINE.*) Catherine. What I know. Can it be
taught? I'll try.

CURTAIN

THE GATES OF SUMMER

Introduction to

THE GATES OF SUMMER

Written in 1953, *The Gates of Summer* was produced in 1956. It is a comedy, but Whiting called it the harshest of his plays. Certainly it is the most cynical, always humorous, but acidly disillusioned and disillusioning.

As in his earlier work, the character who gets closest to heroism is self-conscious about his aspirations. An ex-member of Parliament, John Hogarth sets his sights on a hero's death, fighting Byronically for the freedom of Greece. He has cut loose from his ties in England and sold his assets to finance a rebellion which turns out not to be a popular movement, but a reactionary conspiracy organised by aristocrats. Given £100,000, the elderly Prince Basilios spends it on an elaborate garden party, the idea being to raise funds by charging for admission. But only one guest arrives. Trying compulsively to resolve their conflicts, the characters fail because of the disparity between their ambitions and their abilities.

As in *Marching Song,* we find ourselves in a house situated high above a European capital, but this time the action is set just before – not just after – a world war. This is the summer of 1913. Again we see an older woman struggling with a younger one over a man, and again the main themes are exile, isolation and self-destruction. The older woman, Sophie, left England when she left John Hogarth to marry an archaeologist; John "bought a state of exile" ten years ago by ending an affair with a bishop's wife and uprooting himself.

Like Rupert Forster, John has to make a choice involving death, honour and a woman. He could stay with Caroline, or go north to what, so far as he knows, might be a noble death. Unlike Rupert, though, John is not allowed to act on the decision he takes.

One new theme in this play is the incongruity between the myth of a man's life and its reality. The past John Hogarth is different from the man we meet, and Sophie's memories of him are inaccurate. Dictating her memoirs to an elderly Greek, Cristos, she does not say exactly what she remembers, and he does not write exactly what she says. Sophie is also prepared to interfere with history: knowing a *Times* correspondent, she uses his name on a telegram to the paper, reporting that John has been killed in the mountains, fighting at the head of his troops.

In *A Penny for a Song* there was a touching contrast between the ineffectual grown-ups who were playing soldiers as if they were children and the historical reality of the Napoleonic wars. But this time the historical reality of the 1914 war fails to cast any interesting shadows on the stage action.

Characters

SOPHIE FARAMOND

CRISTOS PAPADIAMANTIS

JOHN HOGARTH

HENRY BEVIS

CAROLINE TRAHERNE

SELWYN FARAMOND

PRINCE BASILIOS

The Gates of Summer started a pre-London tour on 11 September 1956, with the following cast:

SOPHIE,   Isabel Jeans

JOHN,   James Donald

HENRY,   Lionel Jeffries

CAROLINE,   Dorothy Tutin

Director,   Peter Hall

The action of the play takes place in and about a country house in Greece a little way from Athens: the time is the early summer of the year 1913.

ACT ONE

The scene is a room in a country house in Greece, a little way from Athens.

The time is morning of a day in the early summer of the year 1913.

The house is built on two floors, and stands above a valley.

The room has several high windows which allow entrance from a stone terrace. Through these windows can be seen part of an exterior wall which is washed in raspberry colour and contains a small window. A great vine surrounds the house. The floor of the room is stone partly covered by rugs. The ceiling, almost lost in shadow, is painted. There is a main door to the room which stands open showing the wide sweep of a stairway beyond. There is also a small arched entrance from a passage which leads to other parts of the house by way of a few shallow steps.

Within the room it remains cool as yet, and the shadows are only now beginning to shift. The sun strikes through the windows and brings to life in a vivid way several objects in the room – a scarlet shawl thrown over a chair, a piece of jewellery, a gold cross hanging on the egg-shell white wall – and the brilliance of these are marked in the quickening heat.

SOPHIE FARAMOND is standing at the window looking out across the terrace, and down the hill. She is fifty-four years old, and she can stare boldly into the morning sun for she is very beautiful. She has never feared the light: she has never feared anything except, perhaps, the consequences of her vanity.

In a far shadowed corner of the room is CRISTOS PAPADIAMANTIS, a Greek, sixty years of age. He is standing at a tall desk and holds a pen.

SOPHIE turns into the room.

SOPHIE: Put down the pen.
   (*CRISTOS does so.*)
   The man we have been trying to create is coming up the hill. (*She turns to the window.*) John.

(*JOHN HOGARTH has come up the hill, and on to the terrace. He now stands in the window. He has a top coat over his shoulders, and carries a hat and gloves.*)

JOHN: The house stands alone above a wilderness. It's the colour of fruit and looking up the traveller asks, Will it topple? I'll be at the windows on the south side, you said. And it's all true.

SOPHIE: There was a postscript to my letter. It said, Recognise me at once, please.

JOHN: (*He kisses SOPHIE.*) Haven't I?

SOPHIE: Yes.

JOHN: With the best will in the world I couldn't let you know when I'd be here. Have you been patient?

SOPHIE: For ten years. After such a time it would have been natural to send you false instructions.

JOHN: I left Alexandria three days ago and crossed in a boat with a party of olive green pilgrims. I stayed last night in Athens, but didn't sleep because of the song of the cats and the silent mischief of the bugs. So I hired a cart and set off at dawn with your letter in my hand. Here it is. It holds ten years of silence, Sophie. From the day you left England to come out here. Time to go, you said – and go you did. Why?

SOPHIE: I was becoming aware of my age. That's a reason. But you're young – shall I say thirty-six? – and you've left England, never to go back. Or have I misunderstood?

JOHN: No. Everything's been sold up.

SOPHIE: Then I imagine you must be burdened with a great deal of money. What have you done with it?

JOHN: Bought a state of exile.

SOPHIE: Shameful! Not a proper purpose.

JOHN: I'm free. Sophie.

SOPHIE: Again? For how long?

JOHN: Until the end. The first step into middle age did it.

SOPHIE: Who was she?

JOHN: Her name was Ada. You see I can speak of her in the past. She had very short legs, was a comfortable shape and the wife of a bishop. On the night of my thirty-fifth birthday her arms were round my neck, and she was whispering to me. The next morning I began the sale of everything I possessed. When it was done I felt remarkable. Sanctified. I had nothing in the world but money.

(*CRISTOS moves into the room.*)

SOPHIE: This is Mr Cristos Papadiamantis, my secretary. Mr John Hogarth, from England.

(*CRISTOS bows to JOHN.*)

(*To CRISTOS.*) We won't do any more this morning. Go up, please, and make a fair copy as far as we've gone.

(*CRISTOS goes from the room and up the stairs.*)

I spend a few hours every day dictating to Cristos. I'm putting down some of my memories. You'll be able to sharpen my recollection on a number of incidents of the time in England we knew together.

JOHN: Are you writing the truth?

SOPHIE: Yes.

JOHN: Then you're not going to publish.

SOPHIE: Certainly I am. This autumn.

JOHN: That'll upset a lot of people. But I suppose this is a safe distance. The most they can do is hang your publisher.

SOPHIE: You escaped, I see.

JOHN: Without violence to my person, yes. The signal for my going was the baying of the newspapers. There were no tears. Except from that woman shut up in the country. She would be weeping, we can be sure of that, and in a lower room holding a holy book in one hand and biting the nails of the other would be her husband. They're probably still at it, God help them! She tried to lead me to the righteous life, Sophie. That was her only mistake. You know where such excursion must end. On this occasion it was an episcopal four-poster in a cathedral town. The rooks mourned over us through the night.

SOPHIE: I'd hoped he wasn't a provincial bishop.

JOHN: He forgave me like the good man he is, but that wasn't enough for Ada. She had to make a public confession to a national newspaper. Modesty prevents me saying why.

SOPHIE: Then I'll say it for you. She wanted everyone to know how lucky she had been. After all, John, I've always considered myself happy to know you in the drawing-room, so I can appreciate Ada's feelings. There, I'm already speaking of her as an old friend.

JOHN: In the end I took nothing but her teaching to heart and sold up my worldly goods. I've put the proceeds to an ungodly purpose. Which brings me here. Alone.

SOPHIE: The difficulty of exile for a woman is that she can't go unaccompanied. I had to provide myself with an escort at a small church in Kensington on the Tuesday before I sailed.

JOHN: Ah, yes. I'm sorry. How is Selwyn? Where is Selwyn?

SOPHIE: Buried alive at the dig below. You passed the place on the road. Selwyn has been working the excavation for eighteen months. He's found nothing.

JOHN: Is there anything to be found?

SOPHIE: Selwyn is sure of it. There have been several false alarms and then a most unpleasant man has hurried here from the Royal Museum in Berlin. They're putting up money.

JOHN: Has Selwyn found anything under the ground in these ten years of digging?

SOPHIE: Nothing important. For six years we dug over most of the North African desert. Excavations in Egypt rewarded us with a gold commode. And so we came to this place.

JOHN: What's he looking for here?

SOPHIE: He seems to think he may uncover some place of worship of great antiquity. Am I right, Henry?
(She speaks to HENRY BEVIS, who has come into the room.)

HENRY: Quite right, Sophie.

SOPHIE: Henry Bevis is with us, John, as a Special Correspondent to *The Times*. This is Mr Hogarth from London, Henry.

HENRY: From London!
(He shakes hands with JOHN.)
How is that beautiful country of ours?

JOHN: Have you been away from it a long time, Mr Bevis?

HENRY: Yes.

JOHN: I thought so. Well, it was looking very pretty in the spring.

HENRY: And the people?

JOHN: They've never been pretty at any time of year, have they? But I thought they were looking very fit.

SOPHIE: Henry's absence from England isn't voluntary, John. He was sent here to report on whatever is found in that great hole Selwyn is digging. How he's managed to fill a column of *The Times*, once every two weeks I've never understood. Surely, Henry, there must be a limit to the number of ways even you can describe such quantities of mud.

HENRY: It's the suspense, Sophie. No one knows exactly what Selwyn hopes to find.

SOPHIE: I'd have thought the flutter of anticipation even in those small archaeological circles about St James's Square must now be stilled after eighteen months.

HENRY: You mustn't expect quick results in this kind of work, Sophie. Must she, Mr Hogarth?

JOHN: I've no idea.

HENRY: Selwyn has all the patience of an old soldier.

SOPHIE: Yes, I suppose those many years of quite undistinguished service must have taught him that.

HENRY: How unlike you are. Is that the basis for a successful marriage, I wonder?

SOPHIE: Don't brood over me, Henry.

JOHN: Sophie, I've remembered something. When I got out of the cart at the bottom of the hill I left a box at the side of the road.

SOPHIE: One of the men can bring it up later.

HENRY: I'll go down for it.

JOHN: You'll do nothing of the kind. It's very heavy, and that hill is very steep.

HENRY: I'm going down to the dig. I can bring the box back with me. I'll be pleased to do that, Mr Hogarth.

JOHN: Well, thank you.

HENRY: A word: very unwise to leave anything about here. (*HENRY goes out through the window.*)

SOPHIE: Such an old young man. And how the poor creature sweats in this climate. Why did you suddenly remember your box?

JOHN: It was the mention of marriage.

SOPHIE: I don't see any connection.

JOHN: We were on the edge of a discussion. I wanted to avoid it.

SOPHIE: You'll find when you get to know him that it's never difficult to knock Henry off a subject. But he's been meditating on marriage for some weeks now.

JOHN: Must I get to know him?

SOPHIE: Well, how long are you staying?

JOHN: I'll be here two days if everything goes well.

SOPHIE: Why should it go badly? Come here. Yes, there about your eyes – God help you, those are lines of thought. I'd say of recent contemplation.

JOHN: We're well into the twentieth century, Sophie. You're going to have to accustom yourself to a change in the faces of those you love.

SOPHIE: And a change in their habits, it seems. Where are you going from here?

JOHN: When I left Ada curled up and quilt covered for the last time and went back to my rooms I'd decided to sell out. Everything around me – except a bottle of gin – lay cowering beneath the hammer. I stayed alone for two days. The storm had broken about me and Ada. There were no letters except postcards with a single word, usually of a biblical nature. No one came near me but my ancient firelighter. Then, on the second night, there was a shout on the stairs. I thought at first the mob had come. I picked up the poker and went to meet it. Instead of the sanscullottes I found an old man entangled in the curtains of the stairs – caught like a gigantic bat. I freed him. He embraced me. I freed myself. He went on and collapsed like a ruin before the fire and at once began to talk. He used none of the words recently associated with me.

Indeed, he's never heard of Ada, he said. He talked and the words were as fresh to me as his friendliness. He loved me, he said, for I was a son of freedom. He, too, Basilios, was a son of freedom. I was again taken in his arms. He talked through the night. At half-past five I gave him my cheque for one hundred thousand pounds. At half-past seven I gave him my hand and the promise of my services. At half-past nine he left. But there remained on the table a document which made altogether too clear my future commitment to revolution.

SOPHIE: Revolution. So that's the news you've brought me. I think you've been ingenuous. You'll never see your friend again, and certainly not your money.

JOHN: Basilios is a man – the one sex I don't make mistakes about. He'll be here to fetch me as he promised within two days.

SOPHIE: You're very sure.

JOHN: I've reason to be. Basilios talked to me in a language I've known since childhood. Yet until that night I'd never heard it spoken.

SOPHIE: Do you mean Greek?

JOHN: I mean the language of action.

SOPHIE: Am I to expect barricades on my doorstep?

JOHN: No. I shall travel north four hundred miles to the trouble centre. The affair is small enough for me to play a big part. I shall be happy.

(*CAROLINE TRAHERNE comes into the room by the windows. She is twenty-five years old. She carries a large bunch of wildflowers and herbs which are recently gathered.*)

SOPHIE: Do you know John Hogarth, Caroline?

CAROLINE: (*Together.*) Yes.

JOHN: (*Together.*) No.

SOPHIE: Well, yes, or no, this is he. Mrs Traherne, John. My daughter by Selwyn's first wife.

JOHN: How do you do. Have I met you before?

CAROLINE: No. But I know you from Sophie's book.

JOHN: That's very interesting.

(*He at last gently disengages his hand from CAROLINE.*)

SOPHIE: Those are most unsuitable flowers for the house.

CAROLINE: I brought them in to save them from the heat of the sun.

SOPHIE: Save them? But you've uprooted them.

CAROLINE: Well, then, their last hours can be cool and dignified. Unlike Henry, who is staggering about in the sun under an enormous box. (*She goes from the room by the passageway.*)

JOHN: I'd no idea Selwyn had a daughter. Did you know when you married him?

SOPHIE: It was mentioned. She was a child then, of course. In the keeping of some nuns.

JOHN: What's she doing here?

SOPHIE: Recovering from a disastrous marriage contracted seven years ago when she was eighteen.

JOHN: Who was her mother?

SOPHIE: Nobody at all. She lies buried beneath a solitary tree in the Orient. A sacrifice to Selwyn's military career.

JOHN: What did the girl mean when she said that she knew me from your book?

SOPHIE: I didn't know she'd read it.

JOHN: It means, though, that you've written about me.

SOPHIE: Of course. Do you think I could write of those days and forget you? Without you there'd be no story to tell. Let's always remember there was nothing but the years between us then.

JOHN: There's more than age between us now, Sophie. There are the separate ways which brought us here. You came in resignation. I've come in affirmation. That day ten years ago, the day you married Selwyn. I mourned for you then, Sophie.

SOPHIE: You feel I made the one certificate serve for both marriage and death.

JOHN: Everyone does that. No, I mourned the end of an era which you had made so much your own. I think I could have borne it if you'd died – but you married! You became a woman, Sophie. Oh, Sophie!

SOPHIE: It was the morning of a birthday. I awoke very much alone. You were in the country. What were you doing? I forget. No one came near me for hours, it seemed. Then your gift was brought to me. Ah! you were still young at that time to give me birthday presents without flinching. I took off the wrappings and there was the musical box. Something to be given to a child – or to me. I opened the lid and the music began. And with the music the tears. I knew then it was time to go. Selwyn had often called to tell me he was planning this exploration of the past. I'd known him for many years. I'd long admired his amazing spirit. We were of an age and both needed a companion in exile. I proposed marriage that evening, and was accepted.

JOHN: When I came back from the country you were married and gone without a word. No one knew why. All they said was that you seemed serious. I wouldn't believe it.

SOPHIE: Surely that was a time to take something seriously, even if it was only Selwyn. But you – here – now – what excuse have you? At the kindergarten age of thirty-five you're intending to take seriously – what? – a revolt, the rallying cries of manifestos and a mad old man.

JOHN: Yes, all those. And the reason is this: thirty-five – yes, I am – but how do I account for these grey hairs and the fact that I no longer make love without sadness? My contemporaries remain darkly pigmented and continue to go to bed laughing. So you must think of me, Sophie, as one who has also reached a time, if not an age, to be serious.

SOPHIE: Very well. But you mustn't expect me to talk about revolution and freedom. That's not my kind of seriousness.

JOHN: Once you had no seriousness at all.

SOPHIE: In those days. But was there so much to be serious about? No. You could always find something if you went looking for it Like trouble. Why should I have bothered? I was what is called happy. That's nothing to be solemn about. At least, it wasn't when I was young. Perhaps it is these days. I don't know. Now you've an

occupation I expect you look back in horror on the years
we spent in London. I think that's a pity.

JOHN: Not horror. This feeling of sadness for what I loved.
(*CAROLINE has come into the room.*)

CAROLINE: I know very well what you mean. Age doesn't
come into it, Sophie. That's a mistake you would make.
You can be finished at twenty-four.

JOHN: How old are you?

CAROLINE: Twenty-five.

JOHN: And you're finished?

CAROLINE: Yes. Hasn't Sophie told you?
(*HENRY comes through the windows. He is bowed beneath a
large box which he carries on his shoulders.*)

JOHN: Many, many thanks. Are you all right? I feel we
should get it up at once, Sophie. Where am I?
(*SOPHIE points through the main windows to the small
window set in the exterior wall.*)

SOPHIE: You're there.
(*HENRY moves towards the stairs with the box.*)

JOHN: I'd better go with him, I think.
(*JOHN follows HENRY from the room.*)

CAROLINE: Is he staying?

SOPHIE: John? For a while. He's on his way to a revolution.
He seems to think it should begin the day after tomorrow.

CAROLINE: He's on every page of your book, you know.
Even the pages where he's not mentioned. For he's the
time you can't get out of your head.

SOPHIE: How do you come to have seen the book?

CAROLINE: I kissed Cristos and he showed it to me.

SOPHIE: You're corrupt in almost every way.

CAROLINE: Why do people put up with me?

SOPHIE: Your husband didn't.

CAROLINE: Don't be sentimental. You wouldn't have liked
Boy Traherne, either.

SOPHIE: I dislike him intensely for one thing. That is,
running off and making it necessary for you to be here
at this time.

CAROLINE: Do you think he'd be interested in my tragic
story?

SOPHIE: He? Call him by his name.

(*After a considerable pause CAROLINE softly and tentatively says.*)

CAROLINE: John. (*She laughs.*) Ouf! that first time you say a name as a name. Some cold bath, eh? But once you're in – hey! you're in – and it's fine and healthy. John. John! (*She raises her voice.*) John! John!

(*JOHN appears at the window of his room and looks down.*)

JOHN: Yes?

CAROLINE: Nothing.

(*JOHN goes back into the room.*)

The man in the book: the man in the bedroom. Now, then – I've to put them together, haven't I, to make sense?

SOPHIE: To make a man.

CAROLINE: Well, to start with he was born, like the rest. Somewhere in a drawer there'll be faded photographs of a naked baby, which he was, one time. It's always wise to remember that. So things went well, and he began to grow.

SOPHIE: He came to London when he was eighteen. Where did he come from? I've never bothered to ask. Where does love come from? He had money – his mother was an American. He had energy – his father was a Scot. Yet he had no pretensions. He didn't want to do anything with his money or himself.

CAROLINE: And he lived splendidly, at that time.

SOPHIE: Yes.

CAROLINE: What was the secret? The something you know. Tell me. I've an idea he was happy.

SOPHIE: I think he was. Although –

CAROLINE: That's not in your book.

SOPHIE: I shall come to it.

CAROLINE: Come to it now. With me. In your book you call him the first twentieth century man. What do you mean by that?

SOPHIE: He was the only man I knew who seemed perfectly unequipped to face the future. I knew he'd survive.

CAROLINE: Riddles. Good. He's not simple. Good.

SOPHIE: It's an unfortunate fact, Caroline, that the qualities needed for survival as a person are the same unsocial qualities which can destroy an individual, a community, or even a nation. So the lack of moral equipment of the genius and the great criminal are much the same. It's what you haven't got that matters. John's great strength was that he lacked seriousness.

CAROLINE: It's the answer. No unhappiness, in other words.

SOPHIE: And no love.

CAROLINE: Between the weak wail of arrival and the whimper of departure there is not cause for alarm but cause for laughter. Can I see it that way – with him – through him? Can I?

SOPHIE: Wait a minute. I'm speaking of John ten years ago. He's changed.

CAROLINE: A man who believed all that – why should he want to change? Looked at his way, it suddenly becomes worth doing – this hanging around. No one wants to play out the thing seriously, but if it's really a charade – well, then! – how d'you do. (*She looks up at the window.*)

SOPHIE: He left England in all seriousness. He left Ada –

CAROLINE: Ah! she was the great scandal, wasn't she? Ada, you say. Like that. And then tell me he left in all seriousness.

SOPHIE: He was very fond of her.

CAROLINE: Since my husband left me I've become attached to a hot water bottle on cold nights. Seriously? Not at all. A man doesn't give up a country for a flannel bound comforter.

SOPHIE: He didn't. He gave it up to start a revolution. That's the business in hand.

(*HENRY has come down the stairs and is now in the room.*)

CAROLINE: And that's a solemn fact, is it?

SOPHIE: So he says. Is it the heat, Henry?

HENRY: I've been talking to Hogarth.

CAROLINE: Did he make you laugh?

HENRY: Good God, no. He's been telling me the most terrible stories of the people he's going to in the north. I'd never have thought such injustice went on these days.

SOPHIE: He's impressed you, I see.

HENRY: Such sincerity must be impressive.

SOPHIE: (*To CAROLINE.*) You see what I mean? (*She goes from the room and up the stairs.*)

HENRY: Caroline, would you say I'm a sensitive man?

CAROLINE: As a literary gent, Henry, you're a duck.

HENRY: I only ask because sometimes I seem to lack an appreciation of the suffering of others. The conversation with Hogarth made me understand that. It worries me. I know perfectly well that unhappiness exists, but I've never been able to think of a way to do anything about it. You, for example – now, I know you've been very unhappy. When you first came here I tried to help you with my companionship. But it wasn't any good, was it?

CAROLINE: No.

HENRY: I think your kind of unhappiness confused me. I'm very muddled about marriage.

CAROLINE: Who isn't?

HENRY: I am more than most people. What I'm trying to say is this: I don't think I'm big enough to take on a revolution as Hogarth's doing, but I think I could help you. I say, I think I could help you. To be happy – happier.

CAROLINE: All right. Go ahead.

HENRY: Now?

CAROLINE: Well, it depends on what sort of comfort you're thinking of giving me.
(*There is a pause.*)

HENRY: Do you read poetry? I mention this because when I was a boy I was lonely and unhappy and I found it a great help.

CAROLINE: Henry, I need more than a rhymed couplet.

HENRY: That's what I mean. I never seem to be able to suggest anything – helpful. It's this place, I think. Although most of us are English the values seem to be different.

CAROLINE: You miss London.

HENRY: Very much.

CAROLINE: Why don't you go back?

HENRY: I shall, as soon as your father's finished the excavation and I can put in my final article. If he finds something I can really write about – something to which I can do justice – well, it'll make my name. That's what I'm bargaining for. I think I'd better go down to the dig for my morning session now. Care to walk with me?

CAROLINE: No. What do you do down there?

HENRY: Sometimes I do a little sifting, but not often. I don't get on with the workmen.

(*JOHN has come down the stairs and now enters the room.*)

Anyway, that's where I'll be for a while, Caroline.

(*HENRY goes out through the windows.*)

JOHN: Sophie tell me that you've been very unhappy.

CAROLINE: There was a time.

JOHN: You're getting over it.

CAROLINE: Yes. It was nothing. A marriage. He left me. Ran away.

JOHN: I see.

CAROLINE: Do you see it from his point of view or mine?

JOHN: His, I suppose. I'm also running away from a marriage. Not my own. Someone else's.

CAROLINE: He just went into hiding. From what I hear you're making for the open country.

JOHN: I hope so.

CAROLINE: You're looking for more than the heroism of love.

JOHN: I'd say the stoicism of love. Yes, more than that.

CAROLINE: Liberation.

JOHN: Of others. Not myself.

CAROLINE: Have you been talking to Sophie?

JOHN: For a moment. But she insisted on asking a lot of questions, so I came away.

CAROLINE: She thinks you've changed.

JOHN: She's quite right.

CAROLINE: I don't think so.

JOHN: How can you possibly know?

CAROLINE: By remembering what I've read about you. Not only in Sophie's book, but in the newspapers. All show the man you are. Why should you want to change?

JOHN: What are you talking about?

CAROLINE: You. I'm talking about you.

JOHN: Have you been interested so long?

CAROLINE: As long as I can remember. I'm not concerned with the morality of your behaviour in the past. I'm concerned that you're here – now. Why won't you look at me? There. What do you see?

JOHN: I've had the last conversation of this kind in my life!

CAROLINE: Sophie told me her name. It was Ada.

JOHN: Very well, so it was Ada.

CAROLINE: And because of her the London mob threw stones at your windows. That was in the papers. Was she worth it?

JOHN: They'd got it into their heads that I was breaking up something very dear to their hearts: a home. You know how that country domesticates its idols. The main demonstration was a parade past my house of elderly women carrying banners. That went on for some hours. I felt compelled to send them out tea and sandwiches. They leant against the railings eating and drinking and booing whenever I passed a window.

CAROLINE: Women have always felt strongly about you.

JOHN: Women feel too much about everything. That is the dreadful inequality of sex. It was their reserve capacity for actively demonstrating emotion which at last defeated me. Poets are lucky. They can spin out the truth of their passion to at least the length of a sonnet. With my lesser talent I've had to content myself with a brisk action and one short word.

CAROLINE: Which so often led to broken windows.

JOHN: All the best games end in destruction.

CAROLINE: We never get out of the nursery where everything finishes broken up. You played the whole of your life in London that way, didn't you? Without seriousness, because you knew the time would come when you'd have to put your toys away. So better smash them! You were right. You were quite right.

JOHN: How would such behaviour help you?

CAROLINE: If I'd seen my marriage with Boysie – and the breakaway – as you saw your love affairs, then I wouldn't have been unhappy. By the way, I'm not unhappy any more. Why should I be? Throughout my married life I believed that love – you know, the rubnose, softpaw kind – was calculable. It never entered my head not to take it seriously. You, on the other hand, saw it as an incidental. That seems to be reasonable.

JOHN: Is this reasonable? Dawn. London. I wake. It's night within the room until the curtains are drawn back. The bed-covers over my body are heavy as sin. Throw them off! Step freely – ha ha! boldly – to the window. Draw back the curtains. Stare at the sky for a sign. Hmm. It's raining. The policeman at the corner is weeping. The cold strikes me like an unkind reminder. Last night's warrior becomes a goose-pimpled pudding. Cover the poor mockery with a gown. The day must be begun, it seems. Very well, then – good morning. Breakfast. The day's news beside the tray. So, there's energy to engage that still virgin for a start. She gives up her miserable secrets reluctantly, column by column, and the sign is not one of them. Go, light fires! Open the letters of the day. Will one hold the word, the news from another land, the call to action? No. They demand, beg, entreat, abuse – nothing more. Dress. Talk to myself in the looking-glass. Walk out. Meet a man. He complains of my treatment of his daughter. He threatens me with action. Action! Christ, if it were true. He means litigation, which is the English substitute. My interest in him has gone and so, I see, has the sun. Something must be done if only to put in my journal. Well, turn in here. It is a theatre where men knock each other about with wooden swords and die, get up, and bow. The curtain rattles down on the play and the day. Hohum! The sky remains inscrutable – positively unhelpful. Curtain it off with the rest. It is another room – another place. I'm welcome. There's no doubt about it. Here between the sheets there is something to be done with authority, if not with dignity. Let me look at the face before turning away. It smiles, so all's well. Goodnight.

Good morning. Dawn. London. I wake. It's night
within the room until the curtains are drawn back. The
bed-covers over my body – and so on. Day by day by
night-time. Reasonable?

CAROLINE: There is one thing.

JOHN: Tell me.

CAROLINE: The moment of happiness which was in the
smiling face before you turned away.

JOHN: It was never a very intelligent face.

CAROLINE: Nothing to do with it. Always reasonable to
make someone happy.

JOHN: I'm sorry. Not possible now. Sorry. My appointment
is not with you, I'm afraid. It's with a man who took me
by the hand and dragged me from childhood – all those
broken toys, remember – to this present time. Basilios.

CAROLINE: It is a serious business, I see. Why did he
choose you?

JOHN: Some years ago my friends wanted to get me
settled. Before I knew what was happening I found
myself to be a Member of Parliament. It seemed a good
time to make a speech. The motion happened to
concern the Government's attitude to this minority
group under Basilios in the north. They had recently
shot the British Minister, and subjected his wife and
daughter to humiliating proposals which both had
accepted before returning to England.

CAROLINE: One of the lesser perils of our Imperial policy.

JOHN: In a speech to the House opposing reprisals
I suggested the country should be accepted into the
British Empire. It seemed that at the moment of
surrender both ladies had been wrapped in a Union Jack.
No one agreed with me that it was the natives' way of
honouring the flag and the speech was dismissed as an
impertinence. Yet it was a report of that speech in an old
newspaper which brought Basilios to me. The faded
cutting was in his pocket. It remained the one call to
unity and action his country had ever known. Spoken by
me when I didn't know the place was on the map. How
could I resist such an appeal to leadership?

CAROLINE: So the whole thing's a joke, after all. Just a joke, as it was in the past. You don't take it any more seriously than – Ada? – or perhaps me. You haven't changed.

JOHN: I don't want to be unreasonable about this. An incident which begins as a joke can have serious consequences. You've been unhappy, I know, but please don't ask me to console you. Anyway, there would hardly be time, for Basilios will be here before you can say, I love you.

CAROLINE: I love you.

(*SELWYN FARAMOND and HENRY come into the room by the windows. They stop on hearing JOHN's last words to CAROLINE.*)

SELWYN: Then marry her, my dear fellow. Congratulations. Good news. I've been worried about the child. How are you otherwise?

JOHN: Otherwise I'm very well. What on earth are you talking about, Selwyn?

SELWYN: Declaration of love. Made by you both as I came in. Bevis heard it. Yes?

HENRY: Yes.

SELWYN: Never mind. I shouldn't have come in at that moment.

CAROLINE: Why did you?

SELWYN: I want a bath. Be a daughter to me and tell the men to carry up hot water.

(*CAROLINE goes out by the passageway.*)

Dirty work, Hogarth.

JOHN: What?

SELWYN: This digging.

JOHN: Oh, I see what you mean. Yes, it must be.

SELWYN: But I think it will be worth it. I'm sure we're about to uncover something remarkable.

(*He takes a small maquette of a human figure from his pocket and holds it out to JOHN.*)

What do you make of that?

JOHN: (*He takes the figure.*) It's a woman, isn't it?

SELWYN: Yes. One of the workmen found it yesterday. Significant attitude of worship, don't you think?

JOHN: It seems familiar. I don't know why.

SELWYN: If we can get something from this site it will shake them up in London. I want to do the BM crowd in the eye. They've never shown any interest in my work. If it wasn't for the Germans we'd not be able to go on. England's done nothing for the expedition.

HENRY: Are you being quite fair, Selwyn? *The Times* has kept the country informed. Through me.

SELWYN: Hogarth, what's this about you being on your way to some trouble in the north? Is it another of Bevis's fairy stories?

JOHN: No, it's true.

SELWYN: Then do be careful. The political situation in the Balkans has never been so confused. Why are you going? Have you been sent by the Crown?

JOHN: Good God, no! I wanted to leave England.

SELWYN: That's a substantial reason. Some woman, was it?

JOHN: All women. I wanted to get away from the whole business.

SELWYN: There was no need to go to the length of starting a revolution. You could have helped me. Nothing like digging and sifting for keeping the mind off sex.

JOHN: I suppose not.

SELWYN: Bevis has found it invaluable. Haven't you? When I was in the Army and it became troublesome I'd always call a church parade. Made the men rather unhappy turning out so late at night, but it always worked. Still, everyone has their own method.

JOHN: Well, it's a personal problem. Here.

(*He gives the figure to SELWYN.*)

SELWYN: Sophie's pleased to see you, I expect.

JOHN: Yes. We've been talking.

SELWYN: About the old days? She pretends she doesn't miss them. And she pretends very well. Stay on for a while, my dear boy, and keep her amused as you did in the past. And Caroline. She had a bad time before she came here. Married a bastard. Stay. We're not much troubled by the nuisances of London. The weather's good, the local people

are friendly to everyone except Bevis, and we don't have
to be pleasant to each other if we don't want to. As for
women – no worry about them here. They're a simple
good people without the refinements which make life such
hell in London. Stay on, do.

(*CAROLINE comes back into the room.*)

CAROLINE: They're getting your bath ready. The water
will be in by the time you've undressed.

SELWYN: Thank you, Carol. Come up and talk to me,
Hogarth. Have a bath if you like.

JOHN: I'll come and talk. Are you going back to England
when you've finished here?

SELWYN: No. Sophie and I'll never go back. There's some
very interesting work to be done in Asia Minor. I may
join in. Different period, of course. Same digging.

(*SELWYN and JOHN go out of the room and up the stairs.*)

HENRY: I try to make myself believe that I feel such an
outsider because I'm here as an official observer. No more.

CAROLINE: (*She is looking after JOHN.*) He's only a visitor.

HENRY: Hogarth? Yes, but he seems to have the art of
engaging himself at once. I heard enough of your
conversation as I came in to know that he's given you
more comfort in a few words than I've been able to give
in months. I suppose it's the way he said it.

CAROLINE: It's not a matter of words, Henry. That's the
mistake you're making. Read poetry, you said. There
you were off the mark. I went through a poetical
marriage. Boysie knew about every art except one. Life
with him was never too damned beautiful for words.
There were so many to be spoken, sung, whispered,
written, rhymed, scratched on the window pane, carved
into wood and stone – words for everyday use and
casually slung at each other, words for public abuse and
shouted from the housetops, words with single meaning
and words with double meaning, good words, bad
words, holy words and dirty words. And when the day
was over and you'd think the talking would have to
stop – no, there'd always be that dribble of stale words

for explanation of failure, betrayal, misery and horror. Buried beneath, suffocated, dead, was love.

HENRY: Now you listen to Hogarth. Intently.

CAROLINE: Henry, couldn't you take an overwhelming interest in something?

HENRY: I think I could if I tried.

CAROLINE: I don't mean in me. I mean food or politics or God. Or something.

HENRY: Would that help you?

CAROLINE: Not at all. But why should you help me?

HENRY: I cling to that as the one definite purpose I have.

CAROLINE: Nonsense! You're a journalist put down in this place for quite another reason. You're probably the only person I know, Henry, for whom hard work is the solution.

HENRY: My work, yes. Is it shocking to you that the concern of my life is bread and butter?

CAROLINE: Less shocking than your ambitions: to be in love, to be somewhere else than here, to be someone. Think what you'll take on if you achieve all that.

HENRY: I'm not ashamed of my ambitions. And never forget, Caroline, that you can build palaces, even empires, on bread and butter.

(*CRISTOS has come down the stairs and into the room.*)

CAROLINE: What do you want?

CRISTOS: I thought you were alone.

CAROLINE: I can be. Can't I, Henry?

(*HENRY walks out of the room by the windows.*)

CRISTOS: That was unkind. I didn't mean to interrupt you.

CAROLINE: We were only talking about ourselves. Same subject as usual.

CRISTOS: What I'm obliged by custom to call your unhappiness.

CAROLINE: You don't believe it, do you?

CRISTOS: No. Do you?

CAROLINE: Not any more.

CRISTOS: I expect you were angry when your husband left you. Englishwomen are good losers in every game, except marriage.

CAROLINE: Oh damn! Where is he.

CRISTOS: Talking to Selwyn in his bath.

CAROLINE: You know who I mean.

CRISTOS: Apparently I do.

CAROLINE: Have you met him?

CRISTOS: For a moment. I've known a John Hogarth for some months, of course. Very well. (*He holds up two small notebooks he is carrying.*)

CAROLINE: From Sophie's book.

CRISTOS: I'm very interested. Is it the same man?

CAROLINE: Yes, he's the person Sophie's been writing about.

CRISTOS: I know that. Let me put it this way: is it the man in the book you're willing to come down those stairs?

CAROLINE: It's a question of identity. I see what you mean.

CRISTOS: I remember the morning you sat with me reading these books. You were smiling. I found it very disturbing. Sophie and I seemed to have done the job too well! Did you smile when you met the other Hogarth? Not the man Sophie and I put together, but the man of independent action. They're not the same.

CAROLINE: Why tell me that?

CRISTOS: You're English, and so you're likely to prefer a romantic fiction to the real thing. If you were Greek or French – or even German – I'd not be saying this to you.

CAROLINE: It sounds like a warning.

CRISTOS: I mean it to be that.

(*SOPHIE comes down the stairs and into the room.*)

CAROLINE: Can you really believe, Cristos, that I'm still young enough to be in love with a man in a book?

CRISTOS: I wanted to be sure that you're not.

SOPHIE: Now John Hogarth's here I hope I'm not going to find people standing in corners talking about him all the time.

CAROLINE: Cristos was giving me advice.

SOPHIE: Would you like to tell me what it was?

CAROLINE: He thinks that after my misery with Boysie I may be on the look out for an ideal. He's afraid that I've found it in your book under the name of Hogarth. He pointed out that there's a man of that name in the house at the moment. However, I'm not to confuse them. They're not the same. The man in the book's a fiction. According to Cristos.

SOPHIE: That's untrue. My memory's as clear as a spyglass.

(*HENRY comes in through the windows.*)

HENRY: I say, I think somebody responsible should come down to the dig. Something's happened. I'm not quite sure what. One of the workmen has fallen through a hole and disappeared, but there seems to be far more to it than that.

CAROLINE: Selwyn's in his bath.

HENRY: If I could understand what those fellows are talking about it might help.

CRISTOS: I'll come down. I speak the same language as those fellows.

HENRY: So you do. But then you are Greek, aren't you?

CRISTOS: Yes. It's very helpful.

(*HENRY and CRISTOS go out through the windows.*)

SOPHIE: How happy Henry will be if at last that excavation gives up its secret. He'll be able to write this final brilliant despatch we've heard do much about and return at once to London and honour. What will you do?

CAROLINE: By that time I hope to have found someone else to put up with me.

SOPHIE: I suppose you mean John. Will you make your intentions clear to him? In so many words.

CAROLINE: Are you jealous – Mummie?

SOPHIE: A little. Then again I don't think you're good enough for him. I never knew your husband – indeed, I've never met anyone who admitted to doing so – but from what you've told me I'd say he was tolerant and kind, if not very bright. And he left you.

CAROLINE: You, anyway, are not going to let me forget that.

SOPHIE: Not for a moment.

CAROLINE: Well, at least I had the nerve to get married when I was young. Unlike you, who'd never take the risk until you were old enough to enter into this arid married state with Father.

SOPHIE: That's a point. I suppose it does take courage when you're young. Especially when you intend to marry someone called Boysie Traherne.

CAROLINE: What about John Hogarth?

SOPHIE: Darling he'd never marry you. He might pop you under the covers for an hour or two.

CAROLINE: I wouldn't be lonely and unwanted for that little time at least.

SOPHIE: So that's what you're expecting. Have you forgotten? He's here for a different purpose. He's not travelling for pleasure this time. My dear child, it's a fact that men sometimes get sick of us; not individually or personally, but sick of our whole ravening sex. Then they take up soldiering or archaeology, throw themselves into politics or find other things to do which we don't understand – such as revolution. When that happens we haven't a chance. We can fight among ourselves for a man but when we have to get to grips with an idea a man believes to be right then we're beaten. All we can do is to sit back and meditate on past triumphs.

CAROLINE: You're lucky. I never loved anyone but Boysie. I can't meditate on him for the rest of my life.

SOPHIE: Well, Boysie could hardly be described as a triumph, I agree. But you'll find someone worthy of you, Caroline. Goodness knows where, and it won't be John. Remember why he's here. To do his part in something real. He believes in the liberation by revolt of these wretched people. It may seem absurd to us, but it's a fact. Accept it.

CAROLINE: Why start playing soldiers at his age?

SOPHIE: A man always wants to do something positive after a love affair. John's just left Ada, remember. What did Boysie do after he left you?

CAROLINE: He had a nervous collapse.

SOPHIE: That proves my point.

(*JOHN comes down the stairs and into the room.*)

JOHN: Selwyn's a most energetic bather, isn't he? The room's flooded and as a mere spectator I'm soaked to the skin. He saw Henry and the Greek gentleman running down the hill and wants to be told what it's all about.

SOPHIE: Nobody knows at the moment. Henry arrived up here with an account even more garbled than he sends to *The Times*. Pay no attention. We've had such alarms before.

JOHN: I think you should have a word with Selwyn. He's at his bedroom window, stark naked, with a pair of field glasses and an improvised megaphone.

SOPHIE: I'll go up in a minute. John, when are you expecting your friend to come for you?

JOHN: Basilios? In two or three days. Why?

SOPHIE: Couldn't you travel north to meet him?

JOHN: Do you mean at once?

SOPHIE: Well, say tonight.

JOHN: I suppose I could. Are you trying to get rid of me?

CAROLINE: Yes, she is.

SOPHIE: John, we're old enough friends to be frank with each other.

JOHN: Certainly, Sophie. But no friends are old enough to be straightforwardly impolite to each other.

(*CAROLINE laughs.*)

I'd like to stay here for a few days. A little while ago you seemed happy about that. Why have you changed your mind?

SOPHIE: I haven't.

JOHN: Then what have we to be frank about?

CAROLINE: Me.

SOPHIE: I'm so very fond of you, John, and I wouldn't wish anything to take away from your affection for me. Certainly not this arrogant and impertinent child. In other words, I don't want to be blamed for what happens.

CAROLINE: Dear Sophie, always burning her bridges before I come to them.

SOPHIE: I'll go up to Selwyn.

(*SOPHIE goes from the room and up the stairs. JOHN, in silence, moves to the windows. CAROLINE watches him.*)

CAROLINE: You were right to be firm with Sophie. Of course you can stay here as long as you wish.

JOHN: That wasn't the reason. It's not that I very much
 want to stay here. I just want to put off going north for a
 while.

CAROLINE: Why?

(*JOHN does not answer.*)

What's the matter?

JOHN: Selwyn seems to think I may get killed in this
 business.

CAROLINE: Well, don't sound so surprised. Had it not
 occurred to you?

JOHN: It had occurred to me but I didn't think it had to
 anyone else – not seriously.

CAROLINE: But surely that's the point. You can at last be
 taken seriously by others. Why else are you here?

JOHN: Here? This is a strange undisciplined country.
 A good place to be alive in.

CAROLINE: It seems that's not the reason you came.

JOHN: Why did you come? Was it only because your
 father happened to be here?

CAROLINE: Not only that. When I was shut up in a
 nunnery as a child one of my teachers was a Greek.
 She told me wild, unorthodox stories of the country.
 I remembered them when I was alone in London and
 I thought this might be the place to bring me alive
 again. It's done so.

JOHN: I know what you mean. You become aware. Yes? Am
 I right? Aware that you're taking up space and that the sun
 exists to strike down and enwrap you. Aware that you are
 here! Alive, wound up – more! – working, ticking, going.
 Registering something more than a mood. Yes. It's a
 discovery to be reckoned with, I agree. Life is not, after
 all, founded on the meal table, the privy and the bed.

CAROLINE: In this place even those things might take on
 a certain significance.

JOHN: You think it's the element of place?

CAROLINE: Not entirely. It's also because Selwyn talked
 to you. About being killed. With that in mind even the
 most commonplace objects can become charged with
 mystery.

JOHN: I should never have thought of you as a common-place object.

CAROLINE: What did you say?

JOHN: You're confusing me. Are you doing it deliberately?

CAROLINE: I want you to see yourself in the proper light, that's all. As a man who hasn't got all his life before him I think you should.

JOHN: You talk as if I'm condemned.

CAROLINE: There's time for a reprieve. You've only to change your mind.

JOHN: Out of the question. I'm committed to action – on my honour.

CAROLINE: In that case – (*She moves to JOHN and holds out her hand.*) – goodbye. The world will surely go without you. (*JOHN takes her hand: he does not let it go.*) You're doing something which I don't understand, but I suppose is very fine.

JOHN: I'm not one of those men who have to love the country they're prepared to –

CAROLINE: (*After a moment.*) Say fight for. I didn't mean that. I meant it's supposed to be a good thing to give up so much. Everything you've known in such fullness in the past. Good food, sleep, the comfort of whom are gone in this spartan search for an absolute truth in a harsher reality. Great man – almost a saint, you are – yes – for the way of sanctity is the road to the north. (*JOHN is still holding her hand.*)

JOHN: I think you've misunderstood. The pleasures you've talked about had become as bitter to me as any penance. Every one was the harshest reality which I couldn't stomach. For they're only tolerable when they're more than themselves. When the food feeds more than the body, when sleep is more than an escape to a dream and the comfort of women is more than a cushion.

CAROLINE: I see. But tell me something. Did you say to yourself, This is the last time? D'you see what I mean? Take the comfort of women. Did you say to yourself, This is the last kiss, the last embrace? This is not only

farewell to whatshername – Ada – but farewell to all
loving for all time. Did you say that?
(*JOHN takes both her hands in his.*)
Say it now.
(*JOHN is silent.*)
Let the day go. It gets cooler towards the evening. Then's
the time for thought and decision. The smell of the baked
earth comes up from the valley making the scent of the
flowers sour and more understandable. Evening is the time
for straight talking and straight thinking in this country.
The sun goes down and rubs the gilt from the edges. The
senses aren't treacherously attacked by every colour, shape
and sound taking on a form of old happiness. The days in
this place – the days under the sun have all been – have
all happened before. But the nights are new in time – to
newmet people – you'n'me – and they can be used in any
way we – John – please. Please! put off, John – John, put
off telling – to y'self – me – telling whether Ada – a dead
love now – was last – very last time.
(*JOHN pushes her hair back from over her ears and folds his
hands about the back of her neck.*)

JOHN: It was the last chance.

CAROLINE: How – chance?

JOHN: All my life I've treated every opportunity as the last
chance. I've looked – oh, sadly – on each encounter as the
last. But I was cheated. The sun came up and the sun went
down and, damn it, life had to be lived. And opportunity
didn't knock once. It beat a positive tattoo at my door.

CAROLINE: Which every time you opened.

JOHN: It was never shut. (*He kisses her on the forehead.*) But
now the foot of time is edging it to. Soon there'll only be
space in that doorway for the lightest and most frivolous
opportunity to get through. The last – the smallest and
least consequential – will have to stay, I suppose, to
comfort my extreme age for there'll be no getting out.

CAROLINE: My God! Can't you –
(*JOHN kisses her on the mouth.*)
– see? Can't you see – that before you – haven't you
eyes? – oh, yes! you've eyes – before you is not a

quickly closing door. No, John – darling, my new found one: der – fool! there before you are the wide open gates of summer. You've lived only – nothing but – the early months of your year of life. Stay on. I'll not mind – never mind – if you go on from me to another – fairer, she may be – but be aware – beware – not old, not sleeping but now whilst young – of the fairest to hand. Stay. Go on from me – after all if you want to go – on. Go on.

(*JOHN puts his finger against her mouth.*)

JOHN: You're lying. You're saying something you don't believe. That's not good. That's bad. You must – and of course you do – think that you are the last. No going on from you – Caroline – who hold the secret – Caroline – the true ending. So let's have no renunciation from – Caroline. You.

CAROLINE: I don't give up anything – ever. But there comes a time – secret: furtive: upon you before you – no! – know it and a decision has to be made.

(*She kisses JOHN. SELWYN comes down the stairs, crosses the room, and goes out through the windows.*)

You'll not find that in a day's march.

JOHN: I'll not find that in a lifetime's campaigning.

(*They are fast in each others arms.*)

CAROLINE: Ah! my revolutionary. I'll be your marching song. This can be a struggle for freedom worth fighting. So to the barricades which are down – down! – fallen before the uprising. Take the law into your own hands and strike. The tormented are impatient of control.

JOHN: Be still.

CAROLINE: Yes. Yes. Yes.

CURTAIN

ACT TWO

The scene: part of the room of the first act remains showing the windows and the door leading to the stairway.

Now the terrace beyond the window is also revealed.

The time is two days later: evening.

The terrace is a compact area before the house and is enclosed by a low wall. The passage of slippered feet – it is a place of leisure – has given a mirror surface to the mosaic floor. At the centre several steps lead to the pathway going down to the road. The exterior wall containing the small window of JOHN's bedroom is now clearly seen.

A long table with food and drink has been taken out to the terrace.

The harshness of daylight has gone and with the sun low there is an incisive coolness which seems to etch the scene in a most unmisty twilight. It will not be night for some time.

JOHN is alone on the terrace. He is holding a long-barrelled, single-shot practice pistol. A little way from him, and lined on the wall, are various objects: a drinking glass, an orange, a small bottle, a straw hat (HENRY's) a playing card and a cigar. JOHN is using these as targets.

He fires. Not one of the objects is disturbed.

CAROLINE appears at the small window above and looks out to the countryside.

CAROLINE: The dancers! Don't frighten away the dancers. Do you see them? Under the hill. There's been a wedding. One of the workmen. Down there the men and women are making the bond. That slow and heavy circle will tread the pattern into the earth through the night. There's a tribute to love if ever there was one. Can you hear the music? It'll be a thin pipe. Listen.
(*JOHN has reloaded the pistol: he fires.*)

Ah! you don't want to hear. Does that sharp noise comfort
you? Yet you'll not save your life with that kind of toy.
Practise all you can, you'll never shoot your way out.
(*CRISTOS has come down the stairs of the house and crossed
the room. He now stands inside the windows unseen by JOHN
and CAROLINE.*)
Do you still believe the quickest way to someone's heart is
with a bullet? Will you never learn? They're dancing
under the hill. Set your sights a little higher, John, and
you'll see them – dancing the day into the earth – burying
it for ever and ever. Doesn't that mean something to you?

JOHN: No.
(*He fires again. CAROLINE goes back into the room. After a
moment CRISTOS steps out on to the terrace.*)

CRISTOS: I don't want to disturb you.

JOHN: I'm alone.

CRISTOS: I mean disturb your practice.

JOHN: The required number of rounds have been shot off.
I can rest now.
(*CRISTOS pours some wine and takes a glass to JOHN.*)

CRISTOS: I hope you're happy with our local wine.

JOHN: To be quite happy I'd need to be here a few weeks.
It still bites a little.

CRISTOS: You're not intrigued by it to stay on. No, I see
you're not. Unfortunately, it doesn't travel. Like myself.

JOHN: How do you come to speak English so well?

CRISTOS: I went to school in England, and afterwards
lived there for many years.

JOHN: From choice?

CRISTOS: Yes. The place fitted my temperament, for
I think it must be the saddest country in the world.
I long for that perpetual autumn where it is unnecessary –
oh, impossible – to face reality: where every leave-taking
is performed with the grave courtesy of an obsequy:
where the houses look like tombs and the tombs houses:
where the mist of bravely unshed tears softens even the
harshest gesture. Beautiful!

JOHN: Why did you leave?

CRISTOS: My national characteristics failed me. Not being an Englishman I craved something unworthy. I was ruined by a desire for excitement.

JOHN: You mean you found it? In England? Just a minute. This is extraordinary. What did you do? Start a political party? Not that? Surely you were not mad enough to create a work of art.

CRISTOS: Of course not.

JOHN: Women? My dear fellow, you must have known from your public schooldays that Englishwomen were made to purge us by pity and terror.

CRISTOS: Yes. I learnt that at an early age.

JOHN: Then I give up.

CRISTOS: Do you know Epsom Downs?

JOHN: Horse racing. Of course!

CRISTOS: I lost everything. The animal was called Homer II and its liquid eye avoided mine as it was led to the enclosure. It had carried my two thousand pounds into fourth place. I came back here to my only remaining property.

JOHN: I'm sorry. I didn't know this was your house.

CRISTOS: Selwyn rents it from me for the period of the excavation. Yes, it's my house. My position is difficult. I sometimes forget myself and behave very much as a host. Forgive me.

JOHN: It's a charming lapse. Please sit down.

(*HENRY has come up the hill and now steps on to the terrace. JOHN speaks to him.*)

What's happening?

HENRY: They're still trying to get through to the workman who fell into the hole. He seems to have dropped into an underground chamber. He's been there two and a half days now. Selwyn lowered food and wine and some candles to him. But the fellow makes no attempt to get out. All he does is wander about below and shout with laughter.

JOHN: Has he gone mad?

HENRY: We should know later tonight. Selwyn seems to think he can reach the place himself within a couple of hours. Of course, everything's been held up by this marriage of the foreman. About two hundred of his relations are down there at the dig roasting sheep. Have you noticed the dancers?

JOHN: They've been pointed out to me.

HENRY: Queer music. Rather infectious, though. Even I found myself tapping my foot.

CRISTOS: That's because dancing's in your blood, Henry.

JOHN: Henry has dancing in his blood!

CRISTOS: From his mother. She's an actress.

JOHN: Really. Locally?

CRISTOS: No, no. In London.

JOHN: What's she doing at the moment?

HENRY: 'The Feather Duster Girl.'

JOHN: Bevis. You're not Bunny Bevis's boy?

HENRY: Yes.

JOHN: Little Bunny Bevis! You mean you're her flesh and blood?

HENRY: Yes.

JOHN: How extraordinary! I saw her before I left London.

HENRY: Oh?

JOHN: That ageless, bewitching creature! I looked in the night before I sailed. Bunny came on to a scene decorated with enormous flowers. You'd have been proud of her, Henry. The gentlemen of the chorus swept off their toppers and Bunny came through them to the footlights with her eyelids working like shutters, and confided a song to us which must have been written by her worst enemy. (*Spinning an imaginary parasol, he sings.*) I'm the wild wed wose/You didn't pluck fwom your garden!/On your way to your new sweetheart/You chose those silly lilies/And the fwilly daffodilies/To Cawwy on your way/For your wedding day bouquet./But you didn't seem to seeme,/Your only, lonely, dweamy,/Dainty, cherubeamy – ooh! (presto) Little wild wed wose.

(*SELWYN has come up the hill and on to the terrace.*)

SELWYN: Bravo! The latest thing from London, eh?

JOHN: Henry's mother's new song.

SELWYN: Enchanting, ever young thing she is, too.
I remember her when I was quite a boy. She's one of the few women, I'd say, who know exactly what qualities to bring into a man's life to make him happy. Equal parts of gaiety, silence, and plain damned silliness. Not an idea in her head, you know. So refreshing. Funny she's never married. (*He has poured himself some wine.*) This is very pleasant. Where are the women?

JOHN: Dressing.

HENRY: Shall I fetch them?

SELWYN: I think you've missed the point, Henry. My statement that this is very pleasant, and my query as to where the women happen to be are not unconnected. See what I mean?

JOHN: So you hope to get right into the excavation tonight, Selwyn.

SELWYN: Yes. I've left them working on the tunnel. We should know the result of eighteen months work by the morning. You'd better be there, Bevis, standing by with your adjectives when I go in. *The Times* will want a full report.

HENRY: I'm ready for anything. What about the fellow already down there?

SELWYN: I can't get a word of sense from him. Damned fool!

HENRY: Is he still laughing?

SELWYN: Yes. With all respect to your countrymen, Cristos, I've found these workmen inclined to take the whole business rather lightly. I mean, this little fellow falls through a hole into a place where no man has set foot for over two thousand years, and all he does is to wander about giggling like a lunatic. Not only that, but the night we propose to enter the inner chamber the foreman decides to get married. It would have been churlish not to provide wine, but I can't say that I approve.

(*SOPHIE has come down the stairs and into the room. She now comes out on to the terrace.*)

SOPHIE: Will you take me down, Selwyn?

SELWYN: Down, my dear. Do you mean you want to see the digging?

SOPHIE: Certainly not. I want to join the wedding party for a while. I think we should all go. Is the girl pretty?

SELWYN: Not very. She has a heavy moustache.

SOPHIE: Come along, Cristos. You must interpret my best wishes. And John – how can I make you come along?

JOHN: You might drag me by the hair.

SOPHIE: I see. I'm sure I shan't have to persuade Henry with his morbid interest in marriage.

HENRY: I'll come down, certainly.

SOPHIE: We can all do with a little gaiety of this kind. And think how pleased they'll be to see that we're interested.

SELWYN: You'll find it very different, my dear, from the goings-on at Saint Margaret's.

SOPHIE: Nonsense, Selwyn! People the whole world over get married for the same thing.

JOHN: Tell us what it is, Sophie.

SOPHIE: I'd like to give the bride a small gift, Cristos. What do you think would be suitable?

(*SOPHIE, SELWYN and CRISTOS go from the terrace. HENRY remains for a moment to pick up his hat from the wall.*)

JOHN: It's very strange. A simple ritual invented by lawyers and priests can make a woman like Sophie behave in this absurd way. Look out, Henry! In her present mood she might try to engage you to one of the local girls.

HENRY: I very much want to get married, Mr Hogarth. Not, of course, to a local girl, but to someone of my own class.

JOHN: Have you anyone in mind?

HENRY: I had. (*He starts to go.*)

JOHN: (*Calls after him.*) Do you mean Caroline?

HENRY: Yes, I mean Caroline.

(*HENRY goes from the terrace. JOHN stares after him and then sadly looks down the barrel of his pistol. CAROLINE has come into the room. She stands watching JOHN, silently. It is JOHN who speaks.*)

131

JOHN: I know you're there. Come out.

(*CAROLINE stays in the room.*)

CAROLINE: And I know you're there. Alone.

JOHN: Henry wants to marry you.

CAROLINE: He once got as far as telling me what his income is.

JOHN: What is it?

CAROLINE: Eight hundred.

JOHN: Not enough. Why didn't you tell me about him? I've made him unhappy.

CAROLINE: Well, someone had to be made unhappy in this affair. And that's what the Henrys are for. You've made me very happy.

JOHN: Oh, damn you.

(*CAROLINE laughs.*)

Come out here.

CAROLINE: Do you really find comfort in that little weapon? Are you expecting to be attacked*?*

JOHN: Yes.

CAROLINE: From this quarter? Ah! be brave and put it down.

(*JOHN returns the pistol to its case. He walks through the windows into the room. CAROLINE, who is beside the window, quickly puts her arms around his neck. They kiss.*)

JOHN: You're a pest.

CAROLINE: You shouldn't be doing this. But you've a good excuse. It's all anyone wants for such behaviour. For when you left London you didn't know I existed and neatly filled this space. I'll wait, you thought, safe with Sophie.

JOHN: That's what I am doing. Waiting in safety.

CAROLINE: Are you? You meant t'do it. No doubt about it. Wait for your friend before going off to war. You could no more've imagined me, eh, as a friend on the way. Don't look so cross. It's upsetting, I know, to be knocked off y'path to war'n'glory which you'd so carefully plotted, but it's something you've got to get used to. Please!

JOHN: You arrogant and designing –

CAROLINE: Call me names.

JOHN: Later. Why should you think this is any more than an interlude?

CAROLINE: How to pass a night or two in a waiting room without the boredom of loneliness?

JOHN: Just that. How do you know it's more?

CAROLINE: Shall I tell you? Because you've never known anything like this before.

JOHN: This! Each and every one is not only the last chance. It is the first time. And I'm not a man to be detained by novelty. Try again.

CAROLINE: All right. I'm better than any of the others.

JOHN: Who've gone before. Are you.

CAROLINE: I'm just putting the idea in your head. Am I?

JOHN: Yes.

CAROLINE: Then there's your reason for staying on.

JOHN: Oh, no. Not good enough. Unworthy of you, Caroline. I left the best horse I ever had in England. With regret, but I left it.

CAROLINE: Will you leave me – with regret?

JOHN: Of course.

CAROLINE: But you'll leave?

JOHN: I shall.

(*CAROLINE breaks from across the room.*)

Don't go.

CAROLINE: Well, now, you may go it seems yet I must stay. Very well. I've not the cruelty needed to leave you after what we've been through together.

JOHN: Put like that it sounds an ordeal.

CAROLINE: What else? A carrying on of the game? No.

JOHN: Stop answering your own questions and listen to me. I'm an innocent traveller. I mean I'm travelling in an innocent way. I break my journey. You say I didn't know you'd be here. That's true. But I've always been aware of the perils of travel and you're one of them. They attend us on the way.

CAROLINE: Have there been so many on this journey?

JOHN: Enough. I came through Rome: I might have
changed my religion. A man on the boat had a scheme
to make me a fortune: I might have invested. The maid
who brought coffee to my bedside in Alexandria – she
wasn't you, certainly, but she had – ah, well, the sun was
already high. But y'see what I mean. None of these kept
me so why should you? Tell me, squirrel, the ever so
special reason why I should stay with you and not go
north with Basilios.

CAROLINE: Stay with me and you can stay alive with
honour.

JOHN: The word honour should never pass a woman's lips
except in its narrowest and most personal sense. You've
made a monstrous suggestion. If I don't lead this revolt
and stay with you everyone will applaud my courage in
exchanging the trials of revolution for the horrors of
marriage. Is that what you mean?

CAROLINE: I've never spoken of marriage.

JOHN: You will.

CAROLINE: Have you ever been in love?

JOHN: When I was fifteen. She was –

CAROLINE: I don't want to know. What about the others?

JOHN: I've travelled a great deal, you must remember.

CAROLINE: And of all your travelling companions I was
the best. Yes? There! you've a dear face when you relax
your mouth. To smile or to kiss – me.

(*JOHN does so: briefly.*)

Will the man be here tonight to fetch you? I only ask
because I must think what I've to do. What would you
have me do? Travel on? Looking for the encounters
you've tried to avoid. Oh, you – for you the world holds
yourself and humanity. It's the same with everyone who
wants to stir up trouble. Revolution is for men who can't
love. You can, if you'll give yourself the chance.

JOHN: I gave myself every chance in the past. I presented
myself well scrubbed and well dressed, sober and tactful
for the preliminaries. If there was a husband I was
good-natured. The early stages were distinguished by
punctuality and discretion. The mutual pact was sealed

– on my part, at least – with affection and firmness of purpose. Time, Caroline, and time again I was well on my way to being in love with a person.

CAROLINE: That's behaviour. Got no more to do with it than the angle of your hat. You speak of formalities. Didn't you suffer?

JOHN: Horribly. About the fourth week. Oh, to stop playing the dancing ape!

CAROLINE: Poor animal!

JOHN: Yes! You'd blubber over such lack of freedom for your doggies and birdies and dearly sweet gee-gees. But a man? Why, you only bite your finger to stop your laughter. Goad the beast and it will give tongue. Do you recognise human speech? What is it you want to hear? Surely not the beaten, desperate cry: Will you please go away and leave me alone!

CAROLINE: We always go. There's that to be said for us.

JOHN: Go? Yes, but you leave behind a long backward look.

CAROLINE: We have to fight with outdated weapons. We hope the dull edge of remorse stays sharp enough to penetrate the heart.

JOHN: And think of it as only the first thrust of the engagement. For, from longer range, the letters start coming. The small wound caused by remorse must be kept open by the pen. The first letter on parting –

CAROLINE: 'Dear John, Your cruelty to me last night – '

JOHN: Letters stay unanswered. What next?

CAROLINE: A telegram: 'If offended in any way – '

JOHN: At last in person on the doorstep day and night – veiled – or in a carriage across the street – watching. Once even disguised as a washerwoman to be met on the stairs. So it always ends one way. In flight. The last letter speaks to me over the many miles –

CAROLINE: 'Dear John, Your silence tells me that I have failed to please you. Now so far away I shall hope to be remembered as nothing more than a friend of whom in future times of trouble anything may be asked.'

JOHN: That's what it seems to say. It's hard to be sure with the page scarred and blistered by tears. Into the tin box with it. And on. No, Caroline, love can never stand up to the onslaught of your sex. Never.

CAROLINE: And so it has led from one to another until in headlong flight you pass this way.

JOHN: Pass. Yes. Good girl. Pass this way.

(*SOPHIE has returned up the hill on CRISTOS' arm. They come on to the terrace.*)

SOPHIE: Who's in there? Why don't you light the lamps?

(*SOPHIE and CRISTOS move from the terrace into the room. CAROLINE begins to light the lamps.*)

JOHN: Back so soon. What was it like?

SOPHIE: Very disappointing. Even at my age I'd have thought a peasant wedding would be sweetly idyllic. That is nothing of the kind. How could it be when the man is obviously a blackguard and the girl quite distressingly drunk – and ugly.

CAROLINE: You'll have to look elsewhere for your romance, Sophie.

SOPHIE: I shall. Far beyond this house, at least. Cristos, I'd intended to ask you to go to my room and fetch one of my handkerchiefs to give to that poor girl down there, but now I feel sure she'd only blow her great nose on it. Instead, will you go to the kitchen and find an old tablecloth to present with my compliments.

JOHN: You are in a bad temper.

(*CRISTOS goes out.*)

SOPHIE: It's the first time I've walked down that hill. Very tiring.

JOHN: It took a wedding to get you out and about.

CAROLINE: I suppose you insulted them. The wedding pair, I mean.

SOPHIE: Why should you suppose I'd do any such thing?

CAROLINE: Because you're always so damned rude to anyone who disappoints you.

SOPHIE: It would have been difficult, as everything I said had to be translated through Cristos. However, I can speak English and be understood by both of you.

(*CAROLINE begins to go from the room.*)

Where are you going?

CAROLINE: Kitchen. Oil for the lamp.

SOPHIE: The lamp's all right.

CAROLINE: It won't be in a moment. (*She goes out.*)

SOPHIE: So you're staying on with us. I'm very sorry. The sight of you being brought down by Caroline during the last two days has been very painful. I'd hoped it was only a matter of soldier's comfort, but it seems I have to watch your final humiliation. A tacit admission of love.

JOHN: What are you talking about?

SOPHIE: Ah! my dear boy, to be caught by love is one thing: to give it is another.

JOHN: You know, Sophie, you're becoming a contradictory old lady.

SOPHIE: John!

JOHN: You obviously see nothing odd in the fact that you should give your blessing to the lovers down the hill and immediately return to abuse Caroline and me – so much nearer to your heart – in the same situation.

SOPHIE: Then it is true. The night you arrived I saw the lamp in her irresponsible hand go bobbing towards your room. Even then I feared for your safety. Yet I believed you'd break free. We know, don't we, that there's no commitment made in the small hours. Dawn breaks most pacts and the sun burns up all vows. This time, however – well, you're older and you must at least come to rest in someone's bed. I was afraid it would be Caroline's and I was right, it seems. For your daytime behaviour with her has been most revealing. Tragic, I feel, that after all you've been and more important all you've avoided you should end up with that worthless girl.

JOHN: Must I remind you? In London you only knew of such things by letter and through conversation with me. Remember, Sophie, this is the first time you've actually seen the little lamp go bobbing down the corridor. This is no better – ha ! – and no worse than those times in the past. And no more dangerous. I'm not staying.

SOPHIE: You're not? Then why are you letting me say all this?

JOHN: I like to hear you so concerned. You must still be
very fond of me.
(*CRISTOS comes in. He has a cloth folded over his arms.*)
SOPHIE: It's not enough. A cloth. Give the girl a sum of
money as well.
CRISTOS: Certainly. How much?
SOPHIE: All you have on you. Let Selwyn and Henry also
contribute.
CRISTOS: Very well.
SOPHIE: I've been uncharitable. It's not the girl's fault
she's so unpleasant. Come back at one, Cristos. I shall
dictate a chapter at least tonight.
(*CRISTOS goes out to the terrace and down the hill.*)
I'm sorry I made a mistake about you and Caroline.
JOHN: Did you know Henry wants to marry her?
SOPHIE: That's because he's been out here such a long
time. Nothing will come of it.
JOHN: What will happen to her? I'd like her to be happy.
Some day.
SOPHIE: But not today. Not until you're far off. Let her be
happy then.
JOHN: How?
SOPHIE: You're very concerned.
JOHN: Naturally.
SOPHIE: When are you expecting your friend?
JOHN: What? At any moment.
SOPHIE: Tonight?
JOHN: Perhaps. But about Caroline –
CAROLINE: Yes? (*She has come from the darkness of the
passageway.*)
SOPHIE: We were speaking of your future happiness, my
child.
CAROLINE: Were you, darling? What about my present
happiness?
SOPHIE: We thought it problematic –
(*CAROLINE has taken JOHN's arm.*)
– or merely affected. But we can be generous and admire
you for putting a good face on your failure. I suppose you

must have some qualities, Caroline, but I'm surprised that one of them should be to know when you've lost.

CAROLINE: You come of a different – and older – generation than John and I. We're made happy by smaller things of less duration than ever you could be. I suppose you were very beautiful when you were young but I never look at you – knowing you as I do – without thinking that you must have gone yah-yah! gobble – and then sat back emotionally stuffed and sleepy. (*To JOHN.*) Women eating. Do you hate it?

JOHN: Hate it.

CAROLINE: I'll starve. (*To SOPHIE.*) But for me – well, when I've been miserable a smile from a stranger has sometimes been enough. You don't understand that, do you?

SOPHIE: When I was a girl no stranger would have dared to smile at me.

CAROLINE: Poor thing. So what I've known with John is very wonderful. It's not f'rever. But what is? Over f'both of us – tonight? – perhaps we'll see the morning. But I believe not. There, I've taken away your cause for triumph, Sophie. Sorry. You were all ready, I know, to rub my nose in the fact that this man is also leaving me.

JOHN: Would you mind if I waited outside whilst this goes on?

SOPHIE: Not necessary. Please tell Cristos when he comes back that I'm in my room. I'd like you to knock on my door, John, for a moment before you go to shake my hand. That is, if your friend should arrive in the middle of the night. At that time Caroline will undoubtedly be in a position to wish you a long farewell. (*She goes from the room and up the stairs.*)

JOHN: Let me look at you, Caroline. I'd have to know you longer before I could say you're serious.

CAROLINE: If ever there was a time to be serious this is it.

JOHN: I thought you were just maddening Sophie.

CAROLINE: No. You've taught me what you failed to teach the others. But I don't want Basilios to turn up before

morning even now. How will he come? How does a man
go off to war these days? What am I to look for? A
group of silent horsemen on the hill. Is that it?

JOHN: Forgive me. After all that's happened it would be
unbecoming for me to end in a bed.

CAROLINE: I understand perfectly. As a famous man you
must finish up in glory.

JOHN: I'd like to confound my obituaries as they stand
written at the moment.

CAROLINE: You may come through the whole affair
untouched. I hadn't thought of that.

JOHN: I had. It would be just my luck.

CAROLINE: Let's behave as if it wasn't part of the day –
as if it wasn't happening at all. Come on. Here's an
opportunity you've never known. Always before you'd to
be careful – wary – because a word meant being trapped.
But there's no fear of committing yourself with me.
You'll be gone by morning, and there'll be no letters
following after you, I promise.

JOHN: I'm allowed to say honestly and without commitment
that I love you.

CAROLINE: Yes, you're allowed to say that.

JOHN: And having said it –

CAROLINE: You haven't.

JOHN: Having said it I must at once get ready to go. I'm in
an impossible situation.

CAROLINE: I know. (*She holds out her arms.*) Take refuge.
(*JOHN does so.*)

JOHN: I think aloud and you hear my thoughts. What
would it have been? An abject return to England to carve
legal indulgence and tell this story of ours in straight
answers to misleading questions. Your hair smells of
wood smoke: why is that? Marriage and retirement to
the country to give us leisure to begin to hate each other
– your hands are stained with fruit – for having dared to
think we could make each other happy – quite bloodied
over they are: see them – until the time would be when
we'd only find true contentment in our hatred. I know:
my mother and father married – we'd have children to

take sides in our private war – your pulse: racing: oh
dear, yes, it is! – children equally divided to carry on the
battle when we were too old and tired to care. You've
tears in your eyes.

CAROLINE: I know, you fool! Stay with me.

JOHN: What has it been? Discovery without the vulgar need
to stake a claim. Mystery without fear of explanation.
Silence without misunderstanding. We've not used up all
our poetry on each other and been driven to counterfeit.
Your lies amuse me – your unhappiness concerns me –
and your most idiotic mannerisms enchant me. Leave it
so. Be thankful for the horsemen on the hill.

CAROLINE: Stay with me.

JOHN: No.

> (*CAROLINE turns away and goes out on to the terrace
> leaving JOHN alone in the room. CRISTOS has come up
> the hill and on to the terrace. He speaks to CAROLINE.*)

CRISTOS: As a man long since unmarried I'm always
amazed at the savagery attendant upon the simple union
of two good people who are supposed to love each other.
The families of the wedding party are engaged in a
pitched battle. Someone made a comment on the bride's
exact state of chastity, it seems. I'd not have thought it
was a debatable point, as she had two children with her
who cried, Momma, throughout the ceremony. (*He passes
CAROLINE and enters the room.*)

JOHN: Sophie asked me to say that she's in her room
waiting to dictate.

CRISTOS: Thank you. Her memory at this time of day is
too accurate for comfort.

JOHN: Surely that's what you want.

CRISTOS: Accuracy about the past! Mr Hogarth, you speak
like a scholar.

JOHN: Is there another value in reminiscence?

CRISTOS: Certainly. A record of what might have been.

JOHN: In that case, where does the truth get to?

CRISTOS: Now you speak, sir, as if the truth was a
considerable detail. The book will only be read by the
future.

JOHN: Then Sophie's life in London is a myth.

CRISTOS: It will be by the time I've got it on paper.

JOHN: Until this moment I've looked on you as an historian.

CRISTOS: I'm sorry to have misled you. How do you see me now?

JOHN: As an artist, you charlatan. I'm naturally concerned. I play a large part, I'm told, in your forthcoming work.

CRISTOS: You won't suffer, Mr Hogarth. Where in the past your behaviour has seemed irresponsible I've taken care to provide a motive even at the expense of libelling others. Where your actions have appeared cruel or selfish the reader will find an excuse – even if it's only in a footnote. In this work at least, sir, you will be represented beyond your wildest dreams.

JOHN: Thank you so much.

(*CRISTOS goes from the room and up the stairs as CAROLINE returns to the room. Whilst on the terrace she has poured two glasses of wine. She carries one to JOHN and holds it out to him. He takes it.*)

What's this?

CAROLINE: You're going. Let's drink to it.

JOHN: Not at all necessary.

CAROLINE: Now why should it embarrass you to have a woman see you as you see yourself? You are the last of the romantics and carry his accessories. Then you must damned well expect to be treated as such. You can't brood over your pistols and your past, your copy of Malory and your death in battle and have me see you as I see Henry. He's trying to make his way in the world. You're trying to make your way out of it.

JOHN: Very well, darling. If it's going to help you through these last hours by all means take part in my imaginary costume drama. (*He raises his glass.*) To the freedom of man! (*He drinks.*)

CAROLINE: Oh, you did that beautifully! Anyone would've thought it was real. Let me try. (*She raises her glass.*) To the freedom of man! (*She drinks.*) How was that?

JOHN: Not at all bad. There was a note in your voice – militantly feminine – disturbing – might cause alarm in the liberal ranks. Try again.

CAROLINE: No.

(*She takes the glass from JOHN and with her own goes out to the terrace. She throws the glasses far out where they smash on the hillside. She comes back into the room. She speaks.*)

That wine was poisonous.

JOHN: Yes. It wasn't very nice.

CAROLINE: I mean I put poison in it. The wine you've just drunk while we were fooling about. It was toxic.

JOHN: What?

CAROLINE: The wine, darling. I put poison in it.

JOHN: Are you serious?

CAROLINE: You'd have to know me longer before you could say that, so I'll tell you. Yes, I'm serious.

JOHN: Caroline: pull yourself together!

CAROLINE: I'm all right.

JOHN: And stop smiling!

CAROLINE: I'm happy.

JOHN: You're mad!

CAROLINE: No, I'm not. The stuff was in my drink, too.

JOHN: I'm not concerned with you at the moment.

CAROLINE: You must be. We were together in another way. We're together in this. That's right and proper. I'd not do anything for you alone. I love you.

JOHN: So much?

CAROLINE: Oh, so much! Just before we went to sleep last night I asked, How can I make this last for ever? And you said, That's only tomorrow. And suddenly I knew it could be.

JOHN: Give me the facts! The facts!

CAROLINE: Do they matter? Nothing to them. Walking on the hillside with Cristos one day I saw the scarlet berries. We'd been talking of the unhappiness of love, the impossibility of absolute oblivion. Then Cristos took a handful of the berries and told me that many people in this tragic country believed they held the secret. They

143

call them Man's Friend. Cristos threw them away but the day you came I'd happened to be out on the hillside and gathered more.

JOHN: Just give me the facts!

CAROLINE: Do you mean the cook book facts? All right. Place whole in a pan. Cover with boiling water. Simmer on a wood fire. Drain. Keep to hand and when the horsemen on the hill approach use it.

JOHN: A wood fire –

CAROLINE: – yes, it stays in my hair. With the stain on my hands.

JOHN: I think you're lying.

CAROLINE: You'll know I'm not in about eight hours. When you fall asleep. *Mild und leise.*

JOHN: Don't whisper romantic German nonsense to me!

CAROLINE: Why not? Let's show them, John. Let's show this whole damned century with its passion for steam engines and plotting in cellars that there were two people who were unafraid to give themselves up to the oldest passion of all. The beauty and the sacrifices are all in the story books now. I want them as you do to be here in life. You must want it that way or you wouldn't have done the things you have and needed to go off to the north in further search. Sophie called you the first twentieth century man. Live up to it.

JOHN: Give me a chance!

CAROLINE: You'll live for ever in Sophie's book. As you really are. And I shall live with you in history as your last attachment. That makes me all at once want to cry. It's very wonderful.

JOHN: Splendid. Now listen to me, Caroline. I'm very very angry with you. A naughty girl, that's what you've been.

CAROLINE: I thought you'd behave so finely about this. And I'm sure Sophie would expect it, too.

JOHN: You mean I can't rush about the place screaming, Murder!

CAROLINE: Well, you can, but you're going to look silly and most unlike yourself if you make an uproar before Sophie and Henry and Selwyn.

JOHN: I'd certainly quite forfeit Sophie's respect. She'd probably begin to write her bloody book again from the beginning.

CAROLINE: It's a difficult position. I'd be brave and keep quiet.

JOHN: It's all a joke, isn't it, Caroline?

CAROLINE: Believe that, if you want to. It won't do any harm. You've always looked on everything as a joke, so why not this?

JOHN: Oh, my God!

CAROLINE: Everyone thought you'd leave me. As Boysie left me. Won't they be surprised? It's all so simple, too. Why didn't the others think of it, instead of writing you complaining letters?

JOHN: They didn't think of it because they were decent respectable women.

CAROLINE: Poor things! They'll be so mad when they hear about us. So many morning papers to tell them on so many breakfast tables, and so many tears of frustration falling in the porridge. God! I love you looking like that. Let's go upstairs. We've got eight hours or so.

JOHN: Certainly not! You're indecent. You should occupy the eight hours –

CAROLINE: How?

JOHN: I don't know. I don't know.

(*He walks out to the terrace where he at once comes face to face with HENRY who has come up the hill.*)

HENRY: Selwyn's got through to the inner chamber of the dig. He's still there. I've been sent up for some drawing things. He wants to make some sketches.

JOHN: Has he found something interesting?

HENRY: I think it must be. I've not been in yet. Why don't you go down? They've enlarged the entrance. You've only to lower your head.

JOHN: Perhaps tomorrow.

HENRY: Will you forgive me? I must think about my column for *The Times*.

JOHN: Tell me, you're very fond of Caroline, aren't you?

HENRY: I was hoping that matter wouldn't come up again. Do you think it's a fair question, Mr Hogarth?

JOHN: I think so. What do you know about her, that's the point?

HENRY: She makes mistakes.

JOHN: Such as?

HENRY: Believing herself to be emotionally attached to unsuitable men.

JOHN: I suppose you mean in love with me. Has she ever threatened you?

HENRY: With violence? You can't mean that.

JOHN: I do.

HENRY: She's always been most sympathetic.

JOHN: She's never been cruel to be kind.

HENRY: There have been times when she's said or done something she's regretted later.

JOHN: Too late sometimes, I expect. She's mad.

HENRY: Wild? I suppose she is. Yet we'd always forgive her, wouldn't we? Soon after she came here and I suppose I was pestering her she played a joke on me.

JOHN: A joke!

HENRY: It was really nothing – although I might have been killed. We were out riding together. Caroline used to wear boy's clothes for convenience. As an English journalist I was naturally interested in local habits and customs. On this ride we were going down a narrow defile near the coast when we came on a group of men. I wanted to speak to them and Caroline kindly offered to translate. I asked them various questions about their way of life. As I went on I saw the men's attitude become surly and then threatening. I did the best I knew. I held out a sum of money to them. At that they set on me. They dragged me from my horse. Luckily they were unarmed and had only their fists. I called to Caroline to ride off, which she did. I made my way back alone and very much the worse for wear.

JOHN: Hired assassins, I suppose.

HENRY: No, no. Cristos put the police on the case and a few days later they arrested two of the men. They both swore that Caroline had told them I was a wealthy Turk travelling the country buying up young girls – in this case their daughters – for immoral purposes. Caroline admitted that it was true. My innocent questions had been translated into damning demands. Poor child, she cried a little when she asked me to forgive her foolishness.

JOHN: Did you cry, too?

HENRY: I found it very touching that she should have thought those Greeks to have a sense of humour. She quite expected them to join in the joke.

(*JOHN laughs: after a moment.*)

I must get the drawing board.

JOHN: I'd like to speak to Cristos. He's with Sophie. Will you ask him to come down?

HENRY: Of course.

(*He goes into the room leaving JOHN on the terrace and sees CAROLINE sitting alone smoking a cigarette.*)

Hullo, you're there. Can't stop. Must go to my room. They've found something down at the dig, so I must start my last article. Then it will be goodbye, Caroline.

CAROLINE: Goodbye, Henry.

HENRY: I mean when I've finished the article.

CAROLINE: Well, get on with it, my dear.

(*She goes to the window and out to the terrace and speaks to JOHN as HENRY leaves the room and goes up the stairs.*)

Not a satisfactory conversation for you, I'm afraid. Even you could never convince Henry that such a thing as treachery exists. If you shot him dead on the spot his last thought would be, A most unfortunate mishap.

JOHN: The juice of a few berries in a glass of wine can't have any effect.

CAROLINE: Can't they? Look at the effect a few words to some strangers had on Henry when he was being boring.

JOHN: You're a monster.

CAROLINE: There's something you insist on forgetting. I'm with you in this. We'll always be together now. For people to remember.

JOHN: You'll soon convince me that everyone's going to benefit.

CAROLINE: Well, this revolution was a mistake, wasn't it? Things would have gone wrong and you'd have made a fool of yourself and it would have got into the papers and – oh, no, no, it would never have done at all.
(*SOPHIE has come down the stairs and into the room. She calls.*)

SOPHIE: John! Are you there?

JOHN: Yes. (*He moves into the room leaving CAROLINE on the terrace.*)

SOPHIE: Why do you want to speak to Cristos?

JOHN: I need his advice on a local custom I've just encountered. A matter of hospitality.

SOPHIE: He's gone out. Left in quite a temper. About you.

JOHN: Have I upset him?

SOPHIE: No. He was championing you. When he came to my room and picked up his pen I said, Now I shall begin to tell the truth about John Hogarth. He at once put down the pen and said, I'll not be a party to the destruction of a legend which the world will badly need in a few years. A destruction brought about, moreover, by your momentary pique. I answered him sharply. We were about to have a scene when fortunately he left the room. And the house.

JOHN: Can he be found?

SOPHIE: I see no reason for it. I'm capable of writing in my own hand.

JOHN: I meant for myself.

SOPHIE: It's very strange. I once described you as –

JOHN: – the first twentieth-century man. I know.

SOPHIE: Yet Cristos sees you as the true representative of an age which is passing, if not past. He thinks you'll be swallowed up by a world which is going to regret the action and then find its comfort in fairy stories about the man it destroyed. That is your place in history, according to Cristos. A kind of Saint Jack of the Beanstalk. Interesting, isn't it?

JOHN: Very. But at the moment, Sophie, I'm unconcerned with my part in history and deeply interested in my part in the present. So tell me, why did Caroline's husband leave her?

SOPHIE: For none of the usual reasons. They say he was terrified of her. He became very strange towards the end.

JOHN: Go on.

SOPHIE: Is there any more to be said?

JOHN: Nothing, I suppose.

SOPHIE: Then let's change the subject.

JOHN: Certainly. How do you think I'll face up to the enemy.

SOPHIE: In the past you've made your own enemies and been very careful in doing so. You were wise. Friends don't matter, but it's most necessary to have the right enemies one can face with dignity and restraint.

JOHN: I'm speaking of physical danger.

SOPHIE: Oh, that. Well, I hope you won't make a fool of yourself.

JOHN: You feel I should pass into history silent and uncomplaining.

SOPHIE: Of course. You're keeping me in suspense as to what the final chapter of my book is going to be, but under no circumstances can I allow it to be a farce. That's Henry's part.

JOHN: The wealthy Turk.

SOPHIE: Ah! such a disgraceful incident. Lacerated and bruised mercifully beyond recognition for several days. She knew what she was doing. He might have been killed. And the fool still believes it was a joke.

JOHN: The fool!

(*SELWYN has come up the hill and on to the terrace. He speaks to CAROLINE.*)

SELWYN: Success!

(*JOHN and SOPHIE stand listening within the room.*) Success, my dear child, after all these months. Go down and see your old Daddy's crowning triumph. The find that will put our names in the history books. Go down! (*CAROLINE leaves the terrace to go down the hill. SELWYN enters the room to JOHN and SOPHIE.*)

SOPHIE: You've found something.

SELWYN: The most astonishing state of preservation.

SOPHIE: Of what?

SELWYN: An inner room – sixteen feet square or so. Hogarth, my dear fellow, we spoke of a place of worship, remember? Dedicated, we said. It's very much that. A has-relief runs round the four walls from floor to ceiling.

SOPHIE: What does it represent?

SELWYN: Ostensibly man and woman's progress from the cradle to the grave, with overwhelming emphasis on a certain aspect.

SOPHIE: Come, Selwyn. Be brief: be lucid.

SELWYN: A strange experience. I climbed down into the darkness. The little idiot man already there had gone to sleep surrounded by his burnt out candles. The lamps were handed through to me and in their dancing light the still figures on the wall seemed to be animate. For two thousand years they'd remained until I brought them the light which set them performing again their endless love rites. A great moment. To hear a poem of Anacreon spoken by a voice of the time. The young sun-hot bodies joined by the freshly poured wine and playing their games forever to the silent music.

SOPHIE: Selwyn my dear. Selwyn, pay attention. Somehow I feel this is not the correct academic attitude towards what seems to be an important archaeological find.

SELWYN: There was a disturbing impression of youth. Even at that depth the place is warmed by the heat of the sun and there seems to remain the echo of a cry and of laughter and of the last deep silence. All in the inspired graffiti. My God, I'd no idea what I was looking for. Remember the little figure I showed you, Hogarth? Significant attitude, we said, but it meant little. My dear fellow, we were holding the poor creature upside down. Forgive me but you look quite shaken.

JOHN: It's surprising, Selwyn, that you should come all this way and spend all this time and then be pleased to verify a fact of human behaviour which could be observed at ease by visiting any one of a dozen houses in London.

SELWYN: I'm not an anthropologist. I know why you're upset. You left London to free yourself only to come so far and find material proof that the formal pattern of behaviour you wanted to escape was fully developed perhaps beyond your experience over two thousand years ago.

JOHN: I never thought I invented such goings-on.

SELWYN: Distressing, all the same. Now where's that fool Bevis? I sent him up for a drawing board. I must get some of this down on paper for the people in Berlin. My word, the Bloomsbury crowd are going to be mad when they hear about this. (*He has reached the foot of the stairs. He calls.*) Bevis, come down! Come down at once, man! (*SELWYN returns to the room and speaks to JOHN.*) I must set him to work on this article for *The Times*. A detailed and poetic account is what's wanted. Something that will carry a breath of fresh air into a hundred reading rooms. I'm sure the boy can do it if he puts his mind to it.

SOPHIE: He'll do his best.

SELWYN: Why don't you go down, my dear? You'll find it interesting.

SOPHIE: Not tonight. I'm afraid of the path in the dark.

SELWYN: What about you, Hogarth?

JOHN: I'll go tomorrow.

SELWYN: Caroline couldn't wait so long. From the way she ran down the hill you'd have thought there was to be no tomorrow for her.

JOHN: What's that? She's gone?

SELWYN: Like a bird.

JOHN: Selwyn, could you spare me a moment on another matter?

SELWYN: Certainly. What is it?

JOHN: Your family.

SELWYN: What about it?

JOHN: Any insanity?

SELWYN: Hogarth, my excitement and enthusiasm are only natural to a man who's been working in the dark for eighteen months.

JOHN: I don't mean you. Have you – oh, really, this is very delicate – have you observed Caroline?

SELWYN: In passing. Is her behaviour eccentric? The girl has been unhappy in the past, but I don't think there's cause to fear for her mind. You mustn't worry that she'll do herself harm.

JOHN: What about others?

SELWYN: There she resembles her mother: more likely to kill with kindness.

JOHN: Thank you, Selwyn.

SELWYN: Anything more I can tell you?

JOHN: Nothing.

(*HENRY has come down the stairs and he now enters the room carrying a drawing board and a handful of pencils.*)

SELWYN: There you are. What've you been doing?

HENRY: Sharpening the pencils.

SELWYN: Look to your wits. I want a masterpiece from you.

HENRY: Shall we go down?

SELWYN: At once.

(*SELWYN and HENRY go from the room, cross the terrace, and begin the descent of the hill.*)

SOPHIE: John, *pièce touchée, pièce jouée.*

JOHN: What do you mean?

SOPHIE: You know very well. Did you really think the game with her could be ended by knocking over the board?

JOHN: She's coming back. (*He is standing at the window looking down the hill.*)

SOPHIE: When you first came here you wagged your head and talked of my marriage to Selwyn. You made use of your gravest indictment: you said I'd become a woman. Oh, Sophie! Now we have the problem. What am I to gather from your present behaviour? That you've become a man? Oh, John!

JOHN: She speaks to her father. Kisses him. Claps Henry on the shoulder in a comradely way. And laughs. Laughs!

SOPHIE: Why not? She obviously has you for one at a disadvantage. No, no, John, this lack of decision won't do at all. You tell me that you're not staying, yet every word – all those questions! – indicate that you've given up hope of going. Now come along, what's it to be.

JOHN: She's very beautiful – carelessly so – as she walks – sure footed – sure of herself – sure of me – oh, God!

SOPHIE: The game's up, is it? Then let's have the post-mortem.

(*CAROLINE comes on to the terrace from below. JOHN stays at the window between the two women: CAROLINE on the terrace and SOPHIE in the room.*)

CAROLINE: Come out here. The ground under my feet is still warm from the sun.

JOHN: Your father's just told me that you'd not harm anyone.

CAROLINE: I wish I could put you out of your misery.

JOHN: Haven't you?

CAROLINE: I mean by making you understand that it's not a joke.

JOHN: You're beginning to regret it.

CAROLINE: Only when I look directly at you. Look away – like this – to the country and the naked hill waiting for the horsemen – then I don't regret it for a moment. Have you told the old lady?

JOHN: She knows nothing.

SOPHIE: The old lady knows nothing.

CAROLINE: Tell her what's happened. See if you get any sympathy. Go on, have a moment of panic.

SOPHIE: Why don't you walk down and confide in the men, John?

JOHN: Henry Bevis? I don't think so. Did you see the excavation, Caroline?

CAROLINE: Yes. Nothing more than a little dark secret hole in the ground. I looked at it closely. The figures of the men and women are very seriously happy. But, darling, you and I've learnt nothing new in over two thousand years. Mind you, we've forgotten nothing – that's clear enough. So let's be content.

(*A moment's silence.*)

There! did you feel that? The whole land took a deep breath and settled down for the night.

JOHN: I'll take advantage of it. Sophie, earlier this evening in a moment of nineteenth century romantic ardour Caroline put poison in my wine.

SOPHIE: Poison?

JOHN: From the scarlet berries on the hill. Man's Friend, as they're called.

SOPHIE: Oh, you silly girl! Yet it makes a much better ending.

JOHN: For me?

SOPHIE: No. The book, dear boy. Better than the battlefield. Less confusion.

JOHN: Sophie, I love you, but –

SOPHIE: And I love you, John. You're looking quite upset.

JOHN: Is that foolish of me?

SOPHIE: It's surprising. I don't understand. I mean, you came out here with the idea of ending your life on some sordid battlefield among complete strangers. You know how I felt about that. I thought it unwise. But this, John – this fits. Yes, I feel it's much the best way considering your early life. It has a tidiness which is most appealing.

JOHN: I'm glad you're pleased.

SOPHIE: Not pleased, exactly. But there's a feeling of satisfaction.

JOHN: Good. Caroline took the stuff as well.

SOPHIE: That's not important. She'll hardly be mentioned.

(*CAROLINE comes quickly into the room.*)

CAROLINE: Now, look here, Sophie, you've been pretty filthy to me, but that's the dirtiest trick yet. I'm going to be in that book.

SOPHIE: I'll do my best to cram you into an appendix.

CAROLINE: I want the whole story. Nothing less. And I want a portrait. The Sargent, I think. Done when I was sixteen. Don't you dare monkey about with the facts. I loved him more than anyone.

SOPHIE: No, no, Caroline. Your agitated personality would ruin the dying fall of the last chapter. You must be muted.

CAROLINE: I won't be muted!

SOPHIE: Well, at least, dear, don't shout.

JOHN: May I just speak?

(*The two women attend him. There is a long silence.*)

CURTAIN

ACT THREE

The scene is JOHN's bedroom.

The time is later the same night.

The room is almost entirely occupied by a bed which is Byzantine in size and splendour. At the four corners gilded columns whirl giddily to the great canopy above. All around hang damasked curtains of extreme weight. There is a light burning directly over the bed beneath the canopy. The rest of the room is barely furnished by one chair and a small dressing table. JOHN's box is open in a corner. His possessions are spilling out, giving the impression of flight suddenly abandoned.

There is one door to the room and one window.

JOHN is lying on the bed. He is in a state of undress, being only in his shirt and trousers.

There is a knock on the door.

JOHN: Go away!
   (*HENRY comes into the room.*)
HENRY: May I come in?
JOHN: What d'you want?
HENRY: Your advice. How are you feeling? Caroline told me that you've taken something which disagreed with you.
JOHN: Yes. I'm in no state to give advice on any subject.
HENRY: That's a pity. It's really help I need. I'm very worried.
JOHN: I've something on my mind, Bevis, as well as on my stomach and I'd like to be alone.
HENRY: You want me to go away. You mustn't worry. Problems seem so frightening at this time of night. So often they're solved by morning. That's been my experience. But after the sun's down what can you do? I've been walking about the hillside trying to get my mind in order.
JOHN: Have you managed that?
HENRY: No. You see, I've been in the dig with Selwyn.

JOHN: Instructive, I'm told.

HENRY: Mr Hogarth, what on earth am I going to say?

JOHN: Say?

HENRY: About Selwyn's discovery. For *The Times*.

JOHN: I don't know.

HENRY: That's my problem. Shall we deal with it first and then come to you. From the moment I met you I felt there was a sympathetic understanding between us, and that this situation might well come up. When we could be of help to each other.

JOHN: What do you want me to do? I've not seen the place.

HENRY: Well, look at these. They're rough sketches made by Selwyn of the images.

(*He unrolls a bundle of drawings and gives them to JOHN.*)

You see my difficulty.

JOHN: Yes. (*He laughs.*) I see your difficulty. Having to describe these golden children.

HENRY: What line do you think I should take?

JOHN: Ignore them.

HENRY: That's bad journalism.

JOHN: What else is down there?

HENRY: Nothing. It's really too bad! I've waited for this discovery to give me material for my last article, and now look what turns up. If I don't make a success of it I can see myself being stuck in this wretched country for the rest of my life. I've been walking about at my wit's end.

JOHN: You'd best give a straightforward description, I'd think.

HENRY: Look at the drawings!

JOHN: Yes.

HENRY: Help me, Hogarth!

JOHN: Athens: Monday. (Have you a pencil?) The expedition led by Colonel S. F. Faramond (well, come on, man: take it down!) today reached an inner chamber of the excavation. (Shorthand, eh?) The work of eighteen months, as observed by Your Correspondent (that's you) has been successful. The find will disappoint many who had hoped for some revelation of the Periclean age, but will be of interest to those who have never before had any sympathy with archaeological science. (Stop sucking the pencil, Henry. Get it down. Here we go!)

This place – (have you a picture of your ideal reader? I have) – a room stamped down by time under the earth holds, sir, your youth. This place, dedicated to the sparrow and the swan, the rose, the poppy and the lime tree, sacred to Aphrodite, keeps safe the dark girl, the gay brave one in the language of the time, who loved you (so she said) most. Your correspondent has no wish to use these columns for confession or reminiscence but yes, she was known to him.

For she was born to many of us among the raspberry bushes on a hot afternoon in the garden when the younger children laughed and played, but you and I, sir, older (at least fourteen), silent, horribly wiser stayed out of sight: (I speak personally, Henry. You were probably curled up in a theatrical basket) born in the fevered heat on that torrid day with the sun falling out of the sky. She stayed with you growing in beauty and experience as your imagination and longing swept you into manhood. (Were you swept into manhood, Henry? I was. It entailed swimming the length of an ornamental lake at four o'clock in the morning. You're right. Another story). She was so nearly met. There was always the chance of absolute discovery in so many encounters. And yet. And yet.

Where was she? The dark girl with the wit of the sparrow, the viciousness of the swan, the arrogance of the rose, the vulgarity of the poppy and the contentment of the lime tree. Shall we say she was with you until you lost your ambition? Yes, sir, age is responsible for too much. That's agreed. It's responsible, you'll remember, for the loneliness which made you make do with that angel in tweeds across the breakfast table. She's kind to dogs, that one. At the moment she's patting a flat head and believes you to be reading the financial page. Soon she'll go from the room and pat you on the head as she passes. If you're lucky.

Your Correspondent wishes to send a message of hope to
the unloved.

The dark girl, the ideal born in the garden, has
been protected after all. Here, sir, are your boyish
scribblings on the wall, the formal patterns of desire
scratched on the end papers of your Liddell and Scott,
the undergraduate poems and the solitary drinking of
your thirties, all translated to beauty and (God help us,
Henry! Look here) truth. (I'd no idea Selwyn could
draw so well. See that with the hands – so). How foolish
you were, dear reader of *The Times*, to think she was
lost. She was here in every way. Playing the games,
laughing, lying, acting all the scenes and being a
woman. She was in this place. Waiting.

So put the dogs in kennels and send the angel in tweeds
to the committee meeting.

Trains leave daily. From Tunbridge Wells and
Leamington Spa, from Cheltenham and all university
cities, from Baden, Monte Carlo, Venice, Aix, Calais,
and all the places of loveless exile. Bags can be packed.
The pilgrimage can begin.

Yet wait! before you blow the dust from your Gladstone.
With the message of hope must come a warning.

Ah! sir, in two thousand years she has not aged. Her bed
is still a jousting ground: yours is now a place of rest. Her
way of adoration has become a goodnight kiss pecked into
the forehead. There are other differences too painful for
this journal to print.

Wait!

The breath you used to blow the dust from your
travelling bags has left you giddy and confused. Let the
train go. That whistle is the signal for departure, not an
impertinence.

In the Indian night which shrouds all love in seemly
oblivion now, another traces the anagram with an
enfranchised hand.

(*Suddenly.*) Turn to page Six for reproductions of the find
in detail.

HENRY: No, no!

(*There is a knock on the door.*)

JOHN: Nobody here!

(*CRISTOS comes into the room.*)

Hullo. I thought it might be – well, almost anyone else in this damned house.

CRISTOS: I've only just come in. The place seemed deserted. I felt you must have gone. What are you doing?

JOHN: Henry's article for *The Times*.

HENRY: Hogarth, when I'm asked for my help I treat the matter seriously. That is, I've always done so until now. I don't know what your particular problem is, but if you told me you were in the most horrible dilemma known to man I think I'd laugh. Laugh in your face! (*He goes out of the room.*)

CRISTOS: What have you done to upset him?

JOHN: What are we always doing to upset people? You've had a difference of opinion with Sophie, I understand.

CRISTOS: I wouldn't take down the dictation she was giving about you. She meant to rewrite certain passages in the light of her present knowledge.

JOHN: You think that's cheating.

CRISTOS: Oh, the whole thing's a swindle. It depends on who's to be the victim. I don't want it to be you.

JOHN: Why should you try to defend my reputation?

CRISTOS: Forgive me. I'm not. I'm trying to save my own creation.

JOHN: How does it come to be your creation when Sophie dictates?

CRISTOS: I'm making the book from her notes, certainly. You might say that I'm creating a work of fiction from certain established facts.

JOHN: Why doesn't Sophie protest?

CRISTOS: She'd only do that, I think, if she took the trouble to read it. She's not done so yet.

JOHN: At the moment she's in her room writing herself.

CRISTOS: I'm sure she's not. She's too lazy to write in her own hand. Half a line, perhaps. Nothing more. That won't scratch the surface of my central figure.

JOHN: I see. So whatever happens to me can t really affect your legend.

CRISTOS: No. I'll have to observe the practical details, of course. I'm hoping that from the time Basilios arrives you'll begin to live up to the book. That should make my work much easier. I've always preferred the truth.

JOHN: I'd like to help you in that. But I can't. I can only give you the facts and hope that your imagination can translate them to something worthy of your early chapters. I don't think it's possible, for the one end you can't have foreseen is domestic tragedy.

CRISTOS: Not marriage!

JOHN: No, no. Not that. Sometime ago you were walking with Caroline. You were talking of the unhappiness of love.

CRISTOS: We've done that many times.

JOHN: But on this occasion you pointed out a solution. The scarlet berries growing on the hillside.

CRISTOS: As a joke I believe I said –

JOHN: Many people in this tragic country believe those to be the answer. Am I right?

CRISTOS: Something like that.

JOHN: You've been taken at your word. Caroline distilled some of those berries this evening and put the stuff in my wine. And in hers.

CRISTOS: Oh, my God!

JOHN: So it seems as if the story will end here.

CRISTOS: You can't let that happen.

JOHN: Surely it's out of my hands.

CRISTOS: Keep away from her.

JOHN: I am. Too late.

CRISTOS: Your mind must be elevated. Make an effort.

JOHN: There's no point. She says it takes effect in eight hours.

CRISTOS: Less than that.

JOHN: Less? Then I'm dying before your eyes.

CRISTOS: Dying, Mr Hogarth?

JOHN: Yes. From the effect of the poison. Don't distress yourself. I'm calm. What's that noise? Are you laughing?

CRISTOS: Yes. I said to Caroline when she spoke of love, those – the berries – are believed by many to be the answer. Obviously our minds were not in accord.

JOHN: Meaning?

CRISTOS: The effect is mild. Romantic fiction calls it a love potion.

JOHN: An aphrodisiac. (*He looks at the drawings which he holds and then he throws them out of the window.*)

CRISTOS: That's what I meant. I should have remembered that Caroline is apt to see everything in terms of mortality. She thought it was poison. Oh dear, I must tell the poor child at once.

JOHN: No! I'll do that. Later.

CRISTOS: Be gentle. An unexpected return to life can be disturbing.

JOHN: Yes. Yes, I'm understanding that at the moment. Here's the damned thing on my hands again. What do I do with it? Finish packing.

(*SOPHIE comes into the room.*)

SOPHIE: I thought it would do you no harm to have to think on a serious subject for a while. Especially after your frivolous behaviour of the last two days. But I've relented and come to tell you. The wine Caroline gave you was harmless; it has no effect which a day's forced march won't cure.

CRISTOS: Mr Hogarth has already confided in me, and I've put him right on that point.

SOPHIE: Have you, indeed? You're extending your meddling activities beyond his written life now.

JOHN: You knew all the time, Sophie.

SOPHIE: Yes, my dear. The cook has a most comprehensive recipe book. I knew the moment you spoke of Man's Friend. The berries from the hill.

JOHN: That's why you called Caroline a silly girl.

SOPHIE: Well, so she is. The place is overgrown with dangerous herbs which would have polished you off in an instant. But she chose that.

JOHN: Have you thought that it might have been intentional? That she knew what she was doing and lied to me.

SOPHIE: I don't think that's so.

JOHN: I'd like to believe that she meant it.

SOPHIE: Why?

JOHN: Because I'm in love with her.

SOPHIE: You mean you'd like to believe she meant no harm.

JOHN: No, no. I'd like to believe she tried to kill me. It shows a degree of attachment I've never known before.

SOPHIE: Surely there have been several who tried to kill themselves.

JOHN: Oh, yes, several. But only themselves. That was mere selfishness.

SOPHIE: Then the news that you are what everyone else would call all right is not very welcome.

JOHN: Not at all welcome. It makes flight imperative.

CRISTOS: Ah! you're an Englishman. How shall I ever get you truly down on paper for posterity to marvel at?

SOPHIE: You are now writing *my* book.

CRISTOS: My dear Sophie, read it.

SOPHIE: That's what I've been doing for the last two hours. I wasn't able to concentrate myself, so I picked up the manuscript.

CRISTOS: Well?

SOPHIE: You've done a good job of transcription. Nothing more.

CRISTOS: You think the John Hogarth in that book is the man you've been remembering aloud to me?

SOPHIE: Of course. What else? Do you mean I don't know what I've been talking about?

CRISTOS: If you think the man in the book and the man you told me about are the same then yes, I do.
(*CRISTOS goes out of the room.*)

SOPHIE: Don't let me stop you from going on with your packing. I take it you're not waiting for Basilios.

JOHN: No, I must get out of here. It's a very dangerous situation.

SOPHIE: It is, if you've fallen in love with the girl. I was afraid it would happen, but you seemed so sure.

JOHN: I can't go until morning. There's no way of transport.

SOPHIE: Selwyn's been using some mules. You might take one of them.

JOHN: What's the time?

SOPHIE: A little past midnight.

JOHN: Only one person can save me now. Basilios. Why doesn't he come? To be under way through the night rolled in a blanket with the smell of the road dust and weapon oil for company could save me. If he's not here by morning I shall go to meet him.

SOPHIE: I think perhaps that's best. You know I'm not in favour of this insurrection, but I can see it's the only way out.

JOHN: I haven't lost my taste for it. Don't think that. It's not a mere expedient. My affections may now be here in this place but – how can I say this to you? – my duty and my honour are under the open sky in the north.

SOPHIE: Did you hanker after all that during the years in London?

JOHN: I think I must have done.

SOPHIE: You gave no sign of it.

JOHN: Didn't I? But even in those days the American in me wanted to be loved and the Scot in me wanted to be safe, and so began this everlasting and headlong flight. (*CAROLINE has come into the room.*)

CAROLINE: You've always known what you've been running away from, but have you ever paused to think what it is you're running towards? No, for I'm the first person to check you.

SOPHIE: You want him to think about it now?

CAROLINE: Why not? There's the rest of the night.

SOPHIE: Then try, John, try to be all Scot. (*She goes out of the room.*)

CAROLINE: I found these lying on the terrace. (*She is carrying SELWYN's drawings.*) Is this what you've been doing up here alone?

JOHN: It is not. They're your father's drawings of the figures in the dig.

CAROLINE: I thought you might have been remembering past triumphs.

JOHN: Caroline, why did you do it?

CAROLINE: Put the stuff in the wine?

JOHN: Yes.

CAROLINE: Because I can't weather another storm.

JOHN: Another?

CAROLINE: There would have been someone else, darling, somewhere, sometime, after you. You'd have gone and – well, you'd have gone and whatever I'd pretended I'd have been in clear calm water again with no excuse in the world for not sailing on. Yes, I'd have been on my way again smartly answering the helm when – look! it's nothing but a cloud. The sky's full of them. Natural things, like men. What's to be afraid of? That friendly little cloud's to be afraid of. And once again I'm trying to get through the deep waters. Exciting? Yes, it's exciting enough trying to steer a course. But there's panic aboard and Reason, the only unpaying passenger I have, is the first to go over the side. It's frightening when you can't see the sky, and there's no landmark in your past to go by. All swept away, they are. The tempest blows itself out. Nothing lasts for ever, not even bad weather. Some dawn or other it clears and you find yourself a long way out. You're safe. But you're drifting. And you're alone. Reason, the poor soaked fool, humble and ashamed, is fished out, hauled aboard, restored to its seat and at once starts giving advice. You take it and paddle on. This time I wanted to go down with all hands. And with you.

JOHN: It's not going to happen.

CAROLINE: Oh, yes, it is.

JOHN: No, you made a mistake. The berries are harmless.

CAROLINE: But Cristos said –

JOHN: You misunderstood. The stuff has a certain effect.

CAROLINE: What effect?

JOHN: Well, shall we say it strikes at a more private part than the immortal soul.

CAROLINE: I didn't know.

JOHN: Are you sure?

CAROLINE: Of course I'm sure.

JOHN: I'm glad.

CAROLINE: You're glad I thought we'd both be finished?

JOHN: Yes. No one's ever balanced my life so precisely with their own before.

CAROLINE: My God! You love me, don't you?

JOHN: Very much.

CAROLINE: Wait a minute. Have you forgotten? There's going to be a tomorrow after all. Can you say it knowing that?

JOHN: Yes.

CAROLINE: But, John, It's going to be for quite a while. Now say it.

JOHN: A man takes leave of a woman he's loved and an art he's practised in much the same spirit. He loves but he goes. That's what I'm doing now. Both are taken up in a moment of abandon which may occur in the best ordered life. It's difficult to believe that you who occupy little space as a person and the trivial act of writing a poem could in time crowd out the many necessary and amusing ways of living. But it's common knowledge that such is the case. Yet too many men end up as husbands or artists. Sometimes even the ultimate subjection: both.

CAROLINE: So I'm wrong again. It's not to be for quite a while. What's the matter with marriage?

JOHN: I don't know. Ask Boysie.

CAROLINE: He at least tried to make it work. You've never done that.

JOHN: I could make it work perfectly well. But as an arrangement it would be an impossible demand on the genius of the woman.

CAROLINE: Will you marry me, please? So forget Sophie. Go on. Be all Yankee. Will you?

(*SOPHIE has come into the room.*)

SOPHIE: If you delay your answer for a moment, John, there's some business you should attend to. (*She turns to the door.*) Will you come in, please. I found this gentleman waiting below.

(*PRINCE BASILIOS comes into the room: he carries a large black iron bicycle.*)

BASILIOS: Hogarth, my dear child!

(*He casts aside the bicycle and embraces JOHN.*)

JOHN: I'm very pleased to see you, sir. Did you have a good journey?

BASILIOS: No. We feared an ambush of our person.

JOHN: Has your machine brought you all the way?

BASILIOS: No, no. We came by train. Our machine was bought nearby for the emergency.

JOHN: You must tell me about that. First, may I present to Your Highness Mrs Faramond and Mrs Traherne.

BASILIOS: Basilios! We are made happy, Mrs Traherne. The beautiful Sophie engaged our attention and our affection below.

JOHN: Did she, indeed?

BASILIOS: You, Mrs Traherne, are beloved of our great Archistrategos?

CAROLINE: I hope to be, if you mean John.

BASILIOS: Bring him comfort, Madam. Prepare your breasts for his tears. God sent us such little animals for our sorrow. Where shall I find comfort? It is a question which must be settled later.

SOPHIE: Infected with John's enthusiasm we've all waited your coming with impatience, Prince Basilios. When does the revolution begin?

BASILIOS: We are disturbed, shocked to hear such a word come from the mouth of a woman.

SOPHIE: You mean our sex should concern itself only with the status quo ante.

BASILIOS: If you please. When all seems to be lost the world may yet find its salvation in the conservatism of the great regiment of women.

SOPHIE: That sounds strange coming from a famous leader of the people. I must say that remembering your charming conversation and manner downstairs I find it difficult to see you leading a mob of peasants to storm a palace.

BASILIOS: Hogarth, I think, has the same feeling about a lovely woman touched by the mud and blood of politics. He's told you nothing. Have you, my dear?

JOHN: Very little.

BASILIOS: So it seems. Do not think ill of us, Sophie. We do not rise at the head of the people. They have many leaders. No, my darling simpleton. The revolt is to restore the impoverished and unhappy aristocracy of my country. We are a few brothers bound by a belief in a former way of life. When so many today look forward we look back. But such things must not – no, never! – concern you. Now, shoo-shoo, little ones! Hogarth and I must talk in secret. So, shoo! to your prattle and gossip, your novels and embroidery frames. Shoo!

CAROLINE: I think he wants us to go.

SOPHIE: For the first time in my life, Caroline, I feel you're on my side against something.

(*SOPHIE and CAROLINE go out of the room.*)

BASILIOS: No cause to give way to despair before them.

JOHN: You've come with bad news.

BASILIOS: You see it in my face. Yes, my beloved boy, there is bad news.

JOHN: May I be told?

BASILIOS: I left London when I had converted your cheque into gold. There was too much to carry about my person, and so I stored it in a strong box bound with iron. I hired two Germans for my bodyguard.

JOHN: Yet you were robbed.

BASILIOS: Wait! We made the journey across Europe safely. We arrived in my country. At once I called a meeting of the Committee. I spoke to them. I told them of your promises. Many wept. I told them of your donation and the hundred thousand golden pounds were brought in. They were silent. Each man with his own thoughts.

JOHN: This is very moving. Please go on.

BASILIOS: The Archbishop spoke first. Where, he wanted to know, was the money to be kept? He at once suggested the cathedral. I countered this. It was to be kept, I said, under my bed. Hogarth, my dear, I will not even let my bicycle out of my sight in this country. On my way here I stopped by the roadside to perform a natural function. A matter of a moment, but when I returned the machine had been stripped of its pneumatic tyres, as you see.

JOHN: So the money found its way under your bed. Preparatory, I hope, to its original purpose of paying soldiers for the revolt.

BASILIOS: Of course. Yet no sooner was it beneath the bed than I began to receive petitioners. All my old friends. The Archbishop came to ask for a new roof on the cathedral, an aged general wanted new colours for a long disbanded regiment and my brother needed money for his gambling debts.

JOHN: I hope you reminded them of the true purpose of the funds.

BASILIOS: I did, my son. All of them. Except one.

JOHN: A woman.

BASILIOS: So beautiful. So unlike the others. Modest, she came with no demands, but with a proposition. Not for love of politics. For love of me. Precise and smiling she proposed that your money should be spent on a great reception. She told me it was the English way. It is known as charity. Admission would be charged. Your money would be doubled. The Committee of Freedom could sweep to victory. The idea was mad, yes! But I loved her, Hogarth! I listened to her talk but I didn't hear what she said. Before I could bring myself to my senses I found the grounds of my house to be transformed. All had become the setting for an English garden party. Marquees had arrived from the Army and Navy Stores, cakes were sent from Buzzards', a military band was playing Gilbert and Sullivan and my darling was in white organdie with English roses on her arm. I wept, my dear Hogarth. I wept for unutterable joy. The affair cost a fortune.

JOHN: Yet. Yet it was not a success.

BASILIOS: No one came except my beloved. She was heartbroken. Can I say that I was sad? No, I cannot, for it

became my duty to console her. We walked the gardens in
silence until the sun went down and the Chinese lanterns
were lit. The river pageant moved past in splendour for
my lady. My God! Hogarth, never have I loved in such a
way. Her face was to the stars as the firework display was
set off. Later in the ballroom we danced for the first and
last time. The thousand empty drinking glasses rang a
lament for the guests who had never come. But for us the
fiddles sang – and sang until their voices were faint to us
through the empty corridors of the house which led us
dancing to our further sport. When I took her in my arms
the diamonds fell from her hair, her throat and wonder
from her fell down the gown. At that moment, unknown
to me, the mob led by the Committee of Freedom – the
Archbishop, the General and my brother – had stormed
through the gates of the house. Well known to me, alas,
was the fact that the box beneath the bed on which we
played held no more than fifty golden pounds.

JOHN: Just enough to pay your fare here and buy a bicycle.

BASILIOS: Immediate flight was necessary the moment
they broke down the door. Treachery at cock-crow,
Hogarth. It was dawn as I went on foot over the hills to
the south. They may still be at my heels. That's why
I bought the machine.

(*JOHN is sitting at the window in silence.*)

You're angry with me, my son.

JOHN: No. What happened to the lady?

BASILIOS: Being Russian she pleaded diplomatic immunity.
She was kneeling before the Archbishop as I left. Don't be
angry with an old man, Hogarth.

JOHN: Was she beautiful, and were you truly happy?

BASILIOS: She was beautiful, yes, and for the last time
I was truly happy. The last time. For with her hands she
closed the gates of love behind me.

JOHN: I wanted to be sure the money wasn't wasted, that's all.

BASILIOS: Don't forgive me, Hogarth, or I shall weep!

JOHN: Nonsense! There's nothing to forgive.

BASILIOS: Ah! my wonderful boy, you came to bring
freedom to a country, and instead you're content to bring

happiness to an old man. (*He is beside JOHN at the window and he kisses him.*) Call back the women. See, there they walk. Let's be brave before them. Let's show we're not unmanned. (*He calls.*) Come up, my children! Come up, my darlings!

JOHN: Shall I be honest with you, Basilios? I wasn't concerned with the freedom of the country. I wanted freedom for myself. I'd have died in your cause, Basilios, whatever it was.

BASILIOS: My dear boy, you come from a country which has always spoken lightly of dying for the cause. Your great predecessor, Noel Byron, said you remember, If thou regret'st thy youth, why live?/The land of honourable death/Is here: – up to the field and give/ Away thy breath! God took him at his word, though, and fetched him off here.

JOHN: Even Englishmen must expect God to take them at their word sometimes.

BASILIOS: He must love them as he loves all his children. I think more than most for he gave them a special duty. To provide the legends of our time. But a day is coming, Hogarth, when the single man of vision will need more than God on his side. He will also need a party organ*i*sation.

JOHN: You were to provide that in the Committee of Freedom.

BASILIOS: I was only a weak instrument. I failed, Hogarth. Have you anything at all to thank me for?

JOHN: Yes, I think so. You trusted me. That may not seem much to be thankful for at the moment, but it will tell in time. Also you brought me here.

BASILIOS: To the beautiful Mrs Traherne? Shall I be content, my dear?
(*SOPHIE and CAROLINE come into the room.*)
We called you to us as we wish to take our leave. Our conference is done. I can go away content, he tells me.

SOPHIE: It's very late. Won't you stay tonight and go on in the morning?

BASILIOS: As things are it is wiser to travel at night.

CAROLINE: Is John going with you?

BASILIOS: Answer her yourself, Hogarth. See how much happiness can be given in one small word.

CAROLINE: Well? Either yes or no will do.

SOPHIE: I take it there's been some upset in your plans.

BASILIOS: To explain I'd have to talk politics, and you don't want me to do that.

SOPHIE: I don't mind.

BASILIOS: From deep experience I've found that women as beautiful as you, Sophie, should not be allowed even to speak of politics. A woman will always try to do right, and such a philosophy has nothing to do with political life.

SOPHIE: Very well. If the matter is only domestic I'd like to know how much longer we'll have John as a house guest.

BASILIOS: Cherish him. He's a great man. I wish I could tell you of the magnificent part he's played, but I must leave it to history. Now I shall go. Dear Hogarth. Pray don't think me a foolish old man in all things. When we're young it's possible to control the affairs of the state and the affairs of the heart at the same time. Older, one of them must be relinquished. Dear Hogarth.
(*He embraces JOHN.*)
I shall make for the coast. The fishermen are still friendly, they tell me. So a little boat shall carry me off.

JOHN: What will happen to you, sir? Where will you go?

BASILIOS: Where can I go? There is only one place. To Ithaca. To my wife's family.

JOHN: God help you.

BASILIOS: And you, my son.
(*BASILIOS, who has picked up the bicycle, and SOPHIE go out of the room.*)

CAROLINE: I'd say there's nothing left for you but to be happy. Sad, isn't it?

JOHN: And what is there left for you?

CAROLINE: You. Or have you some other commitment of honour to fulfil?

JOHN: No. I've nothing at all. Not even money now. What do you say to that? People always thought I was a rich man. I was not. I had an indulgent mother.

CAROLINE: Could you work?

JOHN: That's unkind.

CAROLINE: I didn't mean it.

JOHN: Yes, you did. You were looking at me as if I'm a pack horse you're about to load. You're not going to send me out to work Caroline. That's one thing nobody's ever suggested.

CAROLINE: Don't get so excited. We shall have to eat.

JOHN: There it is! The voice of the new century. We shall have to eat!

CAROLINE: Sorry. Boysie always left the practical details to me.

JOHN: You talk like a housekeeper.

CAROLINE: Won't that be my position?

JOHN: Now listen to me. For one moment listen to me. When I say that I love you I love you. Why when you hear it you should also hear the clatter of saucepans, the rattle of teacups and the rustle of bills I don't know. For God's sake, why should the mystical union of two souls be celebrated in a kitchen? Is the act of desire now dependent on the price of bedding? Caroline, Caroline, it's too soon to live happy ever after. Too soon.

(*CRISTOS comes into the room.*)

CRISTOS: Sophie's standing on the terrace kissing a strange old man with a bicycle.

JOHN: Never mind. Now that Selwyn's finished at the excavation you'll be seeing the last of her.

CRISTOS: I've been talking to Selwyn about that. It leaves me with a domestic problem.

JOHN: Well, now!

CRISTOS: You see, Selwyn's lease of the house runs only to the end of the excavation. I shall have the place to myself again.

CAROLINE: How much does Selwyn pay?

CRISTOS: Only a nominal sum. It's not that which worries me. I like having people around me. English speaking people. I've explained why to Mr Hogarth.

CAROLINE: Surely the excavation would be of great interest to tourists. It's your land. A small sum for admission. A guide. Me.

JOHN: No, Caroline, no! You're a monster, a fiend! First you domesticate love. Now you're trading it. There is a name for that sort of thing, my girl.

CAROLINE: What are you talking about? I'm only advising Cristos on how not to be lonely.

JOHN: If you can't leave me in peace at least leave those young everlasting lovers down the hill their privacy.

CAROLINE: Now you're talking romantic nonsense.

CRISTOS: Aren't you going to the revolution, Mr Hogarth?

JOHN: No.

CRISTOS: I'm sorry to hear that. What are you doing instead?

CAROLINE: Well, what are you doing?

JOHN: I'll wait for some decision to be made for me.

CRISTOS: That reminds me. Where's Henry? A cable's come for him. From England. A boy brought it from Athens tonight. (*He has taken a cable from his pocket.*)

CAROLINE: What does it say?

CRISTOS: I've not read it.

CAROLINE: Give it to me.

(*She takes the cable from CRISTOS and opens it. She reads.*)
'Cancel further articles on digging stop Proceed incognito to expected trouble centre Bosina stop Membership of secret society taken out for you signed Northcliffe repeat Northcliffe.'

CRISTOS: I don't want that back.

(*CAROLINE is holding the cable out to him.*)
I'll never have enough courage to give it to the poor boy.

CAROLINE: Somebody will have to give it to him.

CRISTOS: He's very fond of you.

CAROLINE: All right. Send him in when he comes back.

JOHN: Are you off to work on your book?

CRISTOS: No, I'm going to bed. Goodnight. (*He goes out of the room.*)

JOHN: There's another person who won't forgive me for
    not living up to his ideals.

CAROLINE: Forget all that. Just be yourself.

JOHN: I've never been anything else. Come here. Don't
    stand so far away.

CAROLINE: But I'm so near I can – (*She kisses him.*)

JOHN: What on earth's going to happen to us? Without the
    benefit of clergy, the sanctity of wealth and even the
    solace of age. No one will receive, respect or love us.
    Worst of all, they'll laugh at us. There's nothing so
    absurd as a man who's given up the world for love.
    They'll look at you and think. Is that it? And you'll have
    to admit it is. Don't go away. I want you where I can lay
    hands on you at a moment's notice.

CAROLINE: I've not moved. I'm in your pocket. This is a
    beautiful house. Sophie, Selwyn and Henry will soon be
    gone. No one would find us here.

JOHN: In a few days the place will be overrun by German
    professors with little trowels. They'd nose out why we
    were here.

CAROLINE: We can lie to them. I can lie in any language.
    Then we'll stay for ever. Cristos will accept the situation
    in no time, and be so proud to have you living there.

JOHN: He's proud to say I've stopped here on my way, but
    he won't be happy if I stay here permanently.

CAROLINE: Every moment makes it obvious that I put the
    wrong stuff in the wine. Tonight could have been so
    simple. Now we shall sit up talking.

JOHN: Caroline, a way has got to be found. You don't seem
    to understand my position. I left England saying that
    I was going to fight for a glorious cause. I made a great
    deal of it. The papers were full of it. A cartoon in *Punch*
    showed me going aboard a ship called *The Rake's Progress*.
    A question was asked in the Upper House; in the Lower
    House there were cheers and counter-cheers. From the
    fuss no one would have thought that I was trying to get
    out of the country. But I did. Only to find the cause is
    lost before I arrive. Now, I'm very sensitive to public
    opinion. How shall I feel when the news gets back to

England that there was nothing but pillow fighting with you in a villa near Athens?

(*SOPHIE comes into the room.*)

SOPHIE: I'm on my way to bed.

CAROLINE: Have you seen Basilios off?

SOPHIE: Yes, poor man. From what he told me he won't see a bed for weeks. He was insistent, John, on the fine part you've played in the revolution. You passed through it, apparently, untarnished and burning bright. His words.

JOHN: You got on well with the old man.

SOPHIE: He has a natural sympathy. I'd be a fool if I didn't see that his sorrow is caused by more than the failure of a revolt. When a man looks into your face, kisses you and whispers, So dies my ambition, he's not referring to a political party. Ah, well, he's gone. But you're still here.

JOHN: Don't let that be a problem any longer.

SOPHIE: I won't. For it's I who'll be leaving now that Selwyn's finished at this dig. Somewhere in Asia there's another piece of innocent ground waiting to be molested by him. Soon he'll be at work again digging up a day that was a thousand years ago, and I, nearby, less fortunate, at work on a mere decade. Yes, the future definitely seems to lie in the past.

CAROLINE: I don't believe that. For you, if you like. But you meant all of us, didn't you?

SOPHIE: Yes. Except, perhaps, Henry.

CAROLINE: Well, as a matter of fact we were talking about our future when you came in.

SOPHIE: You're planning it together?

CAROLINE: (*Together.*) Yes.

JOHN: (*Together.*) No.

SOPHIE: You've both been staggering under the past. You'll double the burden for each other if you share it. Not, as you think, halve it.

JOHN: The problem's not arithmetical, Sophie. It is how I can decently continue after what's happened. If you've any suggestions please tell me. If not, go to bed.

SOPHIE: I've been thinking about it since Basilios left.

JOHN: Any conclusion? For example, how are you going to end your book now?

SOPHIE: About that I could wait no longer. Some decision had to be taken. You'll die on the battlefield, as you wished.

JOHN: How can you? I thought you loved me.

SOPHIE: I do. So I shall end the book that way. It had to be arranged for another reason. You must know that modern readers like the end of a book to be sanctified by marriage. They call it, rather strangely, the happy ending. I've known from the first, of course, that such a resolution would be impossible with you as the main character. So I shall use the best alternative for the lending libraries. You'll die in battle.

JOHN: When?

SOPHIE: Tomorrow morning. I've sent a cable to the Editor of the London *Times*. It says reports from the mountains speak of you falling gallantly at the head of your native troops led in a lost cause. Naturally, I signed myself Henry Bevis. (*She goes out of the room.*)

CAROLINE: How sad! How terribly sad!

JOHN: Is it? I wonder.

CAROLINE: I mean because no one will believe me now when I say we were here together.

JOHN: No, not a soul will believe you.

CAROLINE: Unless, of course, you turn up in London as yourself. With me.

JOHN: I'll not do that.

CAROLINE: I feel as if I've never seen you before. Damn, oh damn and damn! This is what Cristos warned me about. Falling in love with a legend. You're a man. Just a man. Two a penny. That's what you are.

JOHN: Seeing me that way is the penalty of winning, Caro. You've never been anything but a woman to me. I've never asked that anyone I've loved should be more.
(*He lifts CAROLINE in his arms and puts her on the bed.*)

CAROLINE: You mean, however splendid the pursuit, and however corrupt the trickery, I'll end up with a man. Just a man.

JOHN: That's all.

(*JOHN gently pulls on the heavy silken cord and draws the curtains which quite surround the bed. There is a knock on the door.*)

Yes.

(*HENRY comes into the room.*)

HENRY: I want to apologise. I'm afraid the worry about the article made me lose my sense of humour and then my temper.

JOHN: All forgotten.

HENRY: I took another long walk and came to a decision. (*He is a little wild-eyed.*) I'm going to tell the truth about Selwyn's discovery.

JOHN: That's brave of you.

HENRY: Then I shall be called home in disgrace.

JOHN: Yes. Home! Wait a minute.

(*He looks in his pockets. Whilst he is doing so CAROLINE's bare arm comes through the curtains of the bed. She is holding out the cablegram to HENRY. He takes it, staring at the bed. He pulls the cablegram from the envelope. He reads it. Slowly, his face crumples. JOHN has moved to HENRY and now puts an arm round his shoulders. Together, in silence, the two men stand staring down at the cablegram. Then, quietly, JOHN speaks.*)

Do you have a little badge, or something?

(*HENRY shakes his head.*)

Go home. To mother, Incognito. Keep your mouth shut. Your articles will go on arriving. I shall also sign every one Henry Bevis.

(*JOHN gently takes the cablegram from HENRY, and begins to move to the door. CAROLINE speaks from the obscurity of the bed.*)

CAROLINE: May I ask one question? Just one.

JOHN: Yes.

CAROLINE: I want to know. Do we all get what we deserve?

JOHN: Yes. (*He is at the door.*)

CAROLINE: Every time?

JOHN: Yes.

(*JOHN gives a sad smile to HENRY and quietly goes from the room. CAROLINE's arm is still extended between the curtains of the bed. Suddenly, imperiously, she snaps her fingers. Slowly, HENRY moves to the bed and takes her hand in his. There is a pause.*)

CURTAIN

Introduction to

NO WHY
and
A WALK IN THE DESERT

In the summer of 1957, when Peter Hall was artistic director of the Arts Theatre, he was planning a production of Anouilh's *The Traveller without Luggage* in Whiting's translation, and he commissioned Whiting to write a new play as a curtain-raiser. This is how *No Why* came into existence, but Peter Hall changed his mind in favour of an Anouilh double bill, and asked Whiting to translate *Madame de...* His *No Why* was performed on the radio, but was not seen on the stage till 1964.

The least naturalistic of Whiting's plays, it contains echoes of Kafka, Ionesco and Pinter. Locked up in an attic, a small boy is being bullied by members of his family. They come in, one by one, wanting him to confess and ask their forgiveness for something he has done. As in *The Trial*, no specific charge is ever made, and, like Josef K, the boy, Jacob, may have done nothing wrong. None of the family has witnessed the misdeed, which, in any case, seems to have little connection with what they have against him. This is another play about isolation. What matters to the accusers is that Jacob is setting himself apart from them, stonily refusing to share their values.

As in Pinter's *A Slight Ache* and Ionesco's *The Killer*, the silence of one character incites the others to keep talking. They talk about fair play, happiness, goodness, having fun, caring, saying prayers, understanding, the beauty of love, being wicked and repenting, making sacrifices, living for others, freedom and justice. What becomes clear is that whether Jacob is innocent or guilty, the others are all morally reprehensible. He was conceived out of carelessness. His parents' plans for him were determined by their own anxiety and selfishness. The prison-visiting aunt is no more compassionate than the judge-like grandfather. The cousin is glib and hysterical. But the child is defenceless against these ruthless adults who use the notion of goodness as a weapon. The father tries to take

179

away the boy's sense of his own identity. Locking him into the attic overnight, the adult says he'll come back in the morning, "And then I shall hope to find my own little boy."

In some ways, *No Why* prefigures *The Devils*. Evil is masquerading as goodness while society is represented by a group that closes ranks to crush a weak but stubborn opponent whose only power lies in the possibility of refusing to confess. The question Whiting's plays provoke is why the conformists are so desperate to bring the non-conformist into line when he isn't even criticising them. Half-aware of their inadequacy as human beings, they feel he is challenging them by not conforming.

The 60-minute television play *A Walk in the Desert* was written in 1959, and Whiting described it as a rewrite of the stage play *Conditions of Agreement,* which dates from 1948–9. But it is hard to see much in common between the two scripts, except that neither play has a hero, that both are set in provincial cities and deal with moods of violent bitterness, depression and self-destructiveness.

Like Nicholas, Peter is lame. He almost falls short of being a man, while his friend, Tony, feels defeated. Unmarried at the age of 36, and liable to be mistaken for a welfare officer if he goes to local dances, he no longer cares how he passes the time, taking a mild vicarious pleasure in other people's experience. Ultra-serious about amateur acting, Peter's father is inoffensive but stupid, while his mother is well-meaning but ineffectual.

The action centres on a practical joke Peter plays on a girl who is hoping to work for their neighbour and turns up at their house, mistaking it for his. He is a successful writer, and Peter, who is jealous of him, maliciously impersonates him to interview Shirley, taking advantage of his opportunity to subvert her values, deriding the district she lives in and scoffing at her chances of marrying now that she has an illegitimate child.

It was a soldier who made her pregnant, and it was when Peter was in the army that a truck ran over his legs. Her meeting with her lover and his accident are reconstructed in detail through the dialogue. Trying to make her see herself as an outcast from society – like him – he undermines her optimism.

The tension between them can no longer be sustained once she has realised she is in the wrong house, but there is another good sequence when Tony, after watching through the window as she is turned away from the house next door, tries to find out why Peter treated her so badly. He explains it in terms of a compulsion to make himself felt.

When his parents return from an evening of amateur theatricals, it sounds as if Shirley may have drowned herself. The bell of a passing ambulance is heard, and the mother has seen policemen up to their waists in water. But the suspense in relieved when Shirley comes back for the handbag she has left behind: the police were rescuing a cat.

The play ends with a depressed monologue. Talking to his father, who says nothing and understands little of what he hears, except that he is being rejected, Peter describes his isolation, and his account of it is amplified by the depressing images we see on the screen – Shirley and Tony on their way from him, the rainswept town square, a train leaving a platform, a deserted by-pass.

NO WHY

Characters

JACOB
a child

HENRY
his father

ELEANOR
his mother

MAX
his cousin

SARAH
his aunt

AMY
his aunt

GREGORY
his grandfather

FIRST SERVANT

SECOND SERVANT

No Why was first staged as part of a programme of one-act plays, *Expeditions One,* at the Aldwych, London, in July 1964, with the following cast:

HENRY, Tony Church

ELEANOR, June Jago

SARAH, Elizabeth Spriggs

Director, John Schlesinger

The action of the play passes in an unfurnished attic.
Time – the present.

Die Ros' ist ohn' Warum, sie blühet, weil sie blühet,
Sie acht't nicht ihrer selbst, fragt nicht, ob man sie siehet

Angelus Silesius

An unfurnished attic room. Night.

The roof is beamed. There is no window, and the only light comes from a single unshaded electric lamp. There is one door, up centre. The only furniture is an upright chair placed down right centre. The lamp is on a small wood shelf right.

When the curtain rises, a small boy is sitting on the chair. He is in pyjamas. His name is JACOB. Throughout the play, except when indicated otherwise, he looks in front of him, appearing neither to see nor hear anything which occurs.

After a moment the door is unlocked from outside. HENRY, JACOB's father, enters and comes down to the left of the boy.

HENRY: You know why you're here.
  (*JACOB appears to be about to speak.*)
  Shut up. You know why, don't you? Bad boy. I want you to understand. Naughty boy. Say you're sorry. Come on, tell me you're sorry. We all do things we're sorry for. Ask to be forgiven. So much better. For you. For everybody. Makes them happy. Make you happy, too. (*He crosses slowly above the chair to right of it.*) You know you've done a bad thing. A bad thing. Mischief. You've hurt me very much. You've hurt your mother. Yes, your mother, Jake. You've hurt her very much. Make it better, will you? (*He kneels beside JACOB.*) Will you? Say you've done wrong. Look at me, Jake. Say you've been a bad boy.
  (*ELEANOR, JACOB's mother, enters. She cries out.*)
ELEANOR: No! (*She crosses to left of the chair.*)
HENRY: I'm not touching him. (*He gets up.*) I haven't touched him.
ELEANOR: Don't hurt him.
HENRY: I won't hurt him. I'm being very reasonable. Christ's sake, Eleanor, when have I ever hurt him? I've

always been fair. I want him to admit that he's been naughty. Done a bad thing. That's all.

ELEANOR: (*To JACOB.*) Say you're sorry, Jake. Tell Mother you're sorry.

HENRY: It's pride. (*He moves away down right.*)

ELEANOR: Not in a little boy.

HENRY: Stuffed. Up to here.

ELEANOR: (*To JACOB; kneeling by him.*) Listen, Jake. You've done a bad thing. Wicked. No, not wicked.

HENRY: Yes, wicked. (*He returns to the boy.*) We had a nice day today, didn't we, Jake? All of us, together. You enjoyed yourself. Yes, you did. I know you did. I saw you laughing. You were happy. Yes, you were. Quite right. We all wanted it to be a good day. One to remember. For grandfather's sake. And it was. A very good day. (*He pauses.*) Until you did such a bad thing. As your mother says, a wicked thing. Well, it's done. Day's spoilt. Nothing can make it good. No, nothing can make it good now. Pity. Nothing. But you can say you're sorry, Jake. Say you're sorry.
(*Silence.*)

ELEANOR: (*Rising and moving away to left centre.*) He doesn't understand what he's done. He just doesn't understand.

HENRY: (*Crossing above the chair to the right of ELEANOR.*) He may not understand what he's done, but he must understand, I've made it perfectly clear to him, that it was wrong.

ELEANOR: It's not enough. You must understand. You must. I know.

HENRY: You're a fool.

ELEANOR: I want you to explain to him, that's all.

HENRY: You want me to pretend. You want me to end up in the wrong. End up by admitting that I'm the one who's done wrong. Have me confess. Have me on my knees. I know you. Anything for a quiet life. A quiet life. That's what you want.

ELEANOR: No. I just want you to explain to him.
(*Silence.*)

HENRY: (*Returning to left of JACOB.*) Jake, it's easy to go wrong. As you grow up you'll find it's very easy. We can do harm. We can hurt people. But we don't do these things. As you did today. We don't do them because... (*He breaks off and pauses.*)
(*Silence.*)
(*Suddenly shouting.*) Who the hell do you think you are!
(*Silence.*)
(*More calmly.*) Why did you do it? I don't understand. Tell me why you did it.

ELEANOR: He doesn't know.

HENRY: Well, he knows he's shut up. (*To JACOB, crossing above to right of him.*) You know, that, don't you? You know you're being punished.

ELEANOR: We want you to have time to think over what you've done.

HENRY: That's right. Because we love you. We love you very much. We want to forgive you. Let's do that. Say you're sorry.

ELEANOR: You haven't explained. You haven't.

HENRY: I know. You want me down on my knees. To him.

ELEANOR: No, I want –

HENRY: Have I done wrong? Well, have I? You want me to say so. I know. I know what you want.

ELEANOR: (*Moving to left of JACOB.*) – I want him to understand, that's all.

HENRY: There are prisons. (*He crouches down by the chair.*) Jake, listen. Men are shut up all over the world. In prisons. Bad men, wicked men. Men who have done harm. As you did today. They sit by themselves. In little rooms. They walk in circles. In yards. Outside – (*Pointing to the door.*) out there! – are the others. We are the others. We are free. We live good lives. We don't destroy. We're good. We're good, Jake. Those shut up are bad. They're bad, Jake. So bad, some of them, so bad they never get free. They die shut up. Die. Never seen again. No. (*He pauses.*) Say you're sorry, Jake.
(*Silence. HENRY rises and move a pace to the right.*)

ELEANOR: Do you know what I'm thinking about, Jake? (*She smiles.*) I'm thinking about you grown up.

HENRY: Have you forgotten what he's done?

ELEANOR: No. No.

HENRY: Then why are you smiling? Why are you talking about the future?

ELEANOR: Because I want him with me. (*She kneels beside the chair.*) I want you with me, Jake. I shall need you. Always. Never away from me. So please your father. Be a good boy.

(*MAX enters up centre. He is a young man.*)

MAX: (*Moving to the left of HENRY.*) Uncle Henry, Mummy wants to know how long you're going to be?

HENRY: (*Taking MAX's arm.*) Look, Jake, here's your cousin Max.

MAX: (*To ELEANOR.*) Mummy says you could be done with this in no time.

(*ELEANOR rises.*)

HENRY: Now you've always liked Max. Or so it seemed. Aren't you disappointed? Max was going to play the piano and sing some songs. And you were going to be allowed down, Jake. You were going to be allowed down to listen. With the grown-ups.

MAX: (*To ELEANOR; moving above the chair to her.*) Fancy. I'd never have got away with it when I was a kid.

ELEANOR: He doesn't understand.

HENRY: Max will sing some funny songs for us. And you can come down, Jake. When you've said you're sorry.

(*Silence. MAX squats beside JACOB, looking up at him.*)

MAX: Come on, Jakey boy. Don't spoil the party. Gramp doesn't get much pleasure in life. His fun's over. But you've got to be good in some things so's you can be bad in others. Follow? Say you're sorry, you bad lad. Then everything's in front of you. See? Let Max teach you. If you knew what it's all about you wouldn't want to throw it away like this. Come on, you want to grow up, don't you? Then say: I'm sorry.

(*Silence.*)

HENRY: He doesn't care.

MAX: Who does? Let's be honest.

HENRY: He must be made to care.

MAX: Up to you. (*He rises and moves above ELEANOR to up left.*)

HENRY: (*To JACOB.*) You can't win! Not now! Save what you can, you little fool!
(*Silence.*)
(*Loudly; moving in to JACOB.*) I'll put you through hell!
(*Silence.*)

ELEANOR: (*Kneeling to the left of the chair.*) Remember when you were a little boy.

HENRY: That's it. Remember how I taught you your prayers?
(*MAX moves down left.*)

ELEANOR: You remember how they go.

HENRY: Of course you do.

ELEANOR: (*To HENRY.*) Oh, darling, I'm so happy.

HENRY: (*Crouching down.*) Let's try it, Jake. Just a little one to please me. I'll give you a start. Gentle Jesus, meek and mild. Go on from there. (*He waits.*) Well, anyway, you once said them. You said them once. I remember, if you don't. Down on your knees. Now look at you. Look at you now. Breaking a promise to Jesus, that's what you're doing. (*He rises.*) Think of it, Jake. Oh, Jake! To Jesus. How can you do it? How can you?
(*Silence. SARAH enters up centre and moves down to the right of MAX.*)

MAX: Mammy, Jake's being such a naughty boy. Won't say he's sorry for dreadful things he's done. He's damned, sure enough. His daddy promised him to come downstairs and hear me sing and play if he'll confess. But no, he's mum, Mammy. Oh, he's damned.

SARAH: (*Putting her hand on MAX's arm.*) You're a good boy, Max. You never disobeyed your father. When he was alive.

MAX: Oh, Mammy, I loved Daddy with all my heart.

HENRY: This child loves no one. (*He moves away down right.*)

ELEANOR: He loves me!

HENRY: (*Turning.*) You?

ELEANOR: He loves me!

HENRY: (*To JACOB.*) Do you?

ELEANOR: Yes.

HENRY: (*To JACOB.*) Love your mother?
(*Silence. HENRY laughs.*)

ELEANOR: It doesn't need to be said. (*She rises and moves above the chair.*)

HENRY: Which is lucky for you. It never will be.

SARAH: (*Moving a pace to the centre.*) Ah, this child doesn't understand the beauty of love. Pretty pretty. Doesn't understand the pleasure of giving in. I knew it so well! Until my hubbie was taken from me. To wake and find no one to submit to was a terrible thing.

MAX: You've still got me, Mammy.

SARAH: (*Moving back to MAX.*) Yes, darling, I've still got you. (*She fondles him in a disgusting way.*)

MAX: Oo, Mammy, I love you, I love you so.

HENRY: See that, Jake? Hear that? Ashamed of yourself?

SARAH: Darling.

MAX: Oo.

SARAH: Sweet.

MAX: Oo.

SARAH: Kisskiss.

MAX: Oo, loveee.
(*MAX and SARAH kiss. HENRY looks at JACOB.*)

HENRY: I had hopes of you. Even from the start. It was all so romantic. Soft lights and sweet music. Dancing cheek to cheek. I was young When I think of that I could cry. True, I could cry. (*He moves to ELEANOR above the chair, groping for her hand. To her.*) Remember how we planned for him? What should he be like, our son? Should he walk on two legs or on four? We decided two, remember? So his head should be nearer the clouds. You wanted that with your love of pansy poetry. The more feet on the ground the more realistic his outlook, I thought. But you kissed me and I gave in. And he turned out just as our conception of him.

All seemed right. Remember how happy we were? Remember the long winter evenings as we sat reading the school yearbook and careers for boys and he lay farting in his cot? And we laughed and loved him so much. (*He stares down at JACOB.*) That was this little criminal.

ELEANOR: You forget. You exaggerate. We had him in the same way everyone has their boy. More or less. It was late. You were tired. I was nearly asleep. There was nothing strange or wonderful about it. Of course we talked about his school when he was little, and what he might be when he grew up. But only because you worry about money so much. It was all from the very start for our sake, not for his.

(*HENRY lets go of ELEANOR's hand, and moves away right.*)

HENRY: You're taking his part again. This is not the time. If I was as soft as you are you'd have broken my heart long ago. Stand up to the boy!

ELEANOR: (*To JACOB; standing above the chair.*) Are you sorry for what you've done?

HENRY: (*To ELEANOR.*) Are you?

(*Silence. ELEANOR turns slightly upstage.*)

MAX: Mammy, when I was little was I sweet?

SARAH: You were adorable.

MAX: Did you ever have to shut me up like this?

SARAH: Never.

MAX: Not ever?

SARAH: No.

MAX: Did you ever have to give me a little smack?

SARAH: (*After a pause.*) Once.

MAX: Oo, Mammy!

(*AMY enters and comes down centre.*)

AMY: I've had to leave Father down there. It doesn't seem right.

MAX: (*Crossing below SARAH to AMY.*) Does he want to come up?

(*JACOB looks at AMY.*)

AMY: Well, you know what he's like. Hates to miss any fun that may be going. But I can't get the wheelchair up the stairs.

MAX: (*Moving up centre.*) I love Gramp very much. I won't let him be lonely. I won't.
(*MAX goes out.*)

SARAH: That's right, Jake. Look at your Aunt Amy. She's a really good woman.
(*ELEANOR, above the chair, turns downstage again. JACOB looks out front.*)

AMY: No, Sarah.

SARAH: Yes, Amy. A good woman.

AMY: No, Sarah, like little Jake here, I'm a wicked sinner. But I repent. Every time.

SARAH: (*Putting her hand on AMY's arm.*) Oh, you serene and beautiful person. You're wonderful, like – like treacle.

HENRY: No.

AMY: Perhaps I can help. (*She kneels to the left of the chair.*) When I was a little girl, Jake, about your age, I wanted everything in the world for myself. I thought I was beautiful –

SARAH: You were, Amy.

AMY: – talented –

SARAH: You were.

AMY: – and lovable.

SARAH: Wasn't she, Henry?

AMY: And I thought I had a right to everything. I was lost in a dream –

SARAH: Cut it short, Amy. Get to the point. Tell him about your prison visiting. How you tramp the hospital wards. And how you love the lunatics.

AMY: I go to see the prisoners, Jake. Sometimes the condemned men. They often take my hand and ask forgiveness. As you can. Now. Will you?
(*Silence. JACOB does not move.*)
I go into the hospital wards. No sudden death there. A florid growth back to nature. There's a man who is nothing but an enormous mouth, and he always asks my blessing. Will you? (*She pauses.*) In the asylums they run to me. Their darling childish faces are shining with love.

Their trust is so great. One night a young girl lay still.
Moths settled on her open eyes and drowned there. The
insane can learn nothing from me of faith and serenity.
But will you?
(*Silence.*)

HENRY: Don't you understand what your Aunt Amy gave
up to bring comfort to these people? Haven't you any
respect? She's offering her love to you and you won't
accept it.

AMY: It doesn't matter, Henry. (*She rises.*)

HENRY: It does matter, Amy. Is he so proud that he thinks
himself better than the condemned, the sick and the
mad? At least he should recognize the sacrifices you've
made. Oh, Amy, you were such a lovely girl when we
were children. Has it been worth it? Living your life for
others?

AMY: Always, Henry, when others accept it. Not like this
bloody little bastard of yours. This filth.

SARAH: I don't know how you and Eleanor came to have
such a child. How does our lovely, adorable brother
come to have such a child, Amy?

AMY: Perhaps as a curse.

SARAH: From God, darling? They come from God, you
know.

AMY: Of course, Henry, there is the criminal who doesn't
repent. The sick man who dies in silence. The madman
who laughs and turns away. Some don't need others. To
hell with them! (*She moves away up left.*)

HENRY: (*He kneels in front of JACOB.*) Say you're sorry. I'll
do anything. I'll give you anything. Jacob. Listen. You
heard what Amy said. Come back to the family party
before it's too late. Come with me. Please. Darling.
Come back. Come back.
(*Silence. ELEANOR cries out and moves away a pace up
stage. A long silence.*)
Come back.
(*Two SERVANTS enter. They carry GREGORY, JACOB's
grandfather, on a kitchen chair. He is old, a thrown-away*

doll of a man. The SERVANTS set him down centre stage, facing the child. MAX has followed them into the room.)

MAX: Just as you said. He couldn't bear to miss the fun.

(*He crosses above SARAH to down left of her.*)

SARAH: Father! Jake won't say he's sorry.

GREGORY: Does it matter?

(*The SERVANTS stand up centre.*)

ELEANOR: What do you mean? Doesn't it matter? Needn't he say it? Can he come down without saying it?

GREGORY: No. It doesn't matter because it's too late.

ELEANOR: Too late?

GREGORY: Yes. If all criminals got away with saying they're sorry, where should we be?

(*JACOB looks at GREGORY.*)

ELEANOR: He doesn't understand what he's done.

GREGORY: Nobody understands what they do. You sound as if you think that's an excuse. You're a fool. You always were a fool.

HENRY: So I tell her, Father.

ELEANOR: (*To GREGORY.*) Please try and make him say he's sorry.

(*GREGORY and JACOB stare at each other.*)

GREGORY: Why should I? It doesn't matter now. Not when you get to my age. It's not important, I tell you. All that matters is something called – (*He hesitates.*) justice.

(*JACOB looks out front again.*)

MAX: (*To SARAH.*) Oh, he's right. That matters lots. Where'd we be without it?

GREGORY: Has anybody got anything good to say about the boy? No matter how insignificant. Come on, speak up.

ELEANOR: He's always been very sweet to me. Loved me very much.

MAX: (*As if declaiming newspaper headlines.*) Mother's love fails to save child.

AMY: (*Coming down to above left of GREGORY's chair.*) They all love their mother. They cling to the idea. On the scaffold, under the knife. I love mummy.

GREGORY: Remorse. Any sign of it?

HENRY: I'm afraid not. After discovering the crime I went to see him. He was sitting up in bed eating jelly and drinking milk.

GREGORY: Seemed unconcerned?

HENRY: Yes.

MAX: *Distressing scene. Father in box. Admit's sons guilt.*

GREGORY: Has he been in trouble before?

HENRY: He used to wet his bed. He's over it now.

MAX: *Medical evidence causes stir.*

GREGORY: Let's come to the actual crime. Sarah, did you see it?

SARAH: Certainly not. I wouldn't look. I'm not used to such things. Ask Max. I always keep things nice.

MAX: She does, Gramp.

SARAH: I keep off the nasty. So I wouldn't look at what Jake did.

ELEANOR: Then how did you know it was so bad?

SARAH: (*Shouting.*) I read the newspapers, don't I? I know what a man is! (*She points at JACOB.*) That! It ought not to be allowed.

(*MAX protects her, putting his arm round her.*)

GREGORY: Amy, you're used to everything. The whole bag of tricks. Lunacy, sickness, the lot. What's your opinion? How bad was this?

AMY: (*To the left of GREGORY's chair.*) It was unforgivable. In my experience. A crime. An atrocity.

GREGORY: (*To JACOB.*) You hear that? What do you expect us to do? Take you back as our little boy? Our hope and our future. You can't expect that.

MAX: *Judge sums up.*

HENRY: I've tried to explain to him how we live, Father.

GREGORY: Does he understand?

HENRY: I think he understands that the road back is long and hard.

GREGORY: I'm too old to go back, Henry.

HENRY: (*Gently.*) We're talking about Jacob, Father.

GREGORY: Little Jacob. What's he done?

AMY: (*Shortly.*) He exists, Father. Look at him, there in front of your face. He is, Father.

(*GREGORY turns and stares at the child.*)

GREGORY: (*Laughing loudly.*) Jesus Christ. I don't have to find any punishment for you. Take me away.

MAX: *Sensation. Child condemned.*

GREGORY: Take me away.

(*The two SERVANTS lift GREGORY in his chair. AMY moves up left centre.*)

SARAH: You will let Max sing his song, won't you? The one about the commercial traveller's mother-in-law. He's learnt it specially.

GREGORY: Yes, let Max sing his song.

MAX: Oo, thank you, Gramp.

SARAH: (*Turning to MAX.*) If I get a bit tiddly, Max, promise to tuck me up, sweet.

MAX: 'Course, Mummeee.

(*The SERVANTS carry GREGORY from the room. SARAH and AMY exit after them. MAX moves up to the door.*)

ELEANOR: (*To HENRY.*) Let me stay with him.

HENRY: No.

MAX: *Last appeal fails.*

(*MAX goes out. ELEANOR follows him, shutting the door. HENRY and JACOB are left alone.*)

HENRY: When all's said and done there are only two left face to face. The executioner and the victim. And when it comes to that, Jake, when it comes to us, left alone, together, like this, what is there between us? (*He moves slowly above the chair and round to the centre.*) There's no hate. There's no love. There's nothing. Because we recognize each other for what we are. But the executioner comes out of the shed alive. Unfair. Poor devil.

(*Silence. When HENRY speaks again, a second voice is heard. It is HENRY's, amplified and independent. It speaks the following words. HENRY also speaks these words, and he is aware of the voice. Glancing about, he tries to shout it down. He hesitates, falters, catches up again to speak in unison, is borne inexorably along until the last moment.*)

It has to be this way. Because we are good. Out there. (*He indicates the door.*) Good people. Living good lives.

We've repented our existence. We're truly sorry that we are. We're on our knees for being. So we're allowed to go free. We're allowed to go wherever we like all over this little, tiny world. We're not confined. Oh, no. (*He moves down left.*) First of all there's the secure freedom of the womb. There's the freedom of the family. The freedom of loving someone. And more, being loved. And at the end there's the liberty of the tomb. (*Returning to the centre.*) All this could have been yours, Jake, if you'd said you were sorry. Don't you see what you were being offered? How could you be so stubborn? You were being offered what everybody wants. And you refused. (*Silence. The second voice begins. HENRY stumbles after it.*) You brought it on yourself. Look at us now. No feeling, as there should be between father and son. Not even feeling as between two human beings. You in here. And I'm...

HENRY's VOICE: (*Alone.*) Out here.

HENRY: You did it. You did it. First. By the enormity of your crime. Second. By refusing to confess. Confess. You did it. You did it. I wanted to love you so much. I wanted us to be together. I wanted to love you. Now...

HENRY's VOICE: I wish you'd never been born!

HENRY: No!

HENRY's VOICE: I wish you'd never been born!

HENRY: (*In a whisper.*) I wish you'd never been born! (*Silence. A piano begins to play below: a popular tune. There is the sound of laughter.*) (*Alone.*) I'm going down, now. (*He moves above the chair to the shelf right.*) I'm going back to the party. You'll stay up here tonight. You've been a very naughty boy, Jake. You must be punished. I'll come up in the morning. And then I shall hope to find my real little boy. (*He unplugs the electric lamp and moves with it to the door.*) The boy I want to love.

(*HENRY goes out. The door is locked. The piano is being played downstairs. JACOB gets up from the chair. He comes forward and stares into the theatre. He waits, as if for a word. Do any of us speak? No. And if we did, what would we say? JACOB turns and goes up stage into the darkness. The piano plays. The chair falls.*

We get used to the darkness. We see. The child has hanged himself from one of the roof-beams. He swings on the cord of his pyjamas, and the trousers have fallen about his ankles. He looks a useless object: a bag of bones. Cheap meat on a butcher's hook.

The piano and the laughter continue as the curtain falls.)

CURTAIN

A WALK IN THE DESERT

Characters

PETER SHARPE

LAURA SHARPE
his mother

CHARLES SHARPE
his father

TONY COLEMAN
his friend

SHIRLEY FLANDERS
his enemy

A Walk in the Desert was televised by the BBC on 25 September 1960, with the following cast:

PETER, Kenneth Haigh

LAURA, Joyce Heron

CHARLES, Lawrence Hardy

TONY, Nigel Stock

SHIRLEY, Tracey Lloyd

The action of the play takes place in a house in a provincial town in England. The time is the early part of the year.

A small town in the English Midlands.

Distant gasworks seen across polluted meadows. It is winter, early evening. Sunday.

A public park. Goalposts. The statue of some forgotten liberal reformer: bird-stained. Children's swings are tied to the posts in a puritan way. The bandstand drips with recent rain. Puddles.

Distant church bells: evensong.

A canal. It borders the park. Trees overhang. The water is black, reflecting the street lamps which are beginning to show against the sky. The canal is spanned by an iron bridge. Ornate for such a simple crossing, it must be a memorial to someone or something.

Facing the canal, beyond a road, is a row of houses. They are in pairs. They have the solid ugly faces of nineteenth-century prosperity looking into the twentieth century without forgiveness. Steps go up to the front doors: the basement windows have kept their heavy grilles. The brown stone of the houses is stained. The plants in the narrow gardens seem to be dying, although evergreen.

The church bells can be heard. They fade.

A drawing-room in one of the houses. Nothing 'contemporary' here. Haute bourgeoisie: 1930. And for nearly thirty years, until the present day, it has stayed so. Furniture: mahogany. Curtains: velvet. Books behind glass. A wood fire. Winter flowers. Everyone goes soft-footed over the heavy carpets. The clock has a musical strike, hardly audible.

PETER SHARPE is lying on a sofa. He is reading a Sunday newspaper. In a moment he will lower the paper and can be seen to be a young man of twenty-four.

His mother, LAURA, stands at the foot of the sofa looking down at him. She is wearing a hat and coat and is pulling on some gloves.

LAURA: Will you be all right, Peter?
PETER: Yes.
LAURA: We shan't be long, dear.
PETER: Where are you going? Church?

LAURA: No, darling. We're going to the rehearsal. I've told you.

(*PETER drops the paper to the floor: puts his hands behind his head: stares up at his mother.*)

PETER: Of course. The amateur dramatics. Father's self-expression.

LAURA: You mustn't laugh at Daddy. He takes it very seriously.

PETER: What's he acting this time? Hamlet?

LAURA: No. It's a thriller. A whodunnit, as Daddy says. He comes in right at the end. As a detective.

PETER: Does he speak?

LAURA: One line. He makes an arrest.

PETER: Good. Well, it passes the time.

LAURA: What are you going to do?

PETER: Do?

LAURA: This evening.

PETER: I don't know. Tony's coming round.

LAURA: Oh, that'll be nice. I'm so glad that you've got him as a friend. Of course, he's quite a bit older than you.

PETER: Yes.

LAURA: Well, I expect he'll have some idea of what he wants to do.

PETER: I expect so.

(*CHARLES SHARPE, PETER's father, has come into the room. He is carrying a raincoat, a book and a clothes-brush He holds out the brush to LAURA.*)

CHARLES: Give me a brush down, my dear.

(*LAURA takes the brush and begins to do so. PETER has not moved.*)

PETER: Can I hear your line for you, Father?

CHARLES: My what?

PETER: Your line in the play.

LAURA: Now don't tease him, Peter. He's very impressive when he comes in through the French windows and arrests the murderer.

PETER: What happens then?

LAURA: The curtain comes down. It's the end, you see.

PETER: I see.

(*CHARLES has been slowly turning round as his neat dark suit has been brushed. Now he stands staring down at PETER.*)

CHARLES: Well, at least I do something on my Sunday evening, Peter. I know you find our little amateur dramatic club funny, but it's sociable. I meet people. And we have a few laughs.

PETER: And there's the exercise walking to the church hall and back for rehearsals.

CHARLES: Certainly.

PETER: I'm sure there's lots to be said for it.

CHARLES: There's more to be said for it than sticking in the house all day. I don't think you've been off that sofa since the papers came this morning.

(*LAURA has put down the clothes-brush and now comes forward to help CHARLES on with his raincoat.*)

LAURA: Now, Charles, remember…he gets very tired.

CHARLES: I know. But I'm sure there are things you could do, Peter. A hobby of some kind.

PETER: What do you suggest?

CHARLES: I can't suggest. A hobby is a personal thing.

PETER: Like a Woman. For the hours when you're alone. Go to your rehearsal, Father.

LAURA: But you're not going to be left alone, darling. (*To CHARLES.*) Tony Coleman's coming round.

(*CHARLES is into his coat: he pushes the book into a pocket.*)

CHARLES: That's all right, then. Come on, Laura, we shall be late. We'll want an umbrella. It was spitting with rain.

(*CHARLES goes out of the room. PETER glances up at LAURA. She is about to speak, when PETER interrupts.*)

PETER: Have you got any cigarettes?

(*LAURA opens a bag she is holding and begins to look anxiously through it.*)

Oh, not if you've got them in there. They'll stink of powder. I'll smoke Tony's when he comes. You look very nice.

LAURA: Thank you, darling.

PETER: You look absolutely right for a rehearsal of a

thrilling play in the church hall on a Sunday night. How
do you manage it?

LAURA: Well, Daddy likes me to be properly dressed.

PETER: How would he like me, I wonder?

LAURA: He loves you very much, Peter. I know he still
thinks of you as his little boy.

PETER: What?

LAURA: Daddy does. He's disappointed, of course… (*She
suddenly cries out.*) Don't open it in the house!

(*CHARLES can be seen through the open door struggling
with an umbrella in the hall. He looks up, irritably.*)

CHARLES: What do you say?

LAURA: Don't open it in the house. It brings bad luck.

(*CHARLES crosses the hall and goes from sight towards the
front door. PETER looks up at his mother.*)

PETER: Do you really believe that?

LAURA: Of course.

PETER: Well, it may explain quite a lot…

(*In the open front doorway of the house:*
*CHARLES is holding the umbrella open before him. He
snaps it shut and reveals TONY COLEMAN, who has come
up the steps.*)

TONY: Good evening, Mr Sharpe.

CHARLES: Hullo, Tony.

TONY: What on earth are you doing?

CHARLES: My umbrella's broken. Mustn't open it in the
house, you know.

TONY: Bad luck.

CHARLES: Come along in.

(*CHARLES and TONY move into the hall, CHARLES
shutting the door.*
In the hall:
*TONY COLEMAN is thirty-six years old. He takes off his
army-type raincoat and shows himself to be dressed in a tweed
jacket, cord trousers, suede boots, club tie, signet ring: things
like that.*
*As CHARLES is taking TONY's coat from him and putting
it over a chair he says quietly.*)

It's very good of you to come round, Tony. My wife and I appreciate it very much.

TONY: You make it sound as if I'm doing a duty, Mr Sharpe.

CHARLES: Well, in the circumstances...

TONY: You mustn't think of Peter in terms of people visiting him, or being sorry for him. He just wants what we all want. A bit of company, a laugh, some way of passing the time.

CHARLES: Your friendship means a lot to him.

TONY: I'm glad. (*He smiles.*) Can I go in?

CHARLES: Of course.

(*In the drawing-room:*
PETER looks up. He waves. TONY is standing in the doorway.)

PETER: Hullo, Tony.

(*TONY comes into the room. He stands at the foot of the sofa looking down at PETER.*)

TONY: How's the boy?

PETER: (*Smiling.*) I'm all right.

(*CHARLES has come into the room after TONY. LAURA is at a looking-glass letting down a silly little veil from her hat. She can see PETER and TONY in reflection.*)

LAURA: Why don't you both go out, Peter?

TONY: Why not? I've got the car.

(*PETER still stares up into TONY's face. TONY, smiling, stares back with confidence, not shy. LAURA has turned and looks from one to the other. Shut out from the secret understanding between the two men she speaks a little too sharply.*)

LAURA: The air will do you good. Peter, listen! I said...

PETER: I heard what you said. Give me a cigarette, Tony.

(*TONY takes a packet of cigarettes from his pocket and throws it into PETER's lap. CHARLES has come forward.*)

CHARLES: Let them settle their own amusements, Laura. And we must go. (*To TONY.*) I have a rehearsal. The amateurs, you know.

TONY: I often see your name in the paper.

CHARLES: Yes, they're very kind to us. But I shan't be mentioned this time. I've got a very small part.

TONY: Oh, bad luck.

CHARLES: It's the way it goes. Sometimes a big part; sometimes small. Turn and turn about.

TONY: That's the spirit.

CHARLES: Exactly. It's the spirit that counts. The getting together. The – yes, the mucking in.

(*CHARLES stares down at PETER, who is inhaling the cigarette, hand over mouth.*)

I wish I could get Peter to see that.

(*Silence. LAURA has gone to the door. CHARLES turns away and joins her. For a moment they stand together in the doorway. PETER, drawing on the cigarette, stares at them. CHARLES's voice is heard.*)

There's some whisky in the cupboard.

PETER: (*Distinctly.*) Goodbye.

(*PETER's face is seen closely as he watches his mother and father go. The front door is heard to shut. PETER exhales the cigarette: it is a sigh, a release. He is holding out the packet to TONY, who takes it.*)

You're so nice to them.

TONY: Your mother and father? Why not?

PETER: You take them seriously. You don't seem to think the acting, all that make-believe in the church hall, is silly...or sad.

TONY: Is it, old boy?

PETER: Yes.

TONY: Sorry. Don't quite see what you mean. What shall we do tonight?

PETER: Astonish me with a suggestion, Tony.

TONY: What? (*He laughs.*) I say, the Sunday hell's got you, hasn't it?

PETER: No more than usual. No more than any other day of the week. Of course, on Sundays I have to suffer Father. I have to search my conscience. Why don't I *do* something? That question comes up every seven days.

TONY: Well, I expect he worries. He wants you to be happy.

PETER: Happy? Don't be silly. Father doesn't know anything about happiness. He wants me to meet people and chatter, get about best I can, join in, muck in, so that he doesn't have to be ashamed of me. Did he say something about whisky? Give me a hand.

(*TONY holds out both hands to PETER, who takes them. PETER swings his legs down from the sofa. It is apparent that he is crippled in some way. It may very well be that his right leg is artificial from above the knee. The disability is very noticeable as he releases himself from TONY and moves across the room.*)

TONY: Do you want this?

(*TONY is holding out a walking-stick which was underneath the sofa.*)

PETER: No.

(*PETER goes to a cupboard. He opens it and takes out a bottle of whisky. He holds it up to TONY.*)

Feel like it?

TONY: Why not? Let's make it for the road and drive out to the Black Bull. Harold's always good for a laugh on a Sunday night.

PETER: Harold's jokes are like his pub. Dirty, without being gay.

TONY: There's nothing wrong with old Harold. But if you don't want to go...

(*PETER holds up a glass with about an inch of whisky in it.*)

PETER: I never know how much of this stuff it's decent to offer.

TONY: That'll do.

(*TONY takes the glass and adds some soda water which is on the cupboard.*)

I don't see why you should have it in for Harold.

PETER: He's a drunk.

TONY: Well, maybe he does take a bit more than he should, but he's made 'The Bull' the only amusing place to go to for miles around this bitch of a town. You're always saying you hate the place. Why go for somebody who's trying to break it up a bit?

PETER: (*He is drinking: making a face.*) That's not the answer, Tony. It's not an escape to sit in that horrible little bar with Harold breathing over you, and telling you for the hundredth time how he had the local tennis champion in the sports pavilion after winning the mixed doubles ten years ago. The place isn't even an oasis of sin. It's just dull, that's all. But you go, if you want to. I'll be all right.

TONY: I don't really want to go. I just thought it would be somewhere to make for. A sort of place.

(*TONY has wandered away across the room. As he goes he picks up a local newspaper: folds it. PETER is leaning against the cupboard watching TONY with the same intentness with which he looked at his parents.*)

PETER: Tony –

TONY: Um?

PETER: Why do you come here?

TONY: Would you like to see a Western? (*He is reading the advertisements.*) It's called *End of the Trail.* Starts at seven. At the Regal.

PETER: No. I'd rather sit here and have you read *David Copperfield* to me.

TONY: What? Oh, I see, you're being funny.

PETER: Yes. Why do you come?

(*TONY throws down the newspaper and turns to PETER.*)

TONY: Look, old boy, we're what's known as friends. Perhaps I'm a bit innocent in such matters but I've never thought friends needed a reason to see each other.

PETER: You're ducking the question. Go on, answer it. I'm interested.

TONY: I have answered it.

PETER: Then I don't understand. You're very popular in this town. We must ask good old Tony Coleman. I'm sure they're always saying that. If there's any amusement in this God-forsaken place I bet you know where to find it. And...what's the matter?

TONY: Nothing. Go on.

PETER: And yet you come to see me. What about the girls, Tony? You make money out of that estate business of yours. You can afford to take the girls around. Out to the 'Black Bull'. Why don't you?

TONY: Finished?

PETER: Yes.

TONY: I was born in this town. Like you. I grew up in it. Like you. I went to the Grammar School when it was a grammar school, and not the local louts' reformatory. I've always accepted the place as it is...

PETER: Not like me.

TONY: No, not like you. The war took me away, but when it was over I was quite glad to get back and go into the business. And when I was back...yes, there were the girls. I did my share of walking over the Common to the woods past the sports ground, and for the really serious business down to the meadows behind the gasworks. And there were the evenings with the boys, with Harold before he married and took the 'Black Bull', when we went drinking. Nice uncomplicated times.

PETER: Well then, what are you doing here?

TONY: I'm thirty-six, Peter. The girls I went with have mostly married by now. Those that haven't...well, they'd probably catch a nasty chill if they went walking by the gasworks today. As for the chaps...they settled down. Home comforts, you know. Do it yourself. That sort of thing. And I'm left.

PETER: Are you...are you trying to tell me...are you trying to tell me that you're lonely?

TONY: I wandered in to a dance at the Town Hall the other Saturday night. They've been going on as long as I can remember. They were always good for a pick-up. But this time... I was out of my depth. I couldn't have danced that stuff. And they were drinking soft drinks. Didn't seem interested in sex as such. Anyway, the girls were awful. Then one of them asked me if I was a welfare officer. I could have hit her fat pasty little face. (*He laughs.*) No, but really...a welfare officer. I was after creating the social problem that night, not solving it. (*Pause.*) Yes, I suppose I am.

PETER: Lonely?

TONY: It's such a word. Let's say middle-aged, and leave it at that. What shall we do?

PETER: I don't know. I don't know.

(*PETER is sitting on the sofa again, his right leg stuck awkwardly before him. TONY has his whisky glass cradled in his hands and is looking down into it.*)

(*Very quietly.*) I thought you knew people. People as they are today, I mean. I thought you got about.

TONY: Are you disappointed?

PETER: A bit.

TONY: You must ask someone of your own age. Someone like Brian Dickinson. Does he still live next door?

PETER: Yes, he's home again. After all the success and shouting he's come back to Mummy, the bloody fool.

TONY: Just thought of this. Why do you want someone to tell you? You could go about on your own, if you wanted to. Find out for yourself.

PETER: Yes, I could. But, you know, you get more than a sense of embarrassment with this sort of thing. (*He strikes his leg.*) You get a sense of shame.

TONY: Why? It wasn't your fault.

PETER: No, it was what they call bad luck. Did I open an umbrella indoors? Or walk under a ladder? Or smash a mirror? I was brought up to look out for such things.

TONY: It was chance.

PETER: Yes. You happen to be standing in a certain place at a certain time. And all the shut umbrellas and unbroken mirrors can't prevent that. I'd only been in the army a week, you know. I suppose I was the typical National Service idiot, but I was quite enjoying it. I never saw the truck backing towards me. It knocked me flat on my face with the tailboard. I wasn't hurt. Just angry. Then the wheel went over my legs. And the pain... Jesus, that took the anger out of me. I wanted to cry. I passed out.

TONY: Forget it.

PETER: Chance. A summer morning. Two fools in badly fitting uniforms. One learning to drive a truck. The other dreaming. To this day I can't remember what it was so occupied me that I never saw the truck coming. It would be nice to think that it was something important.

For I had a lot of time to fill in later on. Nearly a year in hospital. Everybody was very kind. So kind that I came to hate the word. And the act. That wasn't chance. That was deliberate.

TONY: You suspect kindness. You don't hate it. And you mix it up with pity. Like your father.

PETER: Perhaps.

TONY: You should accept it. Along with the unlucky chance.

PETER: Why should I?

TONY: Because that's the way things go, my dear old boy.

PETER: Why do they go that way?

TONY: Don't ask me. But you see it all the time.

PETER: So I accept it. Now where am I?

TONY: Oh hell. You're just one of the unlucky ones, I suppose.

PETER: And Brian next door is one of the other kind.

TONY: That's right.

PETER: He and I used to play together when we were small. We were born on the same day. That gave a sense of mystery to our friendship which was very satisfying to little boys. And our lives were much the same until our call-up. You know what happened to me. Brian got through untouched. He never even caught a cold in the head. And when he came out he wrote his book. His *funny* book about army life. With its comic sergeant-majors and fatuous officers.

TONY: Yes, I've read it.

PETER: Everybody's read it. And seen the film. And laughed and laughed. Brian's rich and famous. I'm...
(*PETER holds up his glass. He looks at TONY.*)
Shall I have some more of this?

TONY: Why not?
(*TONY takes PETER's glass and his own over to the cupboard to pour the whisky.*)

PETER: I'm left here. Things go on. But how they go on... I don't know about that. And you're no help, it seems. I read magazines and newspapers, and there are the people.

Some of them up to no end of strange things. I pass them in the street. But I don't *know* anybody. News from the World, Tony, that's what you should bring me on Sundays. How the Young Live and Think.

TONY: Damn the young.

PETER: Our Special Correspondent. The Man on the Spot.

TONY: Shut up. Take this.

(*PETER takes the glass of whisky. Drinks.*)

PETER: And every one of them...all the people in the news...are at a certain place at a certain time. Just as I was. Headline! Man Killed in Car Smash. He should have been a moment ahead or a moment behind, in more or less of a hurry. Headline! Old Woman Coshed on Common. She should never have taken the short cut home. Never. Headline! ...

(*The doorbell rings. Silence. The two men glance at each other.*)

See what I mean?

TONY: Who is it?

PETER: I don't know. Let's find out.

TONY: I'll go.

PETER: No, no.

(*PETER pulls himself up from the sofa and begins to move towards the door.*

In the hall:

PETER comes from the drawing-room into the hall. From somewhere in the room behind him a small clock is striking rapidly. TONY can be seen, glass in hand.

When PETER is in the hall the front-door bell rings again. Very strident here. PETER looks up at the bell: it is above the door. Silence. PETER goes to the front door.

He opens it.

In the open front doorway of the house:

A young girl is standing on the steps of the house. She is about twenty. No hat. A raincoat. A handbag held against her body. The street light is behind her casting her face in shadow for the moment.)

GIRL: I've come about the advertisement.

(*She holds out a slip of newspaper to PETER, who takes it. He steps back into the light of the hall and reads the cutting through. He looks up.*)

PETER: Yes, of course. Come in.

(*The girl comes into the hall. Her pretty tilted face can now be seen. Thin, tense body under the neat clothes. Small, red hands.*

She turns in the middle of the hall as PETER shuts the front door.

In the hall:)

GIRL: Through here?

(*She means into the drawing-room. PETER comes forward, shaking his head.*)

PETER: No. Let's go in here.

(*In a darkened room:*

There is a little light from the street lamp, for the curtains are not drawn.

The door opens. PETER comes into the room. He switches on the light. It is one of a pair of small crystal chandelier lights. This is a dining-room, little used. It has the desolation of an unwanted room. A long table, with eight chairs round it like mourners. A gilt-framed mirror over the fireplace. A sideboard set out with silver pieces.

The girl has followed PETER into the room. She stands just inside the doorway. Almost imperceptibly she shivers as the cold of the room strikes her.)

Shut the door.

(*The girl does this, and then moves to the end of the long table, standing beneath the light. PETER has gone to the far end of the room: there is less light here.*)

GIRL: You are Mr Brian Dickinson, I suppose.

PETER: (*After a moment.*) Yes.

GIRL: The writer.

PETER: (*He has been staring down at the newspaper cutting: now he looks up.*) Yes, of course. Have you read my book?

GIRL: No. But I saw the picture. I thought it was ever so funny.

(*A pause. The girl looks down at her distorted reflection in the table top: she traces it with her finger.*)

Well…you say there you want a secretary…temporary …typing and shorthand…apply Sunday, seven o'clock… here I am. I suppose you're waiting to tell me you've already got somebody.

PETER: No.

GIRL: I don't know if I'd suit. I last worked in a coal office. This'd be different.

PETER: Yes.

GIRL: I thought you'd have lots of people applying.

PETER: What's your name?

GIRL: Flanders. Shirley Flanders.

PETER: How old are you?

(*The girl is looking across the table directly at PETER.*)

SHIRLEY: Twenty. What's the matter?

PETER: Nothing. Why?

SHIRLEY: You were looking at me as if…well, I don't know…as if there's something pretty strange about me. Look, you must ask me any questions you want. I've never gone after this sort of job before.

PETER: I've never had a secretary before.

SHIRLEY: Then we both start flat.

(*In the drawing-room:*

TONY is seen. He is standing in the room, smoking a cigarette and drinking whisky. He looks across the room through the open door at the shut dining-room door. He slightly turns his head: there is only a murmur of voices from the other room.

In the dining-room:

SHIRLEY is speaking.)

SHIRLEY: …so, you see, that's the only thing. What hours would you want me?

PETER: It's hard to say. Probably mornings.

SHIRLEY: That'd be all right.

PETER: (*After a moment: quietly.*) Yes, you'll do.

SHIRLEY: But you haven't asked me anything proper.

PETER: What? No. Will you wait here a minute?

(*PETER comes up the room. SHIRLEY watches him.*

In the drawing-room:

TONY looks up as the dining-room door opens. PETER comes from the room and crosses the hall into the drawing-room.)

For a moment SHIRLEY can be seen standing alone, but almost at once the two men move from her line of sight. PETER holds out the newspaper cutting to TONY, who takes it. TONY reads it: looks up.)

TONY: Well? She's come to the wrong house.

PETER: Yes.

TONY: She wants next door. Have you told her?

PETER: No.

TONY: Why not?

PETER: What?

TONY: Why not?

PETER: You're scared of young people, aren't you, Tony? It showed when you told me about the Town Hall dance. And I don't know anything about people of my own age. Not in the last five years. Well, there's one. Aren't you curious?

TONY: No.

PETER: I am. Come on, you wanted something to do. Something for a laugh. Let's interview her.

TONY: How can you?

PETER: She thinks I'm Brian Dickinson. She thinks I write funny books. She thinks I want a secretary. *(He calls.)* Miss Flanders!

TONY: Look here, Peter, what…

(SHIRLEY can be seen in the dining-room across the hall.)

SHIRLEY: Shall I put the light out?

PETER: If you like.

(SHIRLEY reaches out to the switch: darkness beyond her. She comes forward across the hall and into the drawing-room. She stands facing the two men.)

This is Mr Tony Coleman, a friend of mine. He's a business man. Knows all about secretaries. What did you say your first name is?

SHIRLEY: Shirley.

PETER: This is Shirley Flanders, Tony.

TONY: How do you do.

(SHIRLEY nods her head. She is looking from one man to the other, unsure.)

PETER: (*Smiling.*) Sit down.

SHIRLEY: Mr Dickinson, I don't think I'll suit you at all. Much better if I...

(*She half turns to the door.*)

PETER: (*Interrupting her.*) Don't you need the job?

(*The girl stops, turns back, looking at PETER.*)

SHIRLEY: Well, yes...yes, I do.

PETER: Then sit down.

(*SHIRLEY looks around: then goes to an armchair and sits.*)

SHIRLEY: What exactly would you want me to do?

PETER: Well, my working day...let's see. I get up at eight and before breakfast I go for a brisk walk.

(*Almost involuntarily SHIRLEY looks down at PETER's leg: he sees this: pause.*)

I come back, and after breakfast I start work which goes on until lunchtime. It would be very nice if you could come in about nine.

SHIRLEY: Yes, but what would you want me to do?

PETER: Type. Take some dictation. Don't look so worried. It wouldn't be difficult. There'd be letters to answer, of course. Film companies, the publishers, magazine people, and letters from admirers. Fan letters, you'd call them.

SHIRLEY: Well, I could try. I'd do my best. There's just one thing... (*Pause.*)

PETER: What's that?

SHIRLEY: Perhaps it's a bit early... I mean, I don't want you to think...

PETER: Money?

(*SHIRLEY nods her head.*)

I'm prepared to pay you fourteen pounds a week.

SHIRLEY: How much?

PETER: Fourteen. Is that fair?

SHIRLEY: Fair? Why, I didn't expect...

PETER: Would that make you happy?

SHIRLEY: Oh, yes.

(*She suddenly looks like a child. Leans forward, brushes back her hair: intent, smiling.*)

PETER: Good. Well, let's hear something about you. (*To TONY.*) That's what we're waiting for, isn't it?

(*TONY turns away. After a glance at him PETER looks down at SHIRLEY.*)

Go on.

SHIRLEY: I left school when I was fifteen. For a little while I worked in a shop. Woolworth's, actually. But I wanted to better myself, so evenings I went to a secretarial course. Clayton's Commercial College. Opposite the station. Know it? I did quite well, all considered. So when I was seventeen I took this job in a coal office. I was there for about eighteen months. Then I had to leave.

PETER: Why?

SHIRLEY: Personal reasons, if you understand me. But you don't want to hear this sort of stuff. You want to know how many words a minute I can do.

PETER: Not at all. This is just what we want to hear. Carry on.

SHIRLEY: Well, that's all, really. I haven't worked since the coal office.

PETER: Where do you live?

SHIRLEY: Tukehurst Road.

PETER: That's the other end of the town.

SHIRLEY: Yes, the new estate.

PETER: Do you like it?

SHIRLEY: It's all right.

PETER: Surely you don't live alone.

SHIRLEY: Oh no. I live with my Mum and Dad.

PETER: (*Sudden smile.*) Like me.

(*SHIRLEY smiles back at PETER: a moment approaching sympathy between them.*
TONY has come forward.)

TONY: I say, you don't need me here for this. I'll push off.

PETER: No! (*He holds TONY by the arm.*) You mustn't go. It's no fun if you're not here. Ask her a sensible question. Go on.

TONY: (*To SHIRLEY: after a moment.*) Why did you want to better yourself, as you put it?

SHIRLEY: Doesn't everybody?

PETER: No.

TONY: What did you expect to get out of it?

PETER: You thought you'd get away from the horrible place where you live.

SHIRLEY: No, I didn't. It's quite nice.

PETER: Surely you see how ugly it is.

SHIRLEY: But it's modern.

PETER: I know. All those little houses with their desolate little gardens. As embarrassing as a new set of false teeth. And with the same absurd pretensions. 'Parkway', 'Grosvenor Lodge', 'Sorrento', 'Berkeley'. They're inhabited by peasants. Why don't they have the honesty of peasants?

SHIRLEY: I don't know what you're talking about.

PETER: But you must see. Look at the shops there. Full of awful stuff. Look at the sweet shops. Dozens of them. Stuffed with sickening muck.

SHIRLEY: Are you a chapel man?

PETER: No. Why?

SHIRLEY: Just wondered. You seem to be against any fun. (*TONY laughs.*)

PETER: No, I'm not against having fun. It's just...

SHIRLEY: Look, the fun people have at my end of the town is different from your fun up here, I expect. We're another tribe, see?

PETER: Are you defending it?

SHIRLEY: Why not? My Dad, just taking one, worked hard for all we've got. He was out of work a lot before the war. And when I was a baby he was away in the army for six years. He came back here and worked very hard. Now he's foreman, and we have a bit of money. We've got the house – matter of fact, ours is just *Number 23* Tukehurst Road, nothing fancy – and Mum keeps it very nice. You think we spend our money on lots of silly things. Perhaps we do. We haven't learnt yet, you see. It takes a bit of practice when you've only had it a little while.

PETER: Your father's good to you, is he?

SHIRLEY: Yes, he's always been good. I let him down once.

PETER: How?

SHIRLEY: Never mind. I'm going to make up for it.
Anyway, I don't see what all this has got to do with my
being your secretary.

PETER: I wanted to know what sort of background you've
got. You might have to move in a very different society.
Different values. Does that frighten you?

SHIRLEY: No.

PETER: And you might have to travel with me. I mean to
go away a lot.

SHIRLEY: Oh, I couldn't do that.

PETER: Why not?

SHIRLEY: I can't leave the town. I didn't understand you
wanted that. So there you are, it's no good.
(*She stands up.*)

PETER: Wait a minute. You're twenty. Pretty well free to do
as you like. Your mother and father can't expect you to
stay at home for ever.

SHIRLEY: (*Pause.*) I'm not really free.

PETER: Boyfriend?

SHIRLEY: No.

PETER: Then what is it?

SHIRLEY: Something you wouldn't understand.

PETER: Try me.

SHIRLEY: It wouldn't be any good. I'll go.

PETER: No, wait. I think I could arrange for you to work
with me just when I'm in the town.

TONY: Let her go.

PETER: (*To SHIRLEY.*) Would that do?

TONY: Let her go.
(*SHIRLEY has stopped. She looks from TONY to PETER.*)

SHIRLEY: Yes, that'd do.

PETER: Good. Well, come back here and let's discuss it.
The ways and means.
(*SHIRLEY takes a pace or two back into the room, but she
does not sit down.*)
What's the mystery?

SHIRLEY: How do you mean?

PETER: Well, you want the job pretty badly, it seems. Some
time ago you let your father down, you say. And you

can't go away from the town. How do these things add
up? Would you like to tell us?

SHIRLEY: Why not? But if you're expecting ever such a
tragic story – (*She exaggerates the phrase in a mocking way.*)
– you're going to be disappointed. I've got a young baby.

PETER: I see.

SHIRLEY: And I'm not married. (*Pause.*) Never have been.
(*Pause.*) Your face.

PETER: (*Harshly.*) What's the matter with my face?
(*Speaking, he turns sharply away from the girl and almost
falls. He catches hold of the sofa arm for support.*)
God damn this bloody thing!
(*He straightens up, turns, and looks directly at SHIRLEY.*)
(*Quietly.*) So you've got a baby. And you're on your own.
Well, that can't be such an extraordinary thing nowadays.
What's it like?

SHIRLEY: It's a she. And they're no different from other
kids, you know.

PETER: I didn't mean that. I meant what's it like to be…

SHIRLEY: What?

PETER: Never mind. Anyway, that's why you want a job.
This job.

SHIRLEY: Yes. I want to be able to feed and clothe her out
of my own pocket. Dad's been very good, but he's
getting on now and it's not really fair.

PETER: There's something I want to know. Do you feel
you've done wrong?

SHIRLEY: Yes.

PETER: You admit it.

SHIRLEY: Of course I do. Why be surprised? It was not
only wrong, it was silly.

PETER: Are you going to atone for it?

SHIRLEY: I don't think I quite know what that means. I'm
going to make up for it.

PETER: Not the same thing.

SHIRLEY: What I mean is…well, look at you. Somewhere
you collected that leg of yours. But you haven't let it
hold you back. You've gone on and made a success with
your book. Good for you, I say.

PETER: This – (*His leg.*) – wasn't my fault.

SHIRLEY: Your fault? What are you talking about? Things happen. They just happen. I've learnt that by now. Haven't you. (*To TONY.*) Hasn't he learnt it by now?

TONY: It doesn't look like it.

PETER: I was knocked down by an army truck. It wasn't my fault. I just happened to be in a certain place at a certain time. Surely it can't be said that your – your own predicament was brought about in such a casual way.

SHIRLEY: (*She laughs.*) You don't know. You just don't know. I *happened* to be at a dance one Saturday night. I never wanted to go...but what's all this got to do with my interview?

PETER: Everything. Go on.

SHIRLEY: Well, if you want me to. My girlfriend went off and left me. She's good at dancing. I'm not. I was at the café bar...

PETER: Eating ice-cream?

SHIRLEY: I expect so. Can't remember. And this soldier came up. He was only a kid.

PETER: How old were you?

SHIRLEY: Seventeen. He came up and stood beside me. He didn't say anything for ever such a long time. But he stared at me. Then he said – he was Welsh – he said – (*She clumsily imitates.*) – 'May I have the pleasure of this dance, Miss?' I laughed.

PETER: Why?

SHIRLEY: It was a funny old-fashioned way of picking up.

PETER: And that was it.

SHIRLEY: That was it.

PETER: How long did you know him?

SHIRLEY: Two months. Just while he was up at the camp.

PETER: Did you love him very much?

(*Silence.*)

I said, did you love him very much?

SHIRLEY: (*She slowly shakes her head.*) No. I was fond of him. He didn't get on with the other fellows at the camp. He was a long way from home. I was sorry for him, I suppose.

PETER: And that was enough?

SHIRLEY: It looks like it, doesn't it? You see, he never talked much. I didn't either, in those days. Then when he was going away he wanted to make love...and it was the only way I could show him I was fond of him.
(*A pause. Then SHIRLEY says, gently:*)
That's the way it happens. You wouldn't understand, living here like this. But that's the way it happens.
(*TONY has approached PETER, who is looking directly at SHIRLEY. TONY touches PETER on the arm.*)

TONY: Let her go now. Let her go home. (*To SHIRLEY.*) He'll make up his mind and write to you.
(*PETER and SHIRLEY watch each other.*)

PETER: (*To SHIRLEY.*) Do you believe in God?

SHIRLEY: Well, Dad's a Labour man. He doesn't, so the question never came up.

PETER: Then let's start at the beginning. Do you know what sin is?

SHIRLEY: I think so. Doing wrong.

PETER: Right. Who do you hurt most when you do wrong?

SHIRLEY: (*She considers.*) Yourself, I suppose.

PETER: It's an idea. Not generally acceptable, I'd say, but an idea. So you've wronged yourself. In other words, you've been sinful.

SHIRLEY: Look at it like that, yes, I have.

PETER: Do you believe that people who do wrong should be punished?

SHIRLEY: I always got it when I was naughty.

PETER: Have you been punished for this?

SHIRLEY: (*Almost to herself.*) It's not easy. If you want to know. Not easy at all sometimes.

PETER: I can't hear what you say.

SHIRLEY: (*Aloud.*) People. They're funny. The young chaps. Don't go with her. She's got a kid. I know they say that.

PETER: So you are being punished?

SHIRLEY: Well, yes, if it's being left on your own rather a lot.

PETER: Think of the way we should live nowadays.

SHIRLEY: Mind, I've got some good friends.

PETER: You've seen the buses packed to the roof leaving for the country. The holiday camps. The football matches. The dances. The clubs. And you must have heard that voice saying: 'Get together, boys and girls! You don't stand any chance of happiness on your own. No, boys and girls of all ages, it's in big numbers that the gamble's likely to come off. It's not the even chance which makes it today. It's the ten thousand to one chance that does the trick. So get in and win!' And you want to be like that, don't you, Shirley? You want to be in there with the others.

SHIRLEY: I don't want to be different to everybody else, if that's what you mean.

PETER: But you are, and always will be now. Don't go with her. Remember? The young chaps.

SHIRLEY: I'll find somebody.

PETER: No. If you believed in God you could ask forgiveness. But that's no good, is it?

SHIRLEY: Not a bit.

PETER: It's the young chaps' forgiveness you want. And they'll never let you have it.

SHIRLEY: I'll find somebody.

PETER: Never.

SHIRLEY: Some day.

PETER: Look at me. And then say it. We are eruptions on the smooth face of society. It has to be smooth, kept like an old woman's, so as not to alarm. Our cream is soothing for your hands, our paper to your bottom. This will make life easier, velvet-soft; that will make it quieter. Fill your home with the gentle smell of freshly plucked roses. We bring, with our hot drink, the tranquility of death into life. But there are people like us to ruin this vision. The welfare schemes and help in the home try to soothe us out of existence. More is being done every day. The prisons and mental homes get bigger and safer. There is a place for the bastard and a place for the sinner. Kindness is now an official state. It wears a uniform and badges. But where is ordinary human kindness? The thing which passes between men without thought. The kindness of love.

(*SHIRLEY has been staring at PETER. Now, as he goes on, she will look away from him. Soon she will cover her face with her hands and then, when she takes them away, her eyes will be full of tears.*)

For you know perfectly well that no one has given you that sort of kindness. Your father. You say he was good to you, but you only say that because you wish he had been. Really, he's ashamed of you. Remember? Your friends. You haven't got any friends. You can't cart the baby to the palais on Saturday night and so you stay away. Now you pretend you're going to start all over again. You can't. The job, the money, won't alter a thing. You're done for. Like me. Down the High Street we go, you behind your pram and me shuffling and swaying like a drunkard. The wrongdoer and the wronged. Both of us insults to the present perfect way of life.

(*It is now that SHIRLEY looks up. She speaks to TONY.*)

SHIRLEY: He's right, of course. I do pretend. It seemed the only thing. I'm on my own all right, because of what I did. More on my own than any person should ever be. And he means it'll never be different. He's right. This is it. My lot, as Dad says. For always.

TONY: That's not true.

SHIRLEY: (*Suddenly very tired.*) Well, I don't know. All I do know is that you've got to go on somehow.

TONY: Of course you have.

SHIRLEY: That's why I wanted this job. What about it?

(*TONY glances at PETER, giving him a chance to speak. PETER turns away.*)

TONY: There isn't any job.

SHIRLEY: What?

TONY: There's no job here. You've come to the wrong house. This isn't Mr Dickinson. His name's Peter Sharpe.

SHIRLEY: But you both said...

TONY: I know we did. You made a mistake. The house you want is next door. That way.

SHIRLEY: You mean you've been playing some sort of joke?

TONY: Yes.

SHIRLEY: (*A cry.*) Why?

(Silence. PETER has picked up the walking-stick. He stands leaning forward on it, looking down.)

TONY: (*To SHIRLEY.*) Come on. If you go now you may still be in time.

SHIRLEY: They said seven o'clock. I've been here ages.

(SHIRLEY goes to PETER. She stands in front of him, trying to look into his face.)

Why? Why?

(PETER looks up at the girl, almost in surprise.)

PETER: No reason. It just happened to be you. You just happened to be here. No reason. No reason at all.

SHIRLEY: Are you dead, or something?

(She turns away.

In the hall:

TONY and SHIRLEY can be seen coming from the room, leaving PETER alone. TONY brings SHIRLEY into the hall and to the front door. She turns to him.)

He just had to tell somebody, didn't he? And, as he said, I happened to be here. It wasn't personal, was it? Might have been anybody.

TONY: Come on. You must hurry.

SHIRLEY: Answer the question. It wasn't personal, was it?

TONY: Of course not.

SHIRLEY: You see, I want to think the best of him. Nobody could play a trick like that unless they didn't know what they were doing. I suppose he's got some excuse.

TONY: Yes.

SHIRLEY: Have you?

TONY: What do you mean?

SHIRLEY: Why didn't you say something?

(TONY shakes his head. He opens the front door. It has begun to rain. SHIRLEY goes out on to the step. She turns.)

Early on. Why didn't you tell me it was a joke? Because you thought it was funny, I suppose. All right, mister, it's funny to trick me out of a job. I bet you've got one. Now go back and laugh.

(*SHIRLEY turns away and goes down the steps. TONY watches her for a moment, and then he shuts the door. As he moves back into the hall PETER calls from the room:*)

PETER: (*Voice off.*) Well, why didn't you say something?

(*TONY crosses the hall. He does not go back into the drawing-room, but turns into the unlit dining-room.*

In the drawing-room:

PETER is watching TONY as he goes into the room across the hall. PETER calls:)

Where are you going?

(*TONY does not answer.*)

You could have stopped me, if you'd wanted to.

(*TONY has gone from sight.*)

(*PETER shouts.*) Tony!

(*In the dining-room:*

TONY is standing in the bay of the window and pulling the curtain a little aside. Beads of rain are scattered on the darkened window glass, which reflects TONY's face.)

(*Voice off.*) Tony, come here and amuse me. What are you doing?

(*TONY looks out through the window. As he watches SHIRLEY approaches the front door of the next house. All she does will be seen by TONY through the distortion of the rain-covered window and in the fall of light from the street lamp.*)

(*Voice off.*) Come here, Tony.

(*TONY watches through the window. SHIRLEY runs up the steps of the next house and stands at the front door. She rings the bell.*

Music can be heard from the drawing-room: a piano: PETER has switched on a radio.

TONY watches SHIRLEY as she stands at the door. She is quite near, a matter of ten feet or so off. Light falls on her as the door is opened. She speaks to an unseen person: her words cannot be heard. SHIRLEY slowly nods her head as she is answered. Then she turns away into the darkness as the door is shut.

TONY watches her go and then, letting the curtain fall into place, moves away from the window.

In the drawing-room:

PETER is listening to the music. TONY comes in from the hall. The music ends: loud and prolonged applause. TONY switches off the radio. Silence.)

TONY: (*Quietly.*) What have you proved?

PETER: I wasn't trying to prove anything.

TONY: Why do it then? Can I have some more whisky?

PETER: Help yourself.

TONY: Dickinson turned her away. She didn't get the job.

PETER: She'd never have got it anyway.

(*TONY has poured himself straight whisky, and now he turns to PETER.*)

TONY: Explain.

PETER: Analyse, do you mean?

TONY: Oh, balls. Don't use words. Just explain.

PETER: All right. She was standing out there on the steps…
(*He stops.*)

TONY: And…?

PETER: And I saw her…go on, laugh… I saw her as if she was undressed…

TONY: (*Flat statement.*) I'm not laughing.

PETER: I saw her body shrinking from the cold, shrinking from disappointment, withdrawing from love… Don't look at me like that! …and I wanted to hurt her.

TONY: Why?

PETER: (*He imitates.*) Why? That's what she asked. Why? Why? (*Shortly.*) I thought you'd think it was funny. Something to do. Pass the time. You're always talking about it.

TONY: Are you serious?

PETER: Of course I'm serious.

TONY: You're lying.

PETER: What's the matter with you?

TONY: Why did you want to hurt her?

PETER: Oh, shut up. Forget it.

TONY: Not likely. Come here.

(*TONY moves so that he is close to PETER. A pause. PETER turns to look at TONY. PETER is afraid.*)

(*Gently.*) Sit down.

(*PETER sits on the sofa. In a moment TONY will put a cigarette into PETER's mouth, and light it for him. TONY's manner with PETER is patient and not unkind, treating him rather as a frightened child. And PETER's confidence to TONY is childlike. He might be telling of how he woke to see the shadow on the stairs, and how he cried out in the dark many years ago.*)

What got into you?

PETER: (*Staring closely into TONY's face.*) Yes, that's what we say, isn't it? What's got *into* you? What *possessed* you to do it? Leave me alone, Tony. Please.

TONY: No.

PETER: If you live as I do it all goes into your head. All the devils. And it's all thought, no feeling. (*He has groped for this word.*) Saints. Nomads. Me. What other people experience...all that just goes to the head and becomes a possibility. It sometimes gets pretty crowded up there with maybes. I'm trying to explain. That's what you want, isn't it?

TONY: Yes.

PETER: She was standing there on the step. And I didn't feel anything. Some common tart come to the wrong house. Then I saw her...saw her...as I said. And I remembered a song. From years ago. I was once in love, believe it or not. Keep me to the point, for God's sake. So there she was. Enquiring. Unknown. And I wanted her to feel something about me. Recognize me, I suppose.

TONY: You wanted to make an enemy.

PETER: Yes. (*Pause.*) Yes! Something positive. It's not often now that people approach me. Either by chance or wish. There she was. I wanted to be remembered by someone. With hatred? Why not? How can I ask for love? And it was meant to be a joke. At first. This'll make Tony laugh. I remember thinking that. But when she told me about the child it wasn't any good. I found I was talking to one of my own kind. I was talking to myself. And it hasn't made you laugh.

TONY: No.

PETER: Why not? I thought we could have it as a secret between us. The day we…

TONY: You were wrong.

(*TONY has got up and moved away from PETER. It is a sudden movement, as if he cannot stand the physical contact any longer.*)

PETER: And I thought that was the way you saw things. You've never seemed to care about people. You've always seemed so…callous. No, I don't mean that. I mean, offhand.

TONY: Just because I call you old boy, old boy…just because I wear these silly clothes to make me feel good…because of lots of reasons…all right, I drink too much and smoke too much… Filth can still make me laugh…and it's fun to get a rise out of a girl…all right…maybe…that's the way I look to you. All the same, I'm not your kind of criminal.

PETER: Criminal?

TONY: Yes, sweetheart. What you did tonight was criminal. You make an excuse of the accident to your leg. It's got nothing to do with it. If you were active and got around, if Mummy and Daddy understood you, if you were a success like Brian, it wouldn't make any difference. You'd still want to have somebody concerned in some way with you. Perhaps not in your misery, but in something equally trivial, such as your happiness. Yes, with you up and about and she a bit prettier, alone together, you'd probably have made love to her instead of doing what you did. But either way it's a crime. Engaging another person's emotions to prove that you exist.

PETER: What about us, Tony?

TONY: Oh, I gave up long ago. I'm quite happy to drift on the surface of other peoples' lives. I'm always pleased to see almost anybody. Hullo, old boy. How's it go? You don't say so. Tell me more. Tell me all. I'll lend an ear to any deserving cause.

(*Silence. PETER looks up.*

In the hall:

A key is being turned in the lock of the front door.
In the drawing-room:)

PETER: You know what you've just said.

TONY: Pretty well.

PETER: That there's no sort of friendship between us. Nothing that you can't have with anybody. You've just said that, haven't you?

TONY: Yes.

(*In the hall:*

The front door is open. CHARLES and LAURA have come in. It is now raining hard and a sudden gust of wind swings the door as CHARLES stands on the step shaking the umbrella. After a moment he joins LAURA in the hall, shutting the door behind him. LAURA is wiping rain from her face with a little handkerchief, and looking into the drawing-room at PETER and TONY.)

LAURA: (*She calls to them.*) So you're still here. Not gone. (*To CHARLES.*) They're still here.

CHARLES: Oh?

(*CHARLES and LAURA begin to get out of their wet coats. In the drawing-room:*

PETER and TONY are speaking. Their voices are low, the words hurried.)

PETER: Is there nothing? Nothing at all?

TONY: Self-disgust. That I could stand by and not interfere between you and that girl, just let it go on, because I couldn't get rid of my pity for you. Take that, if you want it.

PETER: Do you hate me?

TONY: I don't love you, Peter.

PETER: Then go. Go away.

(*LAURA is coming into the room. She has taken off her coat, but still wears a plastic thing tied over her hat.*)

LAURA: You didn't go out, then. You were right. It's pouring with rain. Set in for the night, I shouldn't wonder. The rehearsal went well. But the roof over the stage began to leak, so we had to give up. Daddy just got his bit in. He's going to be very good. He has such authority. We saw a funny thing on the way home…

(*She stops, staring from PETER to TONY.*)

I haven't interrupted you, have I?

TONY: No.

LAURA: I mean, you weren't in the middle of an important conversation, were you?

TONY: No, we were just gossiping.

LAURA: I'm sure that's not true. Daddy and I have always said what a good mind you've got, Tony. I suppose it comes of being in business. It gives you a sensible and practical approach. That's why we like you to see Peter. He was always a bit of a dreamer, even before his accident. It doesn't do to be too sensitive in this world does it?

TONY: No, it doesn't. I must be going.

CHARLES: (*He has come in from the hall.*) Oh, stay on for a little. What about a drop of this?

(*He means the whisky.*)

TONY: No, thank you, Mr Sharpe.

CHARLES: Peter? (*PETER shakes his head.*) Well, I'm going to. I want to chase that cold out of my head.

(*As CHARLES pours the whisky LAURA suddenly giggles: a very silly sound, indeed.*)

What's the matter with you?

LAURA: I suddenly thought...

CHARLES: What?

LAURA: Of you standing there on the stage just about to speak when – splash! – that water right on your head. And you not moving. Just saying the line as if nothing was happening. (*To TONY.*) Just where he was standing. Such bad luck. They must have that roof seen to.

(*CHARLES has drained the glass of whisky. Now he stares at his wife.*)

CHARLES: I understood you thought I was very good in the part.

LAURA: Oh, you are...

CHARLES: Then why make it sound as if I look a fool?

LAURA: I didn't mean to.

TONY: (*Interrupting: to CHARLES.*) These accidents happen. How do you go about acting a character in an amateur play?

CHARLES: Well, you have to get it right, you know. People are very observant. They'll pick out the smallest detail. For example, you have to look right. Clothes, that sort of thing. Take this policeman I'm doing at the moment. I happen to know one of the fellows down at the station. I've had a word with him.

TONY: Really? That's very interesting.

CHARLES: Goes beyond the play. You can see that. I mean, the information's always useful. How the other chap lives. That sort of thing.

TONY: Yes, it must be.

CHARLES: And as for the play, oh, it's very necessary to get it right. Otherwise, you couldn't believe what you were doing. I get right into it, I must say. While it's going on it all seems more...real, I suppose, than life itself.

PETER: Show us what you mean, Father.

CHARLES: How?

PETER: Do your bit.

CHARLES: I couldn't do it here. Like this.

PETER: Why not?

CHARLES: Well, I haven't got the atmosphere. Got to have the feel of the thing, you know.

PETER: You mean, there's been no crime here. Is that it?

CHARLES: Yes. And the furniture's different... (*To TONY.*) Are you really interested?

TONY: Of course.

CHARLES: The play takes place in a big country house. I'm not exactly sure where it's supposed to be. Somewhere in England. And these people – there are five of them – have been invited for the weekend by this man. They all think they're going to inherit money. Four of them...

LAURA: Who does this belong to?

(*LAURA is holding SHIRLEY's handbag, which she has picked up from the side of the chair.*)

CHARLES: Oh, for God's sake, shut up, Laura! You're always butting in!

(*CHARLES turns again to TONY: speaks to him.*) Four of these people are murdered. Each of them is stabbed to death with a knitting needle. Now one of the characters is an old lady who is always knitting socks. We get a lot of fun out of the fact that it is her needles which keep disappearing. It's all very true to life, though.

TONY: It sounds most exciting.

CHARLES: It is. Then at the end the murderer is discovered by the old lady. She rings me up at the local police station and I come in and make the arrest. Suppose Peter's the man.

PETER: Yes, suppose I'm the man.

CHARLES: Stand there.

(*PETER stands in front of CHARLES. CHARLES turns away for a moment, playing the ostrich, pretending not to be there. Then he turns and approaches PETER.*)

Henry Heber Percy Armitage, I arrest you for the murder of Sylvia Hardcastle. I must warn you that anything you say may be used in evidence.

PETER: I just want to say this…

CHARLES: No, no. That's the end of the play. He doesn't speak.

PETER: There are extenuating circumstances, Inspector. I was very unhappy when I was a child. I hated my father. It's not an unusual excuse, I know. He was never unkind to me. I wish he had been. If he could have been so definite I think I could have loved him. But I was nothing to him. The creature he passed on the stairs, the thing underneath his feet which longed to be kicked, but he had no time even for cruelty. Will that be taken into consideration, sir?

(*A bell can be heard from somewhere in the street. It is the kind which ambulances and police cars use. The sound approaches: passes the house: fades: stops.*
PETER has heard this. He turns to LAURA, holding out his hand for the bag.)

LAURA: (*To CHARLES.*) There goes another car. Or is it an ambulance?

PETER: What's happening out there?

LAURA: We saw it when we were coming home. I wanted to stop, but Daddy wouldn't let me. It was raining...

PETER: But what did you see?

LAURA: It was by the canal bridge. There were several policemen and some people. Peter, who does this bag belong to?

PETER: (*Taking the bag from her.*) Someone called this evening. They must have left it. What else did you see?

LAURA: Not much. Daddy hurried me past. I saw one of the policemen up to his waist in water. They were flashing torches.

CHARLES: There'd been some sort of accident, obviously. No concern of ours.

(*PETER is looking across at TONY, who turns and goes out by the hall to the dining-room. PETER watches him.*)

LAURA: Was it anybody I know?

PETER: (*Turning to her.*) What do you mean?

LAURA: Who called. And left that.

PETER: No. You don't know her. It was a mistake. Wrong house.

(*PETER opens the bag and looks at what is in it. While he does this he continually glances up at the darkened dining-room, where TONY has gone. Then PETER snaps the bag shut and goes across to the dining-room.*

CHARLES and LAURA are left alone.)

CHARLES: What's been going on here? You imagine I don't notice things. I'm no fool.

LAURA: No one suggests that you are. Now sit down. Would you like a hot drink?

CHARLES: Why?

LAURA: For the cold in the head you're going to have.

CHARLES: No. Shut up. Leave me alone. (*Pause.*) That boy...

LAURA: Peter? Our boy?

CHARLES: Yes, Peter. Talking about when he was little. How he hated... (*He cannot say it.*) He meant me. You know that, don't you?

(*CHARLES looks as if he wants to cry: a sudden moment of despair and no comprehension at all. He stares at LAURA: then gives a smile like a whimper.*)

He's got a terrible sense of fun, that boy of ours.

(*In the dining-room:*

PETER and TONY are together at the window. The lights have not been put on. TONY is looking out at the street. PETER is very close to him.)

PETER: What are you thinking? (*He does not give time for an answer.*) It's impossible. Kill herself? She'd never do such a thing. You mean because of what I did? You're mad. Did she go that way? Towards the bridge? Well, if you think it's happened why don't you go out and see? Ask. Find out. (*Pause: PETER follows TONY's look.*) You can't see the place from here.

(*PETER turns away from TONY. He speaks out of the near darkness of the room. Speaks for himself.*)

You're afraid, aren't you? It may be true. There may be a drowned girl pulled from the river lying out there in the rain. Was she heavy enough to go down? I'd not have thought it. You're scared. You're trying to stop it being true by not finding out. But if it's happened it *is* true. The wretched soaked little thing lies on the stones at the moment. But you believe it won't be true until there's some proof. Nothing less than a body. You're the kind of man who is the despair of the Christian church. (*TONY has turned to look at PETER: a moment: suddenly.*) Don't go! (*But TONY has turned away from the window and is crossing the room.*

PETER's face is caught by the light: held.

In the drawing-room:

CHARLES and LAURA turn towards the door as TONY comes into the room.)

CHARLES: Now look here, Tony. I've been having a word with my wife. We agree that it's quite natural for you two boys to have… Are you going?

(*CHARLES sees that TONY has picked up his raincoat as he crossed the hall.*

PETER has followed TONY into the room.)

TONY: Yes. What did you want to say?

CHARLES: My wife and I agree that it's natural for you and Peter to have your differences of opinion. When two people are such close friends of course they sometimes rub each other the wrong way. That's what's happened tonight, isn't it? Now, come on. Be good chaps and make it up. You'll both laugh about this in a week's time, and wonder how it ever could have happened.

LAURA: Yes, it's quite early. There's still time to go out for a drink and a chat. The rain won't worry youngsters like you.

TONY: I'm thirty-six, Mrs Sharpe. And you're wrong. Peter and I haven't quarrelled.

CHARLES: But you haven't said a word to him since we came in. We both noticed it.

TONY: Please let me say goodnight and go.

CHARLES: Peter, I insist that you explain to your mother…

PETER: There's nothing to make up with Tony, Father. We were never friends.

CHARLES: Nonsense.

PETER: It's true. It was an invention of yours. Like most things I possess.

CHARLES: Look, you had your little joke with me earlier on…

PETER: I'm not joking.

(*The doorbell rings. And again, at once.*)

CHARLES: Who the hell's that?

(*CHARLES notices a look between PETER and TONY.*)

Are you expecting someone? (*To LAURA.*) Well, find out who it is.

(*LAURA goes towards the hall and the front door.*)

(*To PETER.*) Why should I invent anything for you? Haven't I always wanted you to go out and about in the real world and be happy? Tell me what's happened. We've always lived quietly. Come on, boy, this can be settled as everything has been settled before, can't it?

(*PETER speaks to CHARLES but watches, with TONY, through the open door to the hall.*)

PETER: Don't make me answer your questions, Father.
We've got to go on living here. Quietly. Together.
Perhaps for a long time. By all means try to make the
people in your play as true to life as you possibly can.
But let us pretend...on each other's behalf...that...
(*LAURA has come back into the room. She stands aside in the
doorway to let SHIRLEY come in.*)

LAURA: This young lady says...

PETER: (*To SHIRLEY.*) You left your bag.

SHIRLEY: Yes.

PETER: Here you are.
(*PETER holds out the bag to SHIRLEY, who takes it. She
opens the bag and looks inside. She seems satisfied.*)

SHIRLEY: Thank you.
(*She is about to turn away and go when PETER speaks.*)

PETER: Mr Coleman – (*He indicates TONY.*) – this is Mr
Coleman remember – he was very worried about you.
(*TONY makes a gesture as if he would stop PETER. It is
ignored.*)
(*To SHIRLEY.*) My mother told him that they were
searching the canal at the bridge, and then he heard the
police cars. Mr Coleman thought...

SHIRLEY: (*To TONY.*) Why can't you people take things as
they are? Look at you now. Inventing a sad story for me.
She ended up in the river. It'd never be like that. Never.
(*SHIRLEY puts her hand on TONY's arm. He does not
move.*)
Still, it was nice of you to be worried. Matter of fact,
it was a cat. It had got trapped in a drain. I stayed and
watched. It was a stray. They got it out all right. It was
starving. They went to a lot of trouble. Got wet. They
wouldn't have done it for me. Not likely. Now they've
taken it away. They're going to destroy it. Somebody
had complained. Its screams were upsetting the
neighbourhood. (*She looks at PETER.*) He's right. No
doubt about it. The place must be kept quiet so that
you and all the other people in this street can die in
peace. Goodnight.

(*SHIRLEY goes out of the room. No one tries to detain her. The front door slams shut behind her. Silence.*)

LAURA: Who is she? I can't believe that she meant...

CHARLES: Be quiet, Laura. I won't have such things discussed in this house. (*A whisper: to TONY.*) You'll stay on and have a little supper?

TONY: No, I must go.

CHARLES: Very well.

LAURA: Shall we see you next Sunday, Tony?

TONY: Well, I was thinking of driving down to the seaside, Mrs Sharpe. I have some people I must see. On business, really...

PETER: (*He has been watching TONY as he struggles.*) Leave him alone, Mother.

TONY: (*Pause.*) No, you won't be seeing me next Sunday.

PETER: Goodbye, Tony.

TONY: Goodbye, Peter. (*To CHARLES and LAURA.*) Goodnight. No, don't bother...

(*This is to LAURA who has made a movement to go with TONY to the door. She stops, and TONY goes out of the room.*)

CHARLES: (*To LAURA.*) Let's have something to eat.

LAURA: All right, dear. What would you like?

CHARLES: Oh, I don't know. Whatever there is.

LAURA: It won't be long.

(*LAURA goes out of the room, quietly shutting the door behind her.*

CHARLES and PETER are left alone. CHARLES has put on reading glasses, and picked up a newspaper. PETER has not moved from where he was standing when TONY left.)

CHARLES: Peter...

PETER: (*Turning to CHARLES.*) Yes?

CHARLES: What exactly was that girl doing here tonight?

PETER: She came to the wrong place. She wanted the Dickinsons. We played a little joke on her, that's all.

CHARLES: A joke, eh? Haha. Was it a good one?

PETER: Not bad.

CHARLES: You always enjoyed a joke. (*He is shaking out the paper.*) When you were a little boy... (*He has folded*

the paper.) ...you couldn't have been more than seven
or eight... (*He has become absorbed in an item of news.*)
...I remember very well...

PETER: (*After a moment.*) What do you remember?

CHARLES: (*He looks up.*) What? (*He stares at PETER as if he
had never seen him before.*) What were we talking about?

PETER: We were talking about me, Father.

CHARLES: Well, go on. I'm listening.

(*CHARLES leans back in his chair, pushing his glasses up
on to his forehead, leaving the newspaper on his knees.*)

PETER: You were saying that I always enjoyed a joke. And
I was going to say that I'm not sure that I enjoy this one.

CHARLES: Something at the moment?

PETER: Yes, something at the moment.

(*CHARLES's eyes are a little wide with concentration as he
stares at PETER. He might be dead. His son's voice is calm,
a man reflecting on a landscape.*)

I mean living in a desert, like this. At one time
I believed that this waste ground must have boundaries.
And I thought that if I made my way towards that limit
I'd at last meet with people. Well, there's been Tony.
And there was Roy and Harry – remember Harry?
– and others. But as soon as I took their hand and
prepared myself to love them, what did I find? They
were not at the beginning of a fertile land, but making
for some other, more believable, place than I had in
mind. So the most we could do was pass each other,
without doing more harm than was necessary.

(*TONY is seen. He is in the street, beside his car.
PETER's voice will continue over this and the following visual
scenes.*

*TONY is pulling on gloves and turning up his coat collar
against the rain. His face, which is closely seen, has relaxed
into tiredness and every year of his age. He pulls on his little
pimple of a cap, and turns to the car.*)

(*Voice off.*) I've heard of people who live in places where
talent and opportunity for a kind of joy in life can
flourish. And I really believe they exist. I don't want to
make the mistake of thinking that all people in all places

are like me. But there are far too many of us. You shouldn't crowd a wilderness. It contradicts its purpose.

(*There is the sound of the car as TONY drives away, leaving the street empty.*

PETER is seen again. He is speaking without bitterness.)

I lost you and Mother many years ago in the hide and seek of childhood. Did we ever meet again?

(*LAURA is seen in the dining-room.*

PETER's voice continues over this.

LAURA is standing by the sideboard. She has a silver-framed photograph in her hand. There are others in front of her. She stares down at them. She looks for something in the fixed faces.)

I think I remember – it was a long time ago – when we…no, I must have dreamt it. We've never met in this place. You're lost a thousand miles from where I am. Sometimes I think I see distress signals fired into the night. But they die out before they can be interpreted.

(*LAURA puts down the photograph. She turns away. PETER is seen again.*)

They say you walk in circles in a desert. Past the tennis club, over the bridge, by the new supermarket, and so down the High Street: round the public lavatories and the preserved market cross, up through the old town – fine view of the gasworks – across the meadows, over the bridge, past the tennis club and back here. And sometimes, raising dust like an army, there is a person. Such as that girl. On the march, believing that by putting one foot before another she makes a track for herself to follow.

(*SHIRLEY is seen walking through the town.*

PETER's voice speaks over this.

SHIRLEY goes forward and lights from shops fall on her. She looks ahead. Her movements are definite and hurried. The rain has made her hair ugly to look at.)

The moment I set eyes on her I knew she was an enemy. She believes in the good land. I don't any more. Not the chance of reaching it, anyway. So I tried to stop her. We fought on shifting ground with no result. Admiring each others' wounds we agreed to call it off. Nothing is even mortal in this place.

(*SHIRLEY has gone from sight down the street.*
PETER's last words are spoken over:
The town square: swept with rain. The station: a train is leaving.)

But it has been some sort of encounter. It's made a landmark, something to catch the eye, like litter on the hills. Something to occupy my mind as I go – forward? – in this labyrinth without walls. Something to remember. Something...

(*A bypass road, lit by sodium lamps and deserted, goes straight into the distance.*)

CURTAIN

THE DEVILS

Introduction to

THE DEVILS

Aldous Huxley's 1952 book *The Devils of Loudon* consists of what he called "variations" on an episode that occurred in a French Ursuline convent during the 17th century. An exorcist was employed to get rid of devils who had apparently taken possession of the nuns. The Prioress was the leader of the demoniacs, and the local parson, Urbain Grandier, was burnt as the sorcerer responsible for the possession. Huxley's premiss was that the human mind is unvarying in its essence, and that we can always choose between unregeneracy and enlightenment, self-assertion and self-transcendence.

For at least twenty years, Huxley had been concerned with the question of what lifts a great man above mediocrity. Describing the "devils" in Georges Clemenceau, the French Prime Minister at the end of the Second World War, he suggested it was a matter of "being, as it were, possessed by more than human spirits". The phoney possession of the nuns could be described as imitation of the demonic in a downward escape from the self. The self is a prison from which saints and mystics escape upwards into spirituality, while baser natures escape downwards into "subhuman or merely human substitutes for Grace". Huxley explains the hysteria of the nuns in terms of sexual starvation, mass hysteria and a patient-doctor relationship with the exorcist, for whom they obligingly provided symptoms that tallied with his diagnosis.

With his theatrical interest in the heroic, John Whiting was no less preoccupied with the question of what it is that empowers some men to reach an exceptionally high level of achievement. He was attracted both to Huxley's terminology and to the story of the Loudun nuns. In 1952 he was working on screenplays, and reading Huxley's book, he thought it would make a good film, but did nothing about it till 1959, when Peter Hall asked him to write a costume play for the first London season of the company which was playing summer seasons in Stratford-on-Avon and was soon to get the name "Royal Shakespeare Company."

It could be said that Paul Southman in *Saint's Day* and Rupert Forster in *Marching Song* are both heroes of Huxleyan self-transcendence. In the new play which Whiting based on Huxley's book, Grandier explores both upward and downward escape routes. When a girl, Ninon, asks whether he wants to be more than a man, he answers: "Of course. Or less."

Grandier never had any contact with the nuns. Though he was invited to become their director, he refused. But emulating their neurasthenic prioress, the frustrated women started dreaming and fantasising about him, becoming hysterical and producing symptoms of what was taken to be diabolical possession. When, encouraged by the exorcist, they denounced Grandier as a magician, Cardinal Richelieu sided with them, and after being imprisoned and tried, the innocent priest was burnt at the stake.

Huxley's explanation of the nuns' behaviour is convincing, but many of his psychological generalisations founder on vagueness about the boundaries of the self. Should the impulses that drive drunkards to drink and mystics to mysticism be regarded as coming from outside the self? If business activities, hobbies and debauched sexuality are all examples of self-transcendence, what is self-assertion?

But Huxley's generalising "variations" seem to have influenced Whiting and his play. With something of the same fastidiousness that made Huxley want to distance himself from the animal ingredients in human nature, Whiting introduces a sewerman who embodies and expresses revulsion against smelly physicality: "Every man is his own drain... Gutters run about him to carry off the dirt." And nothing excites the surgeon, Mannoury, more than dissecting a human head that has been "disassociated from the grosser parts of the body... Think, this is the residence of reason... Isn't it possible that the divinity of man, enclosed in an infinitesimal bag, might rest on the point of my knife?"

The area of Whiting's talent that Huxley nourishes is not the best area. In earlier plays it mattered less if Whiting was schematic in contrasting men who are merely human with the heroes. In *The Devils,* taking most of the unheroic characters from history filtered through Huxley's book, Whiting identifies with them less than usual, and since the clerical accomplices in the destruction of Grandier behaved no better than the laymen, and the noblemen no better than the commoners, the play is populated mainly with villains.

Structurally *The Devils* differs from Whiting's previous plays more than any of them had differed from the others. Being written for a large company, it had to have a large cast. Many of the minor characters seem to have been sketched hurriedly, and the storytelling is cinematic, with short sequences and quick changes of location. In a film it would be easy to move about the streets of London, to shift the action from Ninon's bedroom to the altar of Grandier's church, from the convent to the market, from London to Poitiers, Paris and London. Whiting had previously shown great talent for generating theatrical atmosphere, but the script of *The Devils* does little to create a sense of place, and it is hard for the designer to help: he has to concentrate on keeping the audience informed about where each sequence is situated.

Whiting's Grandier, unlike Huxley's, and history's, turns to self-destruction. He tells the Governor of Loudon: "Politics, power, the senses, pride, and authority, I choose them with the same care that you, sir, select a weapon. But my intention is different. I need to turn them against myself... Living has drained the need for life from me... I am a dead man, compelled to live." This links him to Whiting's other self-destructive heroes, but his world-weariness is not made real for us through action. The love scenes with Philippe are not written as if Grandier is trying to destroy himself, even is she is the daughter of the Public Prosecutor. It is hard to avoid the suspicion that this motive may have been imposed retrospectively.

The closest Grandier gets to upward self-transcendence is in a hubristic monologue about making God. "I created him from the light and the air, from the dust of the road, from the sweat on my hands, from gold, from filth, from the memory of women's faces, from great rivers, from children, from the works of man, from the past, the present, the future and the unknown."

Always at his best in monologues, Whiting gives a good one to the Prioress, who reminds us of Procathren in *Saint's*

Day when she mocks at God's "wretched and sinful children who get above their station, and come to believe they have some other purpose in this world than to die...they do not understand the glory of mortality, the purpose of man: loneliness and death." She has succeeded in destroying Grandier, but this gives her no pleasure.

The attitude of the other nuns never becomes clear. They follow her lead in the ventriloquist act they do with devils' voices in the excommunication scene, but whereas Arthur Miller, in his 1953 play *The Crucible,* shows us exactly how Abigail keeps the other girls under control, Whiting ignores this problem.

But he ends the play brilliantly, evoking a charnel-house atmosphere after Grandier has been burnt at the stake. Mannoury and the chemist, Adam, talk like concentration camp doctors about human fat rendered down by heat to the consistency of candle wax. The Governor and the Chief Magistrate speak drunkenly about couples fornicating in the street and about an old woman with human remains in a basket. Men are fighting for charred bones, and, snatching one of the them, the sewerman offers it to the Prioress: "They want it to cure their constipation or their headache, to have it bring back their virility or their wife. Do you want it for anything?"

Characters

MANNOURY – a surgeon

ADAM – a chemist

LOUIS TRINCANT – the Public Prosecutor

PHILIPPE TRINCANT

JEAN D'ARMAGNAC – the Governor of Loudun

GUILLAUME DE CERISAY – the Chief Magistrate

A SEWERMAN

URBAIN GRANDIER – the Vicar of St Peter's Church

NINON – a widow

DE LA ROCHEPOZAY – the Bishop of Poitiers

FATHER RANGIER

FATHER BARRÉ

SISTER JEANNE OF THE ANGELS – the prioress
of St Ursula's Convent

SISTER CLAIRE

SISTER LOUISE

DE LAUBARDEMONT – the King's Special
Commissioner to Loudun

FATHER MIGNON

SISTER GABRIELLE

PRINCE HENRI DE CONDÉ

RICHELIEU

LOUIS XIII – King of France

LA VRILLIÈRE

BONTEMPS – a gaoler

FATHER AMBROSE

A CLERK

Townspeople, People from the Country, Capuchins,
Carmelites, Jesuits and Soldiers

The Devils was first performed at the Aldwych Theatre, London, in February 1961, with the following cast:

PHILIPPE, Diana Rigg

D'ARMAGNAC, Patrick Allen

GRANDIER, Richard Johnson

BARRÉ, Max Adrian

JEANNE, Dorothy Tutin

DE LAUBARDEMONT, Patrick Wymark

Director, Peter Wood

Designer, Sean Kenny

The action of this play takes place in and near the town of Loudun, and briefly at Paris, between the years 1623 and 1634.

ACT ONE

The streets of Loudun. Day.

A corpse hangs from the municipal gallows. Nearby, a SEWERMAN works in a shallow drain.

People are coming from Saint Peter's Church. ADAM, a chemist, and MANNOURY, a surgeon, among others.

MANNOURY: Shall we go together?

ADAM: By all means.

MANNOURY: Don't catch my sleeve. He spoke as if he were God.

ADAM: Grandier?

MANNOURY: Grandier.

ADAM: Very rousing to the spirit.

MANNOURY: You think so? Hm.

ADAM: So small a town is lucky to have such a caretaker of souls. Did I say that as if I meant it?

MANNOURY: No. There are things, my dear Adam.

ADAM: Things, Mannoury?

MANNOURY: Don't gape. Things said and things done.

ADAM: By the priest? Yes, I've heard.

MANNOURY: Then see.

> (*NINON, a young widow, has come from the church. She goes away along the street.*)

ADAM: With my own eyes.

MANNOURY: I've attended her. Medically.

ADAM: Have you?

MANNOURY: It's not widowhood gives that contentment. That walk.

ADAM: It takes a visit.

MANNOURY: It does.

> (*They have come beneath the gallows.*)

ADAM: Hoo, he dangles.

MANNOURY: What idiot is this?

ADAM: They put him up last night.

MANNOURY: Compelling sight. What resides, Adam?

255

ADAM: I don't understand you.

MANNOURY: What's left, man? After that.

ADAM: Ah, you've something in your head.

MANNOURY: Has he? That's the point. Come to dinner.

> (*ADAM and MANNOURY go.*
> *LOUIS TRINCANT and his daughter, PHILIPPE, have come*
> *from the church.*)

TRINCANT: Fold your hands, child. You walk like a peasant.

PHILIPPE: Who's to see?

TRINCANT: The world. Let it set eyes on a lady.

> (*They have come near the gallows.*)

PHILIPPE: Was he young or old?

TRINCANT: Don't look.

PHILIPPE: You want me to be filled with nice and useful experience, Father, so tell me something: does death unmask the face in heaven?

TRINCANT: A question for a priest.

PHILIPPE: I'm sorry. Let's talk of how my legs move in the dance. And of marriage. And love. Not death. For death smells bad. And there is scent upon a pillow.

TRINCANT: Chatter. Come along. Mind the step.

> (*TRINCANT and PHILIPPE go.*
> *JEAN D'ARMAGNAC, Governor of the town, and*
> *GUILLAUME DE CERISAY, the Chief Magistrate, have*
> *come from the church into the street.*)

D'ARMAGNAC: Grandier seems to have got it into his head that the forces of good are a kind of political party, needing a leader.

DE CERISAY: His mind's been running on such things.

D'ARMAGNAC: Politics? All the same, the terms seem strange coming from a pulpit.

DE CERISAY: So does wit.

D'ARMAGNAC: Yes. I disgraced myself this morning. I laughed aloud. Is that more becoming to the Governor of the town than yawning his way through the sermon, as I used to do before Grandier came here?

DE CERISAY: Have you sent the carriage on?

D'ARMAGNAC: Yes, I thought we'd walk. Tell me –

DE CERISAY: Yes?

D'ARMAGNAC: This is a small town. Can it contain a
    Father Grandier? That proud man. Shall we go this way?
    (*D'ARMAGNAC and DE CERISAY go.*
    The crowd has gone. The church doorway is empty.
    FATHER URBAIN GRANDIER, Vicar of Saint Peter's
    Church, appears. He comes into the street. A bucket of filth
    dredged up by the SEWERMAN splashes his gown.)

SEWERMAN: Sorry.

GRANDIER: It doesn't matter.

SEWERMAN: It's wrong, though. Shit on the holy purple.

GRANDIER: My son –

SEWERMAN: Father?

GRANDIER: Your words suit your condition.

SEWERMAN: How would you have it?

GRANDIER: Otherwise.

SEWERMAN: But I'm a man, sir. A dirty, sinful man. And
    my job is in the drains of the city. Why expect clean
    words from me? Let me oblige you, all the same. I regret,
    sir, splashing your gown with the excrement of the poor.
    Better?

GRANDIER: (*He laughs.*) It'll do.

SEWERMAN: Lovely day. Hot.

GRANDIER: Yes. How can you bear to work down there?

SEWERMAN: Well, I used to keep my mind on higher
    things.

GRANDIER: I'm very pleased to hear it. What were they?

SEWERMAN: My wife and my dinner.

GRANDIER: I see. But now –

SEWERMAN: There's not the need. I've grown used to the
    sink. Nobody can live forty-three years and not have it
    happen. If you were a man, sir, and not a priest, perhaps
    I could make you understand.

GRANDIER: Try, even so.

SEWERMAN: Well, every man is his own drain. He carries
    his main sewer with him. Gutters run about him to carry
    off the dirt –

GRANDIER: They also carry the blood of life.

SEWERMAN: Mere plumbing. Elementary sanitation. Don't interrupt. And what makes a man happy? To eat, and set the drains awash. To sit in the sun and ferment the rubbish. To go home, and find comfort in his wife's conduit. Then why should I feel ashamed or out of place down here?

GRANDIER: Put in that way I can see no reason at all. It must be almost a pleasure.

SEWERMAN: It's clear, sir, that your precious juices will never flow here. As this misguided creature has dripped through his toes all night.

GRANDIER: Don't mock the thing!

SEWERMAN: Sorry.

GRANDIER: He was a man. A young man. Eighteen years old. They brought him to kneel at the church door on his way here. He told me his sins.

SEWERMAN: What were they?

GRANDIER: Being alive.

SEWERMAN: Comprehensive.

GRANDIER: Heinous, it seemed. Manhood led him into the power of the senses. With them he worshipped in total adoration a young girl. But he learnt too quickly. He learnt that only gold can decorate the naked body. And so he stole.

SEWERMAN: And so he hanged.

GRANDIER: He confessed something to me alone. It was not for God to hear. It was a man speaking to a man. He said that when he adorned the girl the metal looked colourless, valueless, against her golden skin. That was repentance. When will they take him down?

SEWERMAN: Tomorrow. When it's dark.

GRANDIER: See that it's done with some kind of decency.
(*GRANDIER goes.*)

DE CERISAY, D'ARMAGNAC, TRINCANT.

D'ARMAGNAC: Provincial life, my dear Trincant.

TRINCANT: You feel it has a bad effect on the art of poetry?

D'ARMAGNAC: Ask De Cerisay.

DE CERISAY: Well, you and I, Trincant, as Public
Prosecutor and Magistrate, are brought close to the
ground by our work. I've always understood poetry to
be an elevated art.

TRINCANT: I assure you that during composition I think
the right thoughts. My mind, if I may put it this way, is
filled with nobility.

DE CERISAY: Why don't you show this latest bunch of
Latin epigrams to Grandier?

TRINCANT: The priest?

DE CERISAY: As a priest his secular senses are well
developed. Make a selection. Submit them. The man is a
scholar.

TRINCANT: Very well. I don't seek praise, but I'll do as
you say. Yes.

(*TRINCANT goes.*)

D'ARMAGNAC: Poor Trincant. He loves the Muses but,
alas, they don't seem to love him. I hope your suggestion
about Grandier was not malicious.

DE CERISAY: Not at all, sir. As with any author, the
greater Trincant's audience the less burden of doubt on
his closer friends.

D'ARMAGNAC: Grandier came to see me this morning.
I was having breakfast in the garden. He didn't know
that I could observe him as he walked towards me.
Vulnerable: smiling. He visibly breathed the air. He
stopped to watch the peacocks. He fondled a rose as if it
were the secret part of a woman. He laughed with the
gardener's child. Then he composed himself, and it was
another man who sat down beside me and talked for an
hour. Where will this other man climb on his ladder of
doubt and laughter?

DE CERISAY: Probably to the highest offices of the church.

D'ARMAGNAC: And the man I saw in the garden?

(*Silence.*)

GRANDIER with NINON. A disordered bed: biretta on the bedpost.

NINON: Tell me.

GRANDIER: Now what do you need to be told? Words are playthings in our situation. Expect music from them, but not sense.

NINON: Don't laugh at me. I never understand. I'm not a clever woman.

GRANDIER: You're too humble, Ninon. It's a female vice. It will never do. Ask your question.

NINON: Why do you come to me?

GRANDIER: That would be a wise question if we were in your drawing-room. As it is –

NINON: There are pretty young girls in the town.

GRANDIER: They didn't need consolation for the untimely death of their husband, the rich wine merchant. That was the reason for my first visit, remember. How many Tuesdays ago was it? I asked you to believe that God loved you, and had you in His eternal care. That the bursting of your husband's heart at the dinner table, when his blood ran with his wholesale wine, was an act of love. That all things, however incomprehensible, are an act of love. But you couldn't bring yourself to believe any of this. Your soul is as tiny as your mind, Ninon, and you had to fall back on a most human gesture: you wept. Tears must be wiped away. How can that be done without a caress?

NINON: I saw you that day just as a man. What's the matter?

GRANDIER: I wish words like that could still hurt me. (*He is putting scent on his handkerchief.*)

NINON: I've never seen you as anything but a man. Do you want to be more?

GRANDIER: Of course. Or less.

NINON: But how can you be a man of God without being a man?

GRANDIER: My dear child, you ask questions out of your time, and far beyond your experience. Your mouth… (*A bell is sounding.*)

NINON: You possess me.

GRANDIER: Go to sleep now. You've been a good little
    animal today. Let the thought of it comfort you. Be
    happy.
    (*GRANDIER goes.*)

ADAM and MANNOURY: a table between them.

MANNOURY: This human head fills me with anticipation,
    my dear Adam.
ADAM: It's a common enough object.
MANNOURY: Every man wears one on his shoulders,
    certainly. But when a head comes into my hands
    disassociated from the grosser parts of the body I always
    feel an elevation of spirit. Think, this is the residence of
    reason.
ADAM: Indeed! Ah, yes. Very true.
MANNOURY: Isn't it possible that one day in the most
    commonplace dissection I might find –
ADAM: What Mannoury? Don't hesitate to tell me.
MANNOURY: I might stumble upon the very meaning of
    reason. Isn't it possible that the divinity of man, enclosed
    in an infinitesimal bag, might rest upon the point of my
    knife? I have dreamed of the moment. I have seen
    myself. I lift the particle, taken from the cerebellum and,
    Adam, I know!
ADAM: What do you know, Mannoury?
MANNOURY: Come, my dear friend, I am speaking in the
    most comprehensive sense. I know – everything. All – is
    revealed.
ADAM: God bless my soul!
MANNOURY: Let's take this thing to your house. We'll
    spend the evening on it.
    (*They begin to go down into the street.*)
    Everyone is speaking of your treatment of the Duke's
    love disease.
ADAM: Yes, I think we're getting on top of it. Too soon to
    be certain.
MANNOURY: Your metallic compound. Does it affect the
    potency?

ADAM: Disastrously. But as I jokingly told the Duke, Science must concern itself with primary causes. It cannot turn its head to observe destructive side issues.

MANNOURY: And never will, we must hope.

ADAM: Is Madam Who Shall Be Nameless delivered?

MANNOURY: Prematurely. The foetus was interesting. It had a tiny cap drawn over its head.

ADAM: Hardly surprising with all this talk about the coachman.

(*They are now in the street. GRANDIER is approaching them.*)

MANNOURY: Look who's coming.

ADAM: Studied indifference, if you please.

GRANDIER: Good evening, Mister Surgeon. And Mister Chemist.

MANNOURY: Good evening, sir.

ADAM: Sir.

GRANDIER: It's been a fine day.

MANNOURY: Yes.

ADAM: It has.

GRANDIER: But now – rain, do you think?

ADAM: The sky is clear.

MANNOURY: It is.

GRANDIER: But it may cloud before night.

ADAM: Indeed.

MANNOURY: Indeed, it may.

GRANDIER: Darken, you know. What have you got in that bucket?

MANNOURY: A man's head.

GRANDIER: A friend?

MANNOURY: A criminal.

ADAM: The body was taken down from the gallows last night.

GRANDIER: (*After silence.*) I hope they didn't overcharge you, in the interest of Science.

MANNOURY: Ninepence.

GRANDIER: Reasonable. A bargain. Let me see. Poor pickle.

ADAM: Yes. Mannoury and I have been discussing the human predicament with this relic as centrepiece.

GRANDIER: I'm sure you said some very interesting things.

ADAM: Well, Mannoury did observe that the seat of reason is situated here.

GRANDIER: How true! But you'll have said that, Adam.

ADAM: I did.

GRANDIER: And we mustn't forget looking down on this pudding that man's fiddledeevinity is what you may say only to the greater purpose of his hohumha.

ADAM: I beg your pardon.

GRANDIER: I quite agree. But I mustn't stay exchanging profundities with you, however much you may tempt me. So goodbye, Mister Surgeon and Mister Chemist.
(*GRANDIER goes. The bell is sounding.*)

MANNOURY: You fell into his trap, Adam. Never engage Mister Clever.

ADAM: He smelled of the widow woman. Filth.

MANNOURY: Of course. He's just come from her.

ADAM: After tickling himself in the confessional with the sins of young girls this morning –

MANNOURY: He consummates himself in the widow's bed this afternoon –

ADAM: And then comes and yawns in our faces.

MANNOURY: Tonight –

ADAM: Tonight he'll spend in some great house. D'Armagnac's, De Cerisay's. Fed, comforted and flattered by the laughter of women.

MANNOURY: What a – I'm so sorry. What were you going to say?

ADAM: I was going to say, What a life!

MANNOURY: So was I.

ADAM: We're never asked to such places.

MANNOURY: I've thought of it often.

ADAM: How do you console yourself?

MANNOURY: By remembering that I'm an honest man doing an honest job.

ADAM: Is that enough?

MANNOURY: What do you mean?

ADAM: Pick up the head and come with me.
(*They go along the street and into a house.*)

GRANDIER enters the church. He kneels at the altar: prays.

GRANDIER: O my dear Father, it is the wish of Your
humble child to come to Your Grace. I speak in the
weariness of thirty-five years. Years heavy with pride
and ambition, love of women and love of self. Years
scandalously marred by adornment and luxury, time
taken up with being that nothing, a man.
I prostrate myself before You now in ravaged humility of
spirit. I ask You to look upon me with love. I beg that
You will answer my prayer. Show me a way. Or let a way
be made.
(*Silence.*)
O God, O my God, my God! Release me. Free me.
These needs! Have mercy. Free me. Four o'clock of a
Tuesday afternoon. Free me.
(*He rises: cries out.*)
Rex tremendae majestatis, qui salvandos salvas gratis,
salva me, salva me, fons pietatis!

*DE LA ROCHEPOZAY, Bishop of Poitiers: Capuchins and
Carmelites.*

DE LA ROCHEPOZAY: I have been alone for many days
now. You will want to know if I have found some kind of
grace. Perhaps, for I am filled with weariness and disgust
at the folly and wickedness of mankind. Is this the
beneficence of God, you ask? It may well be. Let me tell
you the circumstances of the revelation.
Shut in my room for seven days, fasting and at prayer,
I came to see myself as the humble instrument of God's
will. It was a state of such happiness, such bliss and such
abasement that I wished never to return to you. I longed
for this husk to wither away, leaving only the purity of
spirit. But my sense of duty as your bishop forced me to
leave this paradise. I came back to the world.
A priest of Loudun, called Grandier, wished to see me. He
is my child, as you all are, my darlings, and I would wish
to love him. But his handkerchief was scented.

If this man had struck me in the face it would have humiliated me less. The assault on my senses was so obscene that I was in a state of terror. Scent, for a man to whom the taste of water was like fire, and the sound of the birds in the garden like the screams of the damned.

I am very tired. Take these rings from my fingers. Perhaps on your way here from your parish a child smiled at you, or you were attracted by a flower, or the smell of new grass by the road. Did you think of these things with anything but pleasure? One of you may have lost your way and been directed by a stranger. Did you think of it as anything but kindness?

Let me say this to you. There is no innocence, none! Suspect goodness in men, and reject kindness.

For all vanities are an assertion of self, and the assertion of self in Man is the ascendancy of the Devil.

When that handkerchief was flourished in my face this morning I saw it as if in a vision. It became a mighty banner flung across the world, stinking, enveloping, overwhelming our beloved Church in shamelessness and lust. We are in peril!

Take me away. Take me away.

(*DE LA ROCHEPOZAY is led away. FATHER BARRÉ and FATHER RANGIER are left alone.*)

RANGIER: How are things in your part of the world?

BARRÉ: I'm kept very busy.

RANGIER: Is he among you?

BARRÉ: Incessantly.

RANGIER: Can we name him?

BARRÉ: If you want to. Satan.

RANGIER: How is the struggle?

BARRÉ: I shan't give up.

RANGIER: You look tired.

BARRÉ: It goes on day and night.

RANGIER: Your spirit is shining.

BARRÉ: Unbroken, at any rate. But there's never a
    moment's peace at Chinon now. Only the other day

I was conducting a marriage. Everything was going very
well. I had before me a young couple, ignorant,
I thought, but pure. It never entered my head that they
were anything else. I'd reached the blessing, and was
about to send them out to the world as man and wife,
when there was a disturbance at the west door. A cow
had come into the church, and was trying to force its
way through the congregation. I knew at once, of course.

RANGIER: That it was he?

BARRÉ: Say it, Rangier, say it. (*He shouts.*) It was Satan!

RANGIER: You're never taken in.

BARRÉ: Before I could act he had passed from the cow to
the bride's mother, who fell to the ground in a kind of
convulsion. There was the most dreadful confusion, of
course, but I began exorcism at once. There's a couple
that won't forget their wedding day in a hurry.

RANGIER: How did it end?

BARRÉ: The spirit screamed from the church like a great
wind. A kind of black slime was found smeared on the
girl's forehead. She said she'd fallen, but of course
I know better. That's not all. Two days later the husband
came to me and said he'd found himself quite unable to
perform his necessary duty. The usual kind of spell, you
know. I've now started investigations into the whole
family.

RANGIER: This sort of thing must bring a lot of people to
Chinon.

BARRÉ: Thousands.

RANGIER: There's great popular interest in evil nowadays.

BARRÉ: It's certainly helped to offset the sadly declining
attendance at my shrine. The image of Notre-Dame de
Recouvrance.

RANGIER: Well, you know how that's come about.

BARRÉ: Certainly. They all flock to Loudun now. This
Grandier person, who's upset the bishop, is responsible
for that. He touts for his place disgracefully.

RANGIER: There are fashions in miracle-working images,
just as there are in women's hats.

BARRÉ: That's true. But there's a satisfying constancy in
    evil. I must go.

RANGIER: Anything interesting?

BARRÉ: I have to call at a farm. They say that something is
    speaking through the umbilicus of a child. The child
    herself is now in conversation with it, and I'm told the
    two voices have evolved a quite astonishing creed of
    profanation.
    (*BARRÉ and RANGIER go separate ways.*)

*GRANDIER alone. He has a sheaf of poems in his hand. TRINCANT
comes to him.*

TRINCANT: So good of you to call, Father Grandier.

GRANDIER: Not at all. I've brought back your poetry.

TRINCANT: So I see. D'Armagnac holds that any
    insufficiency must be put down to life in the provinces.

GRANDIER: You write them when you get back from the
    office.

TRINCANT: Every day.

GRANDIER: Amid the cooking smells.

TRINCANT: They drift up.

GRANDIER: And the clatter of family life.

TRINCANT: It intrudes.

GRANDIER: And so naturally you achieve – these.

TRINCANT: Put me out of my misery. I want an honest
    opinion.

GRANDIER: You're an important man in this town,
    Trincant. Men in public positions can't expect honesty.

TRINCANT: Speak to me as a poet, not as Public Prosecutor.

GRANDIER: Very well. Your poetry –
    (*PHILIPPE has come in.*)

TRINCANT: What is it?

PHILIPPE: I want my sewing, Father.

TRINCANT: Please take it. (*To GRANDIER.*) This is my
    elder daughter, Philippe. What were you saying?

GRANDIER: I was about to say that your creations – these
    – have great merit. They seem to be moral observations
    of a most uncommon kind.

TRINCANT: Really?

GRANDIER: (*To PHILIPPE.*) Don't you think so? I'm speaking of your father's poetry.

TRINCANT: She's very ignorant about such things. Young girls, you know, dear me. Dancing, music and laughter. Finer things can go hang.

GRANDIER: She should be instructed.

TRINCANT: It's so difficult to find anyone suitable in this town. Unless –

GRANDIER: (*To PHILIPPE.*) Do you speak any Latin?

PHILIPPE: A little.

GRANDIER: That's not enough.

TRINCANT: Unless –

GRANDIER: It's an exact language. Makes it possible to say just what you mean. That's rare nowadays. Don't you agree?

PHILIPPE: Yes, it is.

TRINCANT: Unless you, Father Grandier, would undertake the instruction.

GRANDIER: Of your daughter?

TRINCANT: Yes.

GRANDIER: I'm a busy man.

TRINCANT: Just one day a week. A few hours in the appreciation of finer things. It could be done by conversation. Perhaps the reading of suitable Latin verse.

GRANDIER: Very well.

TRINCANT: Shall we say Tuesday?

GRANDIER: No. Not Tuesday. The next day.

ADAM and MANNOURY: they sit in the pharmacy, beneath a stuffed crocodile and hanging bladders. Light is reflected through bottles which hold malformed creatures.

ADAM: (*He is reading from a small book.*) At half-past five on Tuesday he left the widow's house.

MANNOURY: The man is a machine. Interesting, though. Can sexual response be conditioned by the clock?

ADAM: At half-past seven he was observed in public conversation with D'Armagnac. The subject is in doubt, although Grandier was seen to snigger twice. He dined alone, later than usual, at nine o'clock. A light burned in his room until after midnight.

MANNOURY: I suppose it's possible. I say to a woman: At four-thirty on Tuesday I shall arrive to pleasure you. I do so on the dot for some weeks. It no longer becomes necessary to say that I shall do so. Anticipation speaks for me. Tuesday: half-past four. Usual physiological manifestations. Subject for treatise. Must think.

ADAM: (*He turns a page.*) Discovered at dawn prostrate before altar. Great languor through the morning. A meal at a quarter past two. Sweetbreads in cream, followed by a rank cheese. Wine. Three o'clock: entered Trincant's house for instruction of Trincant's daughter, Philippe.

MANNOURY: Adam, you're a wit.

ADAM: Am I, now?

MANNOURY: Your inflexion on the word 'instruction' was masterly.

ADAM: Thank you.

MANNOURY: But forgive me, my dear friend, if I ask you something. How do we go on? Your observations of Grandier's movements are a marvel. But these are the habits of any man. We shall never catch him on such evidence.

ADAM: You must give me time, Mannoury. We shall never expose him on his habits, certainly. But lust is leading him by the nose. And lust must have a partner. The widow, Ninon? Philippe Trincant? Another? Who knows? But there will be a time. Patience.

SISTER JEANNE DES ANGES alone: kneeling.

JEANNE: I dedicate myself humbly to Your service. You have made me, both in stature and in spirit, a little woman. And I have a small imagination, too. That is why, in Your infinite wisdom, You have given me this visible burden on my back to remind me day by day of what I must carry. O my dear Lord, I find it difficult to turn in my bed, and so in the small and desperate hours I am reminded of Your burden, the Cross, on the long road.

You have brought meaning to my life by my appointment to this Ursuline house. I will try to guide the Sisters of this place. I will do my duty as I see it. (*Silence.*) Lord... Lord, I have had great difficulty with prayer ever since I was a little girl. I have longed for another and greater voice within me to praise you. By Your grace I have come young to this office. Have mercy on Your child. Let her aspire. Meanwhile, the floors shall be swept, the beds neatly made, and the pots kept clean.

(*Silence.*) Mercy. (*Silence.*) I will find a way. Yes, I will find a way to You. I shall come. You will enfold me in Your sacred arms. The blood will flow between us, uniting us. My innocence is Yours.

(*Silence: precisely.*) Please God, take away my hump so that I can lie on my back without lolling my head. (*Silence.*) There is a way to be found. May the light of Your eternal love... (*Whispers.*)

Amen.

(*SISTER JEANNE rises: goes.*)

GRANDIER and PHILIPPE: she is reading.

PHILIPPE: Foeda est in coitu et brevis voluptas, et taedet Veneris statis peractae.

GRANDIER: Translate as you go. Line by line.

PHILIPPE: Pleasure in love is...

GRANDIER: Lust.

PHILIPPE: Pleasure in lust is nasty and short, And sickness...

GRANDIER: Weariness.

PHILIPPE: And weariness follows on desire.

GRANDIER: Go on.

PHILIPPE: non ergo ut pecudes libidinosae caeci protinus irruamus illuc (nam languescit amor peritque flamma); (*Pause.*)

We're not like animals to rush at it,
Love dies there, and the flame goes out.

GRANDIER: Prosaic, but fair. Give me the book. (*He translates.*)

But in everlasting leisure,
Like this, like this, lie still
And kiss time away.
No weariness and no shame,
Now, then and shall be all pleasure.
No end to it,
But an eternal beginning.
My child, why are you crying?

PHILIPPE: I haven't been well.

GRANDIER: Do you find our little lessons too much for you?

PHILIPPE: No, no, I love – I enjoy them very much.

GRANDIER: Well, we've only had six. I thought they might go on say to the end of the year.

PHILIPPE: Of course. As long as you like.

GRANDIER: As long as *you* like, Philippe. They're for your benefit.

PHILIPPE: I want very much to understand. All things.

GRANDIER: All things?

PHILIPPE: There are forces inside me as a woman which must be understood if they are to be resisted.

GRANDIER: What forces, Philippe?

PHILIPPE: Inclinations –

GRANDIER: Go on.

PHILIPPE: Inclinations towards sin.

(*Silence.*)

D'ARMAGNAC stands at a high point on the fortifications of the town. A Council of State. Distant figures: LOUIS XIII, King of France, and RICHELIEU.

RICHELIEU: It is a simple matter to understand, sir. You have that paper upside down. The self-government of the small provincial towns of France must be brought to an end. The first step is to pull down all kinds of fortification. (*GRANDIER has approached D'ARMAGNAC from below.*)

D'ARMAGNAC: So it's the turn of this city.

GRANDIER: Is everything to come down?

D'ARMAGNAC: That's what they want. It's a trick, of course. Richelieu sits with the King in Paris. He whispers in his ear.

RICHELIEU: France must be free within herself if she is to determine her own destiny.

D'ARMAGNAC: Ignorant and crafty provincials like us cannot see beyond the city walls. So we have this order from the Cardinal to tear them down. Will it broaden our view?

RICHELIEU: Such men as your friend D'Armagnac, sir, see with little vision. Their loyalty is to their town, not to France.

GRANDIER: Have they given any reason for this order?

D'ARMAGNAC: When a man's intent on power, as Richelieu is, he can justify his actions with absurdities.

RICHELIEU: Such fortifications provide opportunities for an uprising by the Protestants.

D'ARMAGNAC: Look. An old city. Those walls keep out more than the draught. Those towers are more than ornament. And from that fortress I have tried to administer my small sovereignty with reasonable wisdom. For I love the place.

GRANDIER: You must refuse to destroy it. Will other provincial governors stand against the order?

D'ARMAGNAC: It's very doubtful.

GRANDIER: Shall we?

D'ARMAGNAC: We?

GRANDIER: Let me help you in this matter, sir.

D'ARMAGNAC: Do you mean it? There is a churchman beside the King in Paris. As another, beside me here, do you also want to use this matter for your own ends?

GRANDIER: Conflict attracts me, sir. Resistance compels me.

D'ARMAGNAC: They can destroy you.

GRANDIER: I am weak, it's true. But equal power cannot be conflict. It is negation. Peace. So let me help you with all the passion of my failure.

D'ARMAGNAC: Don't smile. They can destroy you.
> (*DE LAUBARDEMONT, the King's Commissioner, has come to stand below RICHELIEU and the KING. RICHELIEU speaks to him.*)

RICHELIEU: D'Armagnac, the Governor of Loudun, has refused to obey the order. Go to the town. You've served me before. Wait. There is a man. His name is Grandier. He is a priest. Yes, there is a man called Grandier. Remember that.
> (*DE LAUBARDEMONT goes.*)

An unseen woman's voice.

VOICE: Lux aeterna luceat eis, Domine, cum sanctis tuis in aeternum, quia pius est.
> Requiem aeternam dona eis, Domine, et lux perpetua luceat eis.
> (*JEANNE, SISTER CLAIRE OF ST JOHN, SISTER LOUISE OF JESUS, SISTER GABRIELLE OF THE INCARNATION enter.*)

JEANNE: We have suffered a great loss, Sisters. Canon Moussaut was a good old man.

CLAIRE: It is God's will.

LOUISE: God's will.

JEANNE: So we have been taught. All the same, his death leaves us with a problem. We lack a director. The old man served this place well for many years, it's true, but the life of sinful children must go on. Penitents, we must have a confessor.

LOUISE: Have you chosen, Mother?

JEANNE: God will choose.

CLAIRE: We will pray.

JEANNE: Do so. There is a – (*Fit of coughing.*) Don't touch my back! (*Stillness: exhaustion.*) There is a man. His name is Grandier. He is young. I have never seen him, but God has often put him in my thoughts lately. I mean to… (*Silence.*)

CLAIRE: What's the matter?

JEANNE: Claire?

CLAIRE: Why stare at me like that? Have I done something wrong?

JEANNE: (*Seeing the girl.*) No, no. I mean to write to this good man and invite him to be our new director. Grandier. Grandier. It is guidance, you understand. He has been put in my thoughts. Grandier.

CLAIRE: It is God's will.

LOUISE: God's will.

JEANNE: (*Sudden harsh laughter.*) I am tired to death. (*Silence: calmly.*) It is a very excellent and practical solution. He can advise us on the method of education for the children put in our care. He will oversee our spiritual needs. (*Laughter again.*) He can sort out these damned problems of theological progression which muddle me day after day. Yes, it will be a good appointment. Leave me alone.

(*The Sisters go: JEANNE calls back CLAIRE.*)

Claire!

CLAIRE: Yes?

JEANNE: They say I have beautiful eyes. Is it true?

CLAIRE: Yes, Mother.

JEANNE: Too beautiful to close even in sleep, it seems. Go with the others.

(*JEANNE alone.*)

A summer morning. Children playing. Boy and girl. Paper boats sail the pond. Sun shone so hot upon the head that day. Children crouched, staring at each other across the sheet of water. Was it love? Flick. A toad upon a slab. Croak. Boy, head to one side, smiling, gentle voice whispering over the water: Look. Speak to your brother, Jeanne. There. Green brother. Hophop. Speak to him, Jeanne. (*Laughter: silence.*) God, forgive my laughter. But you haven't given me much defence, have You?

(*JEANNE goes to a window and opens it. She stares down through the grille upon:*)

A street. There is a market stall. People of the town are coming and going, buying and selling. Children. A cart passes. A song is heard.

GRANDIER comes through the crowd. He is in full canonicals, magnificent, golden, in the dying light of day. His tread is quick, confident and gay.

JEANNE cries out.

The sound is not heard by the crowd, but GRANDIER stops. He looks around him, into the faces of the crowd, wondering which man or woman could have been moved to such a cry of agony in the middle of such careless activity. GRANDIER goes on by way of ascending steps.

JEANNE is writing. Rapid, angular hand, ornamented.

The street. ADAM and MANNOURY are among the crowd. They come forward.

MANNOURY: The first thing to do is to draw up some kind of document.

ADAM: An accusation against Grandier.

MANNOURY: Exactly. We know about his debauchery.

ADAM: Profanity.

MANNOURY: And impiety.

ADAM: Is it enough?

MANNOURY: It'll have to do.

ADAM: For the time being.

MANNOURY: We'll present the paper to the Bishop.

ADAM: It must be properly done.

MANNOURY: Of course. Framed in correct language, decent to handle –

ADAM: Something's just occurred to me.

MANNOURY: Oh?

ADAM: What a lot of criticism we middle classes come in for just because we like things nice. I'm sorry. Go on. What will the document say?

MANNOURY: Say? (*Pause.*) We shall have to decide.

ADAM: It's not important.

MANNOURY: No. Just the means.

ADAM: We must keep the end in sight.

MANNOURY: Always.
  (*They go.*)

A confessional: GRANDIER and PHILIPPE. They speak in whispers throughout.

GRANDIER: When was your last confession, child?

PHILIPPE: A week ago, Father.

GRANDIER: What have you to tell me?

PHILIPPE: Father, I have sinned. I have suffered from pride.

GRANDIER: We must always be on guard.

PHILIPPE: I finished some needlework yesterday, and I was pleased with myself.

GRANDIER: God allows us satisfaction in the work we do.

PHILIPPE: I have been in error through anger.

GRANDIER: Tell me.

PHILIPPE: My sister teased me. I wished her – elsewhere.

GRANDIER: You're absolved. Anything else? (*Silence.*) Come now, others are waiting.

PHILIPPE: I've had unclean thoughts.

GRANDIER: Of what nature?

PHILIPPE: About a man.

GRANDIER: My child –

PHILIPPE: In the early hours of the morning...my bedroom is suffocatingly hot... I've asked them to take away the velvet curtains...my thoughts fester...and yet they are so tender...my body... Father...my body... I wish to be touched.

GRANDIER: Have you tried to suppress these thoughts?

PHILIPPE: Yes.

GRANDIER: Are they an indulgence?

PHILIPPE: No. I have prayed.

GRANDIER: Do you wish to be saved from this? (*Silence.*) Answer, child.

PHILIPPE: No! I want him to take – no, possess – no, destroy me. I love you. Him. I love him!
  (*GRANDIER comes out from the box: compassion. After a moment he draws aside the curtain and PHILIPPE is seen. They stand facing each other.*)

276

DE LA ROCHEPOZAY. ADAM and MANNOURY humbly before him.

DE LA ROCHEPOZAY: I have considered this document you have presented against the priest, Grandier. He is known to us as an impious and dangerous man. A few months ago we ourselves suffered insult and humiliation by his presence. But this is neither here nor there. What is your complaint?

MANNOURY: We feel, my lord bishop, that Grandier should be forbidden to exercise the sacerdotal function.

DE LA ROCHEPOZAY: What is your profession?

MANNOURY: I'm a surgeon.

DE LA ROCHEPOZAY: Would it amuse you if I came and instructed you in your business?

MANNOURY: I'm always prepared to take advice.

DE LA ROCHEPOZAY: Don't talk like a fool. This grubby and ill-composed document tells us nothing we did not know about the man. Vague and yet somewhat hysterical accusations concerning lonely widows and amorous virgins are all that I can find here. I'm not prepared to conduct the affairs of this diocese on the level of a police court.

ADAM: He has powerful friends.

DE LA ROCHEPOZAY: Stop whispering. What did you say?

ADAM: Grandier is protected by his friends.

DE LA ROCHEPOZAY: What are their names?

MANNOURY: (*To ADAM: a nudge.*) Go on.

ADAM: D'Armagnac. De Cerisay. Others.

DE LA ROCHEPOZAY: I'll accept your reasonable intentions in coming here. Although, God knows, if there's anyone I distrust it's the good citizen going about his civic duty. His motive is usually hate or money. But I will not accept your opinions, your advice, nor, for a moment longer, your presence.

(*ADAM and MANNOURY go.*)

(*To his attendant.*) It is vital that the Church should be protected from the democratic principle that every man must have his say. Those two probably spoke the truth, but they must not be allowed to think that they influence our judgement in any way.

JEANNE alone: a book of devotions. Night. CLAIRE comes to her.

CLAIRE: This was just delivered at the gate.
　　(*JEANNE takes a letter from CLAIRE, breaks it open, and reads.*)
JEANNE: He has refused.
CLAIRE: Father Grandier?
JEANNE: (*She reads aloud.*) My dear Sister: It is with great regret that I must refuse your invitation to become Director of your House. The pressing duties I have in the town would not allow me the time to devote my energies to the advantage of your Sisterhood. I very much appreciate all you say of my qualities and...
　　(*JEANNE tears the letter across and presses it to her body.*)
Thank you, Sister.
　　(*CLAIRE goes.
JEANNE alone.*)
What is this divine mystery? Let me see. Let me see. (*Laughter.*) I was about to address myself to God in this matter. Habit. Habit. It would never do. No. It must be to Man.
(*She whispers the name:*) Grandier.
You wake up. Dawn has broken over others before you. Look at the little grey window. Then turn. She lies beside you. The attitude is of prayer or the womb. Her mouth tastes of wine and the sea. Her skin is smooth and silky, rank with sweat. The native odours of her body have exhausted in the night the scents of day.
(*PHILIPPE, naked, is seen making love with GRANDIER. They will continue to be seen in the touching formal attitudes of passion throughout JEANNE's words.*)
Look down at her. What do you feel? Sadness? It must be sadness. You are a man. Ah, now she stretches her arms above her head. Are you not moved? This is not the sophistry of a whore, whatever you may pretend. She

shifts her legs, entwines them, lays a finger on your lips and her mouth upon her finger. She whispers. Those words were taught. She only repeats the lesson. Such filth is love to her, and the speaking of it is an act of faith. (*Sudden laughter.*) What was that you did? Stretching out to clutch the falling bed-clothes. Was it to cover your nakedness? Is there modesty here?

(*Silence: in wonder.*) How strange. Can you laugh, too? That's something I didn't know. Pain, oblivion, unreason, mania. These I thought would be in your bed. But laughter…

How young you both look. Quiet again.

The girl is heavy in your arms. She yawned, and you have taken up the shudder of her body. You tremble, in spite of yourself. Look, the sun is breaking up the mists in the fields. You're going to be engulfed by day. Take what you can. Let both take what they can. Now.

Now.

(*She weeps.*) This frenzy, this ripping apart, this meat on a butcher's slab. Where are you? Love? Love? What are you? Now. Now. Now.

(*JEANNE falls on her knees, convulsed. GRANDIER and PHILIPPE can no longer be seen.*)

(*Suffocated, young voice.*) O my God, is that it? Is that it?

(*Darkness.*)

D'ARMAGNAC, DE CERISAY, DE LAUBARDEMONT.

DE LAUBARDEMONT: It's not a question of compromise. I'm here as His Majesty's Special Commissioner, but I have no power to negotiate. I'm sorry, D'Armagnac.

D'ARMAGNAC: You know, Laubardemont, grown men in this country are getting a little tired of the father figures which keep arising, so we are told, for our own good. France may very well be looked on as a woman, and submissive, but she's not a baby.

DE LAUBARDEMONT: I'm inclined to agree with you. But I'm not here for argument. I simply brought a message.

D'ARMAGNAC: An order. Pull down the fortifications.

DE LAUBARDEMONT: That was the message. What answer may I take back?

D'ARMAGNAC: That I refuse.

DE LAUBARDEMONT: I have a curious feeling.

D'ARMAGNAC: Fear?

DE LAUBARDEMONT: No, no. Just that you've been influenced in this decision. And that there is pressure behind your obduracy.

D'ARMAGNAC: The decision is entirely mine. As governor of the town.

(*GRANDIER approaches.*)

D'ARMAGNAC: Do you know Father Grandier?

DE LAUBARDEMONT: I've heard of him.

D'ARMAGNAC: Well, this is he.

DE LAUBARDEMONT: (*Turning.*) Ah, Father. Can't you bring your influence to bear on the Governor in this matter of the demolition. As a man of peace I'm sure you want it brought about.

GRANDIER: As a man of peace, I do. As a man of principle, I'd prefer the city walls to remain standing.

DE LAUBARDEMONT: I see. Well, I seem to be alone in this. If you change your mind, and I earnestly hope you will, I shall be in Loudun for a few days.

(*DE LAUBARDEMONT goes.*)

D'ARMAGNAC: Look at him, Grandier.

GRANDIER: A funny little man.

D'ARMAGNAC: My dear fellow, we are all romantic. We see our lives being changed by a winged messenger on a black horse. But more often than not it turns out to be a shabby little man, who stumbles across our path.

A cloister. JEANNE and FATHER MIGNON, a foolish old man, walking together.

JEANNE: We are all of us so happy, Father Mignon, that you've been able to accept. We shall look forward to having you as our director for many years to come.

MIGNON: You're very kind, my child. You have a direct
simplicity which an old man like myself finds very
touching.

JEANNE: There are many problems in a place like this.
I shall need your advice and guidance.

MIGNON: Always at your disposal.

JEANNE: For example, nearly all the Sisters here are young
women I think you'll agree that youth is more exposed
to temptation than age.

MIGNON: That's so. I remember when I was a young man –

JEANNE: I have myself –

MIGNON: What's that?

JEANNE: I was about to say that I have myself recently
suffered from visions of a diabolical nature.

MIGNON: In living close to God one becomes a natural
prey to the Devil. I shouldn't worry about them too much.

JEANNE: I can speak about this in the daytime. But at
night –

MIGNON: It is a well-known fact, my dear, that the spirit is
at its weakest in the small hours.

JEANNE: Yes. I managed to resist the vision. Several hours
of prayer and I was myself again. But the visitation –

MIGNON: Visitation?

JEANNE: The dead Canon Moussaut, your predecessor,
came to me in the night. He stood at the foot of my bed.

MIGNON: But this was a visit of love, my child. Moussaut
was a good man. You were fond of him. Did he speak to
you?

JEANNE: Yes.

MIGNON: What did he say?

JEANNE: Filth.

MIGNON: What's that?

JEANNE: He spoke filth. Dirt. Jeering, contemptuous,
hurtful obscenity.

MIGNON: My beloved Sister –

JEANNE: He was not in his own person.

MIGNON: What do you mean?

JEANNE: He came to me as another. A different man.

MIGNON: Did you recognise this man?
JEANNE: Yes.
MIGNON: Who was it?
JEANNE: Grandier. Father Grandier.
　　(*Silence.*)
MIGNON: My dear, do you understand the seriousness of
　　what you're saying?
JEANNE: (*Calmly.*) Yes. Help me, Father.

GRANDIER: *in the pulpit.*

GRANDIER: ...For some lewd fellows go about the town
　　and speak against me. I know them. And you will know
　　them when I say that Surgery and Chemistry go hand in
　　hand, vermination against the wall. They have borne false
　　witness. They spy. They sneak. They snigger. And the first
　　sinful man was called Adam, and he begot murder. Why
　　do they pursue me? I am not sick!
　　If they be here, in this holy place, let them stand before
　　me and declare their hatred, and give the reason for it.
　　I am not afraid to speak openly of what they attempt to
　　discover secretly. If they be in this church let them stand
　　before me. (*Silence.*) No, they are in some hole in the
　　ground, scratching, so that more venom may come to the
　　surface, and infect us all; distilling bile in retorts;
　　revealing lust, envy and blight with the turn of a scalpel.
　　(*During this DE LAUBARDEMONT, with two attendants,
　　has approached, listened and moved on.*)
　　O my dear children, I should not speak to you so from
　　this place. And I should not speak to you in bitterness as
　　your pastor.
　　Do they provoke me to anger? saith the Lord: do they
　　not provoke themselves to the confusion of their own
　　faces?

The pharmacy: ADAM and MANNOURY.

ADAM: It's after ten o'clock. Would you believe it?
MANNOURY: Well, we have had a nice talk.

ADAM: Have we got anywhere?

MANNOURY: Somebody at the door.

ADAM: Can't be.

MANNOURY: Is.

(*ADAM opens the door. DE LAUBARDEMONT stands there.*)

ADAM: No business. Shut.

DE LAUBARDEMONT: My name is Jean de Martin, Baron de Laubardemont. I am His Majesty's Special Commissioner to Loudun.

ADAM: Can I help you?

DE LAUBARDEMONT: I hope so.

(*DE LAUBARDEMONT comes into the shop.*)

I am visiting the town for a kind of investigation.

MANNOURY: (*Carefully.*) We are both honest men.

DE LAUBARDEMONT: I know. That's why I'm here. I've always found in cases like this that there are perhaps two incorruptible men in the town. Usually close friends, professional men, middle class, backbone of the nation. Deep civic interest. Patriotic. Lost sons in a war. Happily married. Managing to make ends meet in spite of taxation. Austere lives, but what they have they like to be nice. Gentlemen, am I right?

ADAM: Quite correct.

DE LAUBARDEMONT: Good. I want you to tell me all you know about a man called Grandier. Father Grandier, of Saint Peter's Church.

ADAM: My dear Mannoury, at last!

GRANDIER and PHILIPPE: a secluded place.

PHILIPPE: I must go home now.

GRANDIER: Yes.

PHILIPPE: I don't like walking through the streets at night. Dogs bark. Listen, they're at it now.

GRANDIER: I wish I could come with you. I would like – oh, words, words!

PHILIPPE: What is it?

GRANDIER: Come here. Gently. I want to tell you –

PHILIPPE: Yes?

GRANDIER: You know the love-making –

PHILIPPE: Yes.

GRANDIER: I want to tell you, Philippe. Among the clothes dropped on the floor, the soiled linen, the instruction, the apparatus, the surgery – among all this there is a kind of passion of the heart.

PHILIPPE: I know. It is love. Human love.

(*Silence.*)

GRANDIER: You understand it that way?

PHILIPPE: I think so.

GRANDIER: Do I love you?

PHILIPPE: I believe so.

GRANDIER: Then what comfort can I give you?

(*Silence.*)

PHILIPPE: I am a simple person. I see the world and myself as I have been taught. I am deeply sinful, but my love of God has not deserted me. It is said by Man that those in our state should stand before God. I believe this to be right. And I would not be afraid to declare myself to Him with you beside me, even in our transgression, for I believe Him to be good, wise and always merciful.

(*Silence.*)

GRANDIER: You shame me.

The pharmacy. DE LAUBARDEMONT, MANNOURY, ADAM. They have been joined by MIGNON.

MIGNON: I couldn't get any more out of the prioress. I can prove nothing. She may be just an hysterical woman.

ADAM: Does it matter?

MIGNON: I'd very much like you, as a surgeon, Mannoury, and you, Adam, as a chemist, to be there.

DE LAUBARDEMONT: May I attend as a disinterested party?

MIGNON: Certainly. If this is a genuine case, the more the – (*He stops.*)

DE LAUBARDEMONT: Were you going to say merrier?

MIGNON: I've sent a message to Father Barré, at Chinon. He's our great local expert in these matters.

MANNOURY: I shall be only too happy to give you any medical advice, Father.

ADAM: And I'll comment on any chemical or biological manifestations.

MIGNON: She already complains of a spasmodic but acute swelling of the belly.

ADAM: Fascinating!

MANNOURY: Not unusual. Sense of false pregnancy. Known it before. Nothing to do with the Devil. Wind?

DE LAUBARDEMONT: Conjecture is useless. It'll soon be morning.

Dawn. JEANNE at prayer beside her simple bed.

JEANNE: Please God, make me a good girl. Take care of my dear father and mother and look after my dog, Captain, who loved me and didn't understand why I had to leave him behind all that time ago. Lord... Lord, I would like to make formal prayers to You, but I can only do that out of a book in the chapel. (*Silence.*) Love me. (*Silence.*) Love me. Amen.

(*JEANNE gets up and goes from the room to a great open space where stand:*

DE LAUBARDEMONT, MANNOURY, ADAM, MIGNON, RANGIER and BARRÉ. JEANNE approaches them.)

BARRÉ: Let me deal with this. Good morning, Sister. Are you well?

JEANNE: I'm very well, thank you, Father.

BARRÉ: Excellent. Will you kneel down?

(*JEANNE does so. BARRÉ goes to her.*)

(*Sudden shout.*) Are you there! Are you there! (*Silence: to the others.*) They never answer at once. Afraid of committing themselves. (*To JEANNE.*) Come now, declare yourself! In the name of Our Lord Jesus Christ –

(*Suddenly JEANNE throws back her crooked head and peals of masculine laughter pour from her open, distorted mouth.*)

(*With satisfaction: to the others.*) Always does the trick.

JEANNE: (*Deep man's voice.*) Here we are, and here we stay.

BARRÉ: One question.

JEANNE: Pooh!

BARRÉ: Don't be impudent. One question. How did you gain entry to this poor woman?

JEANNE: (*Deep voice.*) Good offices of a friend.

BARRÉ: His name?

JEANNE: Asmodeus.

BARRÉ: That's your name. What is the name of your friend?

(*JEANNE is swaying on her knees. She gives inarticulate cries which gradually form themselves into the word:*)

JEANNE: Grandier! Grandier! Grandier!

(*Deep, sullen laughter.*)

CURTAIN

ACT TWO

Saint Peter's Church. Night.

GRANDIER is at the altar. PHILIPPE kneels below him.

GRANDIER holds up a salver. Speaks:

GRANDIER: Benedic, ✠ Domine, hunc annulum, quem nos in tuo nomine benedicimus, ✠ ut quae eum gestaverit, fidelitatem integram suo sponso tenens, in pace et voluntate tua permaneat, atque in mutua caritate semper vivat Per Christum Dominum nostrum.

PHILIPPE: Amen.

(*GRANDIER sprinkles the ring with holy water, and then, taking the ring from the salver, comes down to kneel beside PHILIPPE.*)

GRANDIER: With this ring I thee wed: this gold and silver I thee give; with my body I thee worship; and with all my worldly goods I thee endow.

(*GRANDIER places the ring on the thumb of PHILIPPE's hand, saying:*)

In the name of the Father: (*Then on the second finger, saying:*) And of the Son: (*Then on the third finger, saying:*) And of the Holy Ghost: (*Lastly on the fourth finger, saying:*) Amen.

(*And there he leaves the ring.*

GRANDIER mounts the altar steps.)

Confirma hoc, Deus, quod operatus es in nobis.

PHILIPPE: A templo sancto tuo, quod est in Jerusalem.

GRANDIER: Kyrie eleison.

PHILIPPE: Christe eleison.

GRANDIER: Kyrie eleison.

PHILIPPE/GRANDIER: (*speak together.*) Pater noster –

(*– and their voices whisper into silence.*)

A street.

The SEWERMAN is sitting at ease. He holds a cage with a bird in it. GRANDIER and PHILIPPE come from the church.

PHILIPPE: We should step out into the sunlight. Bells should tell the world about us. It shouldn't be night. And as quiet as this. Dear God, my husband, kiss me.

(*They kiss.*)

SEWERMAN: So it's done. I saw you go into the church.

GRANDIER: It's done. And well done. Does the bird sing?

SEWERMAN: Not its purpose. Tongueless.

GRANDIER: Do you carry it for love?

SEWERMAN: An idea which would only occur to a good man. Or one careless with hope. No, I carry the thing so that it may die, and I live. He's my saviour. Who's yours?

GRANDIER: You –

SEWERMAN: Blaspheme?

GRANDIER: Yes.

SEWERMAN: Sorry. You know the pits at the edge of the town? Where even your beloved here sends in my buckets. Well, there are days when the place gives off poison. So I always approach it with this creature on a pole before me. His many predecessors have died in the miasma. When this happens I know it's no place for me. So I let the drains run foul for a day or two, and I spend my time catching another victim to shut up here. You'll understand what I mean.

(*Silence.*)

GRANDIER: I have put my trust in this child. She is not a victim.

SEWERMAN: Just as you say.

GRANDIER: Come now, even at this hopeless hour you must admit more passes between human beings than the actions which provide you and the laundry with a job.

SEWERMAN: I'm not arguing.

GRANDIER: There is a way of salvation through each other.

SEWERMAN: Are you trying to convince me?

GRANDIER: I'd like to.

SEWERMAN: What about yourself? Has the little ceremony in there done the trick?

GRANDIER: It has given me hope.

SEWERMAN: Hope of what?

GRANDIER: Hope of coming to God by way of a fellow
  being. Hope that the path, which taken alone, in awful
  solitude, is a way of despair, can be enlightened by the
  love of a woman. I have come to believe that by this
  simple act of committal, which I have done with my heart,
  it may be possible to reach God by way of happiness.

SEWERMAN: What was that last word?

GRANDIER: Happiness.

SEWERMAN: I don't know what it means. You must have
  made it up for the occasion. It's getting light.

PHILIPPE: I must go.

SEWERMAN: Yes. They mustn't find the bed empty. On
  the other hand, they mustn't find it too full.

PHILIPPE: (*To GRANDIER.*) Speak to me.

SEWERMAN: Say it.

GRANDIER: I love you, Philippe.
  (*PHILIPPE goes.*)

SEWERMAN: Speaking of love, some very odd things are
  going on up at the convent.

GRANDIER: So I'm told.

SEWERMAN: It seems your name is being bandied about
  by the crazy ladies.

GRANDIER: We must pity them.

SEWERMAN: Will they pity you, that's the point?

GRANDIER: What do you mean? They're deluded.

SEWERMAN: What were you, a few minutes ago, with that
  girl?

GRANDIER: I was in my right mind, and I knew what
  I was doing. You may mock me, my son, if you wish.
  What seems to you a meaningless act, the marriage of an
  unmarriageable priest, has meaning for me. The lonely
  and the proud sometimes need to avail themselves of
  simple means. I, too, have made fun of the innocent
  before now. Your debasement has given you an unholy
  elevation. From your superior position be kind, be wise.
  Pity me. Pity me.

SEWERMAN: All right. Let's hope the good women of
  Saint Ursula's will do the same.

Daylight.

JEANNE, on her knees. Facing her, BARRÉ, RANGIER and MIGNON.

BARRÉ: Exorcise te, immundissime spiritus, omnis incursio adversarii, omne phantasma, omnis legio, in nomine Domini nostri Jesus Christi, eradicare et effugare ab hoc plasmate Dei.

(*RANGIER and MIGNON come forward. RANGIER splashes holy water: MIGNON lays on the stole. Asmodeus, in a deep voice, speaks through JEANNE.*)

JEANNE: (*As Asmodeus.*) You gentlemen are wasting your time. You're soaking the lady, but you're not touching me.

BARRÉ: (*To MIGNON.*) Give me the relic.

(*MIGNON hands BARRÉ a small box. It is applied to JEANNE's back.*)

Adjure te, serpens antique, per judicem vivorum et mortuorum...

JEANNE: (*As Asmodeus.*) Excuse me.

BARRÉ: ...per factorum tuum, per factorum mundi...

JEANNE: (*As Asmodeus.*) I'm sorry to interrupt you.

BARRÉ: Well, what is it?

JEANNE: (*As Asmodeus.*) I don't understand a word you're saying. I'm a heathen devil. Latin – I suppose it is Latin – is a foreign language to me.

BARRÉ: It is customary to carry out exorcism in Latin.

JEANNE: (*As Asmodeus.*) Hidebound, that's what you are. Can't we continue our earlier conversation, which interested me so much, about the sexual activities of priests?

BARRÉ: Certainly not!

JEANNE: (*As Asmodeus.*) Is it true that men of your parish... (*Insane giggles.*) ...is it true that they... Bend low. Let me whisper.

(*As herself.*) O dear God, release this thing from me.

(*As Asmodeus.*) Be quiet, woman. You're interrupting a theological discussion.

(*As herself.*) Father, help me.

BARRÉ: My dear child, I'm doing all I can.

(*BARRÉ takes RANGIER and MIGNON aside: speaks to RANGIER.*)

The wretch thinks I'm defeated.

JEANNE: (*As Asmodeus.*) You are.

BARRÉ: He seems at the moment to be lodged in the lower bowel. Are Adam and Mannoury here?

RANGIER: They're waiting. In there.

BARRÉ: Ask them to get ready, will you. Consecrate the water, while you're about it.

(*RANGIER goes out through the small, low door. BARRÉ turns to JEANNE.*)

My beloved Sister, it must be extreme measures.

JEANNE: What do you mean, Father?

BARRÉ: The fiend must be forced from you.

JEANNE: Is there any way but exorcism?

BARRÉ: Haha! They say the Devil takes residence only in the innocent. It's true in this case, it seems. Yes, child, there is another way. (*He shouts.*) Do you hear me, Asmodeus?

VOICE: (*Of Asmodeus. Is it JEANNE's voice?*) Mercy. Mercy.

BARRÉ: (*A scream.*) Nonsense!

(*Silence.*

RANGIER comes out from the inner room.)

My dear boy, you look quite pale. The use of such methods in our job distresses you. Wait till you've been at it as long as I have. Anyway, the Church must keep up with the times. (*To JEANNE.*) Come, my dear Sister. Through that little door. There lies your salvation. She looks like a child, doesn't she? Touching. Um. Go along, now. Pretty, pretty. A few steps.

(*JEANNE moves forward towards the small door.*)

Let the power of good propel you. Not much further. There!

(*JEANNE is standing in the doorway staring into the small, dark room – and then at once she is struggling in BARRÉ's arms, a howling animal.*)

(*Powerful: confident.*) Help me, Rangier!

(*RANGIER comes to BARRÉ, and together they hold the woman.*)

JEANNE: No, no! I didn't mean it!

BARRÉ: Too late, Asmodeus. Do you expect mercy now, after your blasphemy and filth against Our Lord?

JEANNE: Father! Father Barré, it is I speaking to you now, Sister Jane of the Angels –

BARRÉ: Ah, Asmodeus, you spoke with many voices.

JEANNE: But it's I, Father. Beloved Mother of this dear convent, protector of little children –

BARRÉ: Silence, beast! Let's get her in there, Rangier. Are you ready, Adam?

ADAM: (*From within.*) Quite ready.

(*BARRÉ and RANGIER carry the struggling woman into the room. The door slams shut. MIGNON, left alone, gets down on his knees and begins to pray.*

There is a scream from JEANNE inside the room: it dissolves into sobs and laughter. MIGNON prays louder. His empty, excited little voice ascends to nothingness.)

D'ARMAGNAC, DE CERISAY and GRANDIER move into the foreground.

DE CERISAY: The devil, it seems, departed from the woman at two o'clock precisely.

D'ARMAGNAC: What about the others?

DE CERISAY: The Fathers are working on them now.

D'ARMAGNAC: Same method?

DE CERISAY: No. It seems that after the Prioress more normal methods of exorcism are proving successful. A little holy water – applied externally – a few prayers, and the devils go.

D'ARMAGNAC: Then we can hope for some peace.

DE CERISAY: I don't know.

D'ARMAGNAC: Can't you do something if it starts again? As Magistrate. I'd say such goings-on constitute a civil disorder.

DE CERISAY: I saw Barré and Rangier the other day and questioned the legality of their methods. Next time the convent door was shut in my face. I put myself in a difficult position if I use force against priests. They've asked me to be present at an interrogation of Sister Jane. I'm on my way there now.

D'ARMAGNAC: (*To GRANDIER.*) You know your name is constantly being mentioned in this affair.

GRANDIER: Yes, sir.

D'ARMAGNAC: Wouldn't it be a good thing to take steps to clear yourself?

DE CERISAY: Have you offended this woman in some way?

GRANDIER: I don't know how that's possible. I've never seen her.

DE CERISAY: Then why has she chosen you as the devilish perpetrator?

GRANDIER: You look frightened, De Cerisay. Forgive me.

D'ARMAGNAC: You're the one who should be frightened, Father. There was a case some years ago – I forget the man's name –

GRANDIER: I don't, poor devil. There have been many cases, sir.

D'ARMAGNAC: You're in danger.

GRANDIER: Of death? But surely not by a farce such as the convent's putting on. Come, sir, death must be more magnificent, more significant for a man of my kind.

D'ARMAGNAC: How did these other men end?

GRANDIER: At the stake. But they were ridiculous and obscure. Proper matter for sacrifice, that's all.

DE CERISAY: D'Armagnac and I will give you any help we can, Father.

GRANDIER: Can't I talk either of you out of this? When I came here this morning I heard the stories on the streets. I laughed. I thought you'd be doing the same. Is the possession genuine?

DE CERISAY: Not from the evidence I have. As I say, I shall see the woman today. I'll let you know what happens. But you haven't answered my question. Why should it be you?

GRANDIER: Secluded women. They give themselves to God, but something remains which cries out to be given to Man. With the truly pure in heart it can be given in the form of charity, but for the weaker members it is not so easy. It's sad. Very sad, indeed, when you think about it. Imagine being awakened in the night by a quite innocent dream. A dream of your childhood, or of a friend not seen for many years, or even the vision of a good meal. Now, this is a sin. And so you must take up your little whip and scourge your body. We call that discipline. But pain is sensuality, and in its vortex spin images of horror and lust. My beloved Sister in Jesus seems to have fixed her mind on me. There is no reason, De Cerisay. A dropped handkerchief, a scribbled note, a piece of gossip. Any of these things found in the desert of mind and body caused by continual prayer can bring hope. And with hope comes love. And, as we all know, with love comes hate. So I possess this woman. God help her in her terror and unhappiness. God help her. (*To D'ARMAGNAC.*) Now, sir, the business I called on. I've the new plans for your garden summer house. Will you come and see them? I've revised and modified the frivolity of the design. As you wished.

(*GRANDIER and D'ARMAGNAC go. DE CERISAY stares after them for a moment, and then moves on to enter –*)

A high-ceilinged room, furnished with two small beds. One is occupied by JEANNE. BARRÉ, RANGIER and MIGNON are present. Also ADAM and MANNOURY. A CLERK sits writing.

BARRÉ: Dear Sister in Christ, I must question you further.

JEANNE: Yes, Father.

BARRÉ: Do you remember the first time your thoughts were turned to these evil things?

JEANNE: Very well.

BARRÉ: Tell us.

JEANNE: I was walking in the garden. I stopped. Lying at my feet was a stick of hawthorn. I was sinfully possessed by anger, for that very morning I'd had cause to admonish two of the Sisters for neglecting their duties in the garden. I picked up the unsightly thing in rage. It must have been thorned, for blood ran from my body. Seeing the blood, I was filled with tenderness.

RANGIER: But this revelation may have come from a very different source.

BARRÉ: All the same – (*To the CLERK.*) Are you getting this down?

JEANNE: There was another time.

BARRÉ: Tell us.

JEANNE: A day or two later. It was a beautiful morning. I'd had a night of dreamless sleep. On the threshold of my room lay a bunch of roses. I picked them up and tucked them into my belt. Suddenly, I was seized by a violent trembling in my right arm. And a great knowledge of love. This persisted throughout my orisons. I was unable to put my mind to anything. It was entirely filled with the representation of a man which had been deeply and inwardly impressed upon me.

BARRÉ: Do you know who sent those flowers?

JEANNE: (*Long silence: quietly.*) Grandier. Grandier.

BARRÉ: What is his rank?

JEANNE: Priest.

BARRÉ: Of what church?

JEANNE: Saint Peter's.

(*BARRÉ turns to stare in silence at DE CERISAY.*)

DE CERISAY: (*Quietly.*) This is nothing.

(*BARRÉ turns back to JEANNE.*)

BARRÉ: We are unconvinced, my dear Sister. And if our conviction remains untouched I do not have to remind you that you face eternal damnation.

(*JEANNE suddenly throws herself across the bed: she utters grunts like a small pig: she grinds her teeth: she disorders the bed. The men draw back from her. JEANNE sits upright, staring at them.*)

(*With great urgency.*) Speak! Speak!

JEANNE: It…was…night. Day's done!

BARRÉ: Yes?

JEANNE: I had tied back my hair, and scrubbed my face. Back to childhood, eh? Poor Jane. Grown woman. Made for – for…

BARRÉ: Go on.

JEANNE: He came to me.

BARRÉ: Name him!

JEANNE: (*At once.*) Grandier! Grandier! The beautiful, golden lion entered my room, smiling.

BARRÉ: Was he alone?

JEANNE: No. Six of his creatures were with him.

BARRÉ: Then?

JEANNE: He took me gently in his arms and carried me to the chapel. His creatures each took one of my beloved sisters.

BARRÉ: What took place?

JEANNE: (*Smiling.*) Oh, my dear Father, think of our little chapel, so simple, so unadorned. That night it was a place of luxury and scented heat. Let me tell you. It was full of laughter and music. There were velvets, silks, metals, and the wood wasn't scrubbed, no, not at all. Yes, and there was food. High animal flesh, and wine, heavy, like the fruit from the East. I'd read about it all. How we stuffed ourselves.

DE CERISAY: This is an innocent vision of hell.

BARRÉ: Ssh! Go on.

JEANNE: I forgot. We were beautifully dressed. I wore my clothes as if they were part of my body. Later, when I was naked, I fell among the thorns. Yes, there were thorns strewn on the floor. I fell among them. Come here.
(*She beckons to BARRÉ, who leans towards her. She whispers and then laughs.*)

BARRÉ: (*Bleakly.*) She says that she and her sisters were compelled to form themselves into an obscene altar, and were worshipped.

JEANNE: Again.
(*Again she whispers: laughs.*)

BARRÉ: She says demons tended Grandier, and her beloved sisters incited her. You'll understand what I mean, gentlemen.
(*JEANNE again draws BARRÉ to her. She whispers frantically, and gradually her words become audible.*)

JEANNE: ...and so we vanquished God from his house. He fled in horror at the senses fixed in men by another hand. Free of Him, we celebrated His departure again and again. (*She lies back.*) To one who has known what I have known, God is dead. I have found peace.

(*Silence. MIGNON has fallen on his knees and is praying. BARRÉ takes DE CERISAY by the arm. As they speak they will move far from JEANNE and the others.*)

BARRÉ: This was an innocent woman.

DE CERISAY: That was no devil. She spoke with her own voice. The voice of an unhappy woman, that's all.

BARRÉ: But the degraded imagination and filthy language she used in other depositions. These cannot spring unaided from a cloistered woman. She is a pupil.

DE CERISAY: Of Grandier?

BARRÉ: Yes.

DE CERISAY: But the man swears he's never been in the place.

BARRÉ: Not in his own person.

DE CERISAY: There must be some way of proving what she says. Will you let my people into the house? They will conduct an investigation on a police level.

BARRÉ: Proof? Three of the Sisters have made statements saying that they have undergone copulation with demons and been deflowered. Mannoury has examined them, and it's true that none of them is intact.

DE CERISAY: My dear Father, I don't want to offend your susceptibilities, but we all know about the sentimental attachments which go on between the young women in these places.

BARRÉ: You don't wish to be convinced.

DE CERISAY: I do. Very much. One way or another.

(*DE CERISAY goes. BARRÉ turns. MANNOURY and ADAM are approaching.*)

ADAM: Well, there, now.

MANNOURY: Fascinating.

ADAM: Unusual.

MANNOURY: Must say. Hell can't be as dull as some people make out. Haha! What?

ADAM: Such things.

MANNOURY: You know, I think a privately printed testament of this case might have quite a sale. Shall we write it up?

ADAM: Let's.

(*They have approached BARRÉ.*)

BARRÉ: Have you examined her?

MANNOURY: Yes. I'll let you have my report later.

BARRÉ: Can you give me anything to go on, meantime?

MANNOURY: As a professional man –

ADAM: He speaks for me.

MANNOURY: I don't like to commit myself.

BARRÉ: Even so –

MANNOURY: Well, let's put it this way. There's been hanky-panky.

BARRÉ: Don't mince words. There's been fornication!

MANNOURY: Rather!

BARRÉ: Lust! She's been had!

ADAM: I'll say.

BARRÉ: Thank you, gentlemen. That's all I need. Look.

(*They are silent. GRANDIER is walking in the distance.*
BARRÉ, MANNOURY and ADAM go.

GRANDIER approaches. PHILIPPE comes quickly to him.)

PHILIPPE: They said you were at the Governor's house.

GRANDIER: I've just come from there. What's the matter?

PHILIPPE: I want to know. Was I restless last night? I had to leave you before it was light. I went as quietly as I could. Did I disturb you? It's important that I should know.

GRANDIER: I can't remember. Why is it important?

PHILIPPE: You can't remember.

(*She gives a sudden, startling, harsh laugh.*)

GRANDIER: Walk to the church with me.

PHILIPPE: No.

GRANDIER: Very well.

PHILIPPE: There's no need to go into the confessional to say what I have to tell you. I'm pregnant.

(*Silence.*)

GRANDIER: So it ends.

PHILIPPE: I'm frightened.

GRANDIER: Of course. How can I own the child?

PHILIPPE: I'm very frightened.

GRANDIER: And there was such bravery in love, wasn't there, Philippe? All through the summer nights. How unafraid we were each time we huddled down together. We laughed as we roused the animal. Remember? Now it has devoured us.

PHILIPPE: Help me.

GRANDIER: And we were to have been each other's salvation. Did I really believe it was possible?

PHILIPPE: I love you.

GRANDIER: Yes, I did believe it. I remember leaving you one day – you had been unusually adroit –

PHILIPPE: O God!

GRANDIER: I was filled with that indecent confidence which comes after perfect coupling. And as I went I thought – yes, solemnly I thought – the body can transcend its purpose. It can become a thing of such purity that it can be worshipped to the limits of imagination. Anything is allowed. All is right. And such perfection makes for an understanding of the hideous state of existence.

PHILIPPE: Touch me.

GRANDIER: But what is it now? An egg. A thing of weariness, loathing and sickness. So it ends.

PHILIPPE: Where is love?

GRANDIER: Where, indeed? Go to your father. Tell him the truth. Let him find some good man. They exist.

PHILIPPE: Help me.

GRANDIER: How can I help you? Take my hand. There. Like touching the dead, isn't it? Goodbye, Philippe. (*GRANDIER goes.*)

The pharmacy. ADAM, MANNOURY and MIGNON.

There is a harsh cry from BARRÉ as he appears at the top of the stairway. He moves like a drunken man. The others scatter in alarm.

BARRÉ: I was denied entrance to the convent tonight. By armed guards.

MIGNON: My God, my God, what's wrong?

BARRÉ: The Archbishop has issued an ordinance against further exorcism or investigation.

MIGNON: Never!

BARRÉ: It was done at the request of De Cerisay and D'Armagnac. What's more, the Archbishop's personal physician – that rationalist fool! – got hold of the women without my knowledge. He examined them, and gave it as his opinion that there was no genuine possession.

MIGNON: What shall we do? Oh, what shall we do?

(*BARRÉ comes down into the room.*)

BARRÉ: De Cerisay sees it as an act of justice. He doesn't understand that such things play straight into the hands of the devil. Allow reasonable doubt for a man's sin, and the devil snaps it up. (*He shouts wearily.*) There can be no reasonable doubt in sin. All or nothing!

MIGNON: Of course. Of course. Justice has nothing to do with salvation. Sit down. Sit down.

BARRÉ: My life's work is threatened by a corrupt archbishop, a liberal doctor and an ignorant lawyer. Ah, gentlemen, there'll be happiness in hell tonight.

(*Silence.*)

MANNOURY: Are we done for, then?

ADAM: Seems so.

MANNOURY: All up.

ADAM: Dear me.

MANNOURY: Pity.

MIGNON: Let us pray.

ADAM: I beg your pardon?

MIGNON: Let us pray.

ADAM: What for?

MIGNON: Well, let me think –

ADAM: Right you are.

MIGNON: I know!

ADAM: Yes?

MIGNON: Let us pray that the Archbishop has a diabolic vision...

BARRÉ: (*To MANNOURY.*) I shall go back to my parish.

MIGNON: (*To ADAM.*) ...of a particularly horrible nature...

BARRÉ: (*To MANNOURY.*) There's work for me there.

MIGNON: (*To ADAM.*) He's an old man, too. Perhaps we can frighten him to death.

BARRÉ: Be quiet, Mignon. You rave.

MIGNON: Don't leave us.

BARRÉ: I must.

MIGNON: You're naturally a little depressed by this setback. But we'll find a way.

BARRÉ: No. The Archbishop's ordinance has made evil impossible in this place. For the moment. But the ordinance doesn't apply in my parish, and you can be sure that Satan is trumpeting there. I must answer the call.

MIGNON: We shall miss you very much.

BARRÉ: My dear friend, a whisper from hell and I shall be back.

D'ARMAGNAC and DE CERISAY at a table. GRANDIER formally approaches them.

GRANDIER: I believe I must thank you, De Cerisay, for having this persecution stopped. Very well. I do so now.

DE CERISAY: I acted for you, Father, but not entirely on your behalf. The circus up at the convent was beginning to attract a lot of unwelcome attention to the town. It's my job to keep some sort of order in the place.

D'ARMAGNAC: You don't make it easy for your friends, Grandier. Trincant has told me about his daughter. You have your whores. Why did you have to do this?

GRANDIER: It seemed a way.

D'ARMAGNAC: A way to what?

GRANDIER: All worldly things have a single purpose for a man of my kind. Politics, power, the senses, riches, pride and authority. I choose them with the same care that you, sir, select a weapon. But my intention is different. I need to turn them against myself.

D'ARMAGNAC: To bring about your end?

GRANDIER: Yes. I have a great need to be united with
God. Living has drained the need for life from me. My
exercise of the senses has flagged to total exhaustion.
I am a dead man, compelled to live.

D'ARMAGNAC: You disgust me. This is a sickness.

GRANDIER: No, sir. It is the meaning and purpose.

D'ARMAGNAC: I'm not one for sophisticated argument,
but tell me something. I can see that the obvious short-
cut, self-destruction, is not possible. But isn't creating the
circumstances for your death, which is what you seem to
be doing, equally sinful?

GRANDIER: Leave me some hope.

D'ARMAGNAC: The hope that God will smile upon your
efforts to create an enemy so malignant as to bring you
down, and so send you – up?

GRANDIER: Yes.

D'ARMAGNAC: I've a letter here from Paris. It should
make you happy. By supporting me in this matter of
the fortifications you have made an excellent enemy.
Richelieu. So far the King is standing with me against
the Cardinal. But should the King fail or falter this
city will come down, and you will probably have your
wish, for you are deeply implicated. All the same,
I shall continue to protect you from what I think to be
a most dreadful course, and a most blasphemous
philosophy.

GRANDIER: It is what I seek, sir. Don't hold it from me.
Think what it must be like. I reach the end of a long
day. I am warm, fed and satisfied. I go home. On the
way I stare at a stranger across the street, perhaps a
child. I greet a friend. I lie looking down on the face of
a sleeping woman. I see these with wonder and hope,
and ask myself: Is this, perhaps, the means to my end?
And I am denied.

(*GRANDIER suddenly hides his face in his hands.*)

O my God, my God! All things fail me.

D'ARMAGNAC: Afraid, Grandier?

GRANDIER: Yes. Yes. Yes. Forsaken.

The convent garden. JEANNE and CLAIRE are sitting on a bench.
LOUISE and GABRIELLE are on the ground at their feet. Two
lay sisters stand nearby. Great stillness.

LOUISE: What shall we do, Mother?

JEANNE: Do?

LOUISE: People are taking their children away from us.

JEANNE: Who can blame them?

CLAIRE: There's no one to help. We have to do all the
housework ourselves. It's very tiring.

JEANNE: (*Sudden laughter.*) Why don't you ask the devils to
lend a hand?

CLAIRE: Mother!

GABRIELLE: I've taken in a little washing and sewing.
I hope you don't mind, Mother.

JEANNE: Sensible girl. When hell fails to provide one can
fall back on hard work, eh?

GABRIELLE: I know you've never liked us to do menial
tasks.

JEANNE: I said it diminished women in our vocation. (*She
laughs.*) Did I say that?

GABRIELLE: Yes.

(*Silence.*)

LOUISE: Mother –

JEANNE: Yes, child?

LOUISE: Why has the Archbishop forbidden Father Barré
to come and see us any more?

JEANNE: Because the Archbishop has been told that we are
foolish and deluded women.

LOUISE: Mother –

JEANNE: Yes?

LOUISE: Have we sinned?

JEANNE: By what we've done?

LOUISE: Yes. Have we mocked God?

JEANNE: It was not the intention.
But to make a mockery of Man. That's a different
matter!
For what a splendid creature he makes to be fooled. He
might have been created for no other purpose. With his

head in the air, besotted with his own achievement, he
asks to be tripped. Deep in the invention of mumbo-jumbo
to justify his existence, he is deaf to laughter. With no eyes
for anything but himself, he's blind to the gesture of
ridicule made in front of his face.

So, drunk, deaf and blind, he goes on. The perfect subject
for the practical joke. And that, my sisters, is where the
children of misfortune – like me – play a part. We do not
mock our beloved Father in Heaven. Our laughter is
kept for His wretched and sinful children who get above
their station, and come to believe they have some other
purpose in this world than to die.

After the delusions of power come the delusions of love.
When men cannot destroy they start to believe they can
be saved by creeping into a fellow human being. And so
perpetuating themselves. Love me, they say over and
over again, love me. Cherish me. Defend me. Save me.
They say it to their wives, their whores, their children,
and some to the whole human race. Never to God. These
are probably the most ridiculous of all, and most worthy
of derision. For they do not understand the glory of
mortality, the purpose of man: loneliness and death.

Let us go in.

On the fortifications. Night.

*D'ARMAGNAC and DE CERISAY enter from different ways. They
are wrapped against the rain, and they shout above the wind.*

DE CERISAY: D'Armagnac, are you there?

D'ARMAGNAC: The horseman fell at the gate. They found
these papers, scattered.

DE CERISAY: What are they?

D'ARMAGNAC: The King has gone back on his word.
Richelieu has won. The town fortifications are to come
down. It is to be a little place. I shall have no more
power than a tradesman.

(*GRANDIER has appeared far below them.*)
Is that the priest?

DE CERISAY: Yes. (*He shouts.*) Grandier!

D'ARMAGNAC: He will suffer. (*He shouts.*) Grandier!

GRANDIER: What's the matter?

D'ARMAGNAC: The Cardinal has moved against us.

DE CERISAY: The King has lost his nerve.

D'ARMAGNAC: All this is to come down.

DE CERISAY: You are mentioned –

D'ARMAGNAC: We shan't stand here much longer.

DE CERISAY: – named for your resistance.

D'ARMAGNAC: You are in danger.

GRANDIER: Thank God.

D'ARMAGNAC: What do you say? I can't hear you. Are you mad? Is he mad? Let's go down.

(*D'ARMAGNAC and DE CERISAY go. GRANDIER kneels. The wind and rain sweep about him.*)

GRANDIER: Heavenly Father, You have restored strength to my enemies, and hope to Your sinful child. I give myself into the hands of the world secure in the faith of Your mysterious ways. You have made the way possible. I understand, and I accept. But You work beyond a curtain of majesty. I am afraid to raise my eyes, and see. Reveal Yourself. Reveal Yourself.

(*His voice is lost.*)

Stillness.

DE LAUBARDEMONT and MIGNON.

DE LAUBARDEMONT: We shall have to act quickly.

MIGNON: Yes. Yes.

DE LAUBARDEMONT: I must start for Paris tonight.

MIGNON: So soon?

DE LAUBARDEMONT: Can it be done in the time?

MIGNON: We must try.

DE LAUBARDEMONT: Sort out your thoughts on the subject.

MIGNON: I've been reading it up. There was the appalling Gauffridy case. In Marseilles, twenty years ago. The priest bewitched and debauched several Ursulines –

DE LAUBARDEMONT: We don't need precedents. We need results. Here and now. Call them in.

(*MIGNON leads JEANNE forward. They are followed by CLAIRE, LOUISE, GABRIELLE and the two lay sisters. DE LAUBARDEMONT stands apart.*)

MIGNON: My beloved sisters in Christ, I am only a foolish old man who hasn't much time left on this earth to do God's will –

DE LAUBARDEMONT: Well then, get on with it.

MIGNON: My children, do you trust me?

JEANNE: Of course, Father.

MIGNON: As your spiritual instructor, do you trust me?

JEANNE: Always.

MIGNON: Very well. I am deeply disturbed by this sudden cessation of diabolical manifestations in you. Dreadful stories are being put about in the town and farther afield. They say you were not truly possessed by demons, but that you were playing parts, making a mockery both of your sublime state, and your superiors in the Church.

JEANNE: That is what we were told by the Archbishop's doctor. He talked about hysteria. The cry from the womb.

MIGNON: But as a good woman it was up to you to prove him wrong. Oh, assure me that it was true. You were possessed.

JEANNE: It was true. We were possessed by hell.

MIGNON: And the instigator, the foul magician –

JEANNE: Grandier! Grandier!

THE SISTERS: Grandier! Grandier!

MIGNON: But now I fear for you in another way. The evidence is all against you. The silence of the devils condemns you.

(*Silence.*)

You see, they do not speak. There is no proof of your virtue. Ah, my sisters, this stillness presages your eternal damnation. I fear for you. I dread. Forsaken by God and forsaken by the Devil you stand in the most desolate limbo forever. I beg you, consider your position.

JEANNE: Father, we are afraid.

MIGNON: And well you may be, my child.

JEANNE: Don't leave us!

MIGNON: What else can I do? I will pray for you.

> (*MIGNON turns away towards DE LAUBARDEMONT.*)

JEANNE: (*As Leviathan.*) May I put in a word?

MIGNON: God be praised! What is your name?

JEANNE: (*As Leviathan.*) Leviathan.

MIGNON: Where are you lodged, unholy thing?

JEANNE: (*As Leviathan.*) In the lady's forehead.

> (*As Beherit.*) I am in the woman's stomach. My name is
> Beherit.
>
> (*As Isacaaron.*) Isacaaron speaking. From under the last rib
> on the left.

CLAIRE: (*As Elymi.*) I am here. (*Another voice.*) And I.

LOUISE: (*As Eazaz.*) And I. (*Another voice.*) And I am here.

> (*Clamour of diabolical voices. Derisive laughter: grunts,
> squeals, howls. DE LAUBARDEMONT moves to MIGNON.*)

DE LAUBARDEMONT: Well done. Barré must be got back
from Chinon. He must begin exorcism at once. In public.
A representative of the Court will attend. See to it.

> (*DE LAUBARDEMONT goes. MIGNON runs forward,
> shouting.*)

MIGNON: Open the gates! Open the gates!

> (*A crowd floods into the palace. Men and women of the town.
> The SEWERMAN. ADAM and MANNOURY. TRINCANT.
> A dwarf. A creature. A trumpeter. Laughing women. Dogs.
> Children climb to points of vantage and look down.*
>
> *Below: the Sisters laboriously perform their antics. JEANNE
> is on her hands and knees, snuffling the ground. CLAIRE has
> the skirts of her habit over her head, exposing herself in a dull
> promenade. LOUISE and GABRIELLE are locked in an
> embrace, making a beast. And from all of them come the hoarse,
> masculine cries of diabolic voices: inarticulate, whining,
> commanding, a dissonance of obscenity.*
>
> *The townspeople are very amused. They point out especially
> delectable gestures to each other. Some urge the Sisters to
> greater excesses. A lay sister, agile as a tumbler, is applauded.
> A party has settled down to eat and drink and watch.*)

Thunder of bells from Saint Peter's spire.

BARRÉ enters in glory. He carries a gold, jewelled crucifix, which twists and glitters in his nervous hands. RANGIER comes from another way. Three Carmelites from another. MIGNON approaches them. All meet.)

BARRÉ: I have been sent for.

MIGNON: Yes. Yes.

BARRÉ: The triumph of good!

MIGNON: It is. Yes.

BARRÉ: De Cerisay –

MIGNON: Bah!

BARRÉ: D'Armagnac –

MIGNON: Filth!

BARRÉ: Are they here?

MIGNON: No.

RANGIER: Dare not show their faces.

BARRÉ: The triumph of good! I am in love with the words. I must say them again. It is the triumph of good!

(*A lay sister is scrabbling at BARRÉ's feet.*)

Peace, Sister.

(*BARRÉ lays on the crucifix. It has no effect, so he savagely kicks the woman aside.*)

RANGIER: The King's man is here.

BARRÉ: Who have they sent?

RANGIER: Prince Henri de Condé.

BARRÉ: One of the blood!

RANGIER: No less.

BARRÉ: Excellent. (*He shouts.*) Constables!

(*Archers enter, and press back the crowd. Near silence. The archers range themselves against the crowd, isolating the Sisters.*)

JEANNE: (*As Leviathan in a loud voice.*) Where is the enemy?

BARRÉ: (*In great exaltation.*) I am here.

JEANNE: (*As Leviathan.*) Who are you?

BARRÉ: I am only a humble man. But I speak for the Lord Jesus Christ.

(*A terrible scream from JEANNE (as Leviathan). Babel of voices from the other devils. Delight of the crowd.*)

Mignon: water, a missal, the stoles, the ciborium, the
saint's fingernail, the piece of the true cross. Let me have
them all.

MIGNON: God's armoury! It's here.

(*The Carmelites have brought forward and are arranging the
relics.*)

BARRÉ: I must prepare myself.

(*BARRÉ falls on his knees: prays. The crowd is silent.
HENRI DE CONDÉ enters. This exquisite and handsome
sodomite is supported by painted boys. He regards BARRÉ for
a moment: speaks.*)

DE CONDÉ: I don't wish, my dear Father, to disturb your
devotions and I would never suggest that a member of
the royal family took precedence over God...all the
same...

BARRÉ: (*He has got to his feet.*) I'm at your service, sir.

DE CONDÉ: Thank you. These are the raving women,
I take it.

BARRÉ: All of them are possessed by one or more devils.

DE CONDÉ: And the instigator is a man of your own
people?

BARRÉ: A priest, yes.

DE CONDÉ: You don't seem amused.

BARRÉ: Amused?

DE CONDÉ: Never mind.

BARRÉ: If you'll take your place, sir, I'll proceed.

DE CONDÉ: Very well.

(*DE CONDÉ goes to a prepared part nearby, and sits
overlooking the scene. The boys play around him like
butterflies.
The Sisters are now in an untidy heap, exhausted, mere
rubbish on the ground. BARRÉ is robing and preparing
himself with the help of MIGNON and RANGIER.
DE CONDÉ draws one of the boys to him.*)

These are women, darling. Look well. Vomit, if you wish.
Man is born of them. Gross things. Nasty. Breeding
ground. Eggs hatch out in hot dung. Don't wrinkle your
little nose, pet. Take this scent. Some men love them.

The priest, Grandier, for example. He's picked the
gobbets from the stew. He's –
(*DE CONDÉ whispers in the boy's ear. The child's eyes widen.*
DE CONDÉ laughs.
BARRÉ has come forward.)

BARRÉ: With your permission, sir, I'll begin.

DE CONDÉ: Please do so.

BARRÉ: But first I have a declaration to make. This, sir –
(*He holds up the ciborium.*) – contains the holy Eucharist.
(*BARRÉ places the ciborium on his head and kneels.*)
Heavenly Father, I pray that I may be confounded and
that the maledictions of Dathan and Abiram may fall
upon me, if I have sinned or been at fault in any way in
this affair.

DE CONDÉ: A very commendable gesture. Bravo!
(*BARRÉ rises, and goes towards JEANNE.*)

BARRÉ: Leviathan! Leviathan!

JEANNE: (*As Leviathan: sleepy.*) Go away.

BARRÉ: Rouse yourself.

JEANNE: (*As Leviathan.*) You bore me.

BARRÉ: In the name of Our Lord Jesus Christ –

JEANNE: (*As Leviathan.*) Don't keep bringing that impostor's
name into the conversation.

BARRÉ: It disturbs you, eh?

JEANNE: (*As Leviathan.*) I don't tolerate fools gladly. All
that talk about love. It has a softening effect on the
character. And what's more, the fellow wasn't a
gentleman.

DE CONDÉ: Reverend Father –

BARRÉ: Yes, sir?

DE CONDÉ: I notice that you don't speak to these creatures
in Latin, as is usual. Why is that?

BARRÉ: They're not conversant with the language. You'll
understand, sir, that there are uneducated as well as
educated devils.

DE CONDÉ: Quite.

JEANNE: (*As Leviathan.*) I haven't travelled much.
(*Deep laughter, taken up by the other devils.*)

BARRÉ: Listen, Filth –

JEANNE: (*As Leviathan.*) You're always so personal.

BARRÉ: I'm going to speak a name to you. Grandier!

JEANNE: (*As Leviathan.*) Oh, that's a sweet noise. Do it again.

BARRÉ: Grandier!

JEANNE: (*As Leviathan.*) Yes, I like that.

BARRÉ: You know him?

JEANNE: (*As Leviathan.*) We serve him. Don't we?

CLAIRE: (*As Zabulon.*) Yes.

JEANNE: (*As Isacaaron.*) We do. We do.
(*As Beherit.*) Grandier! Grandier!

LOUISE: (*As Eazaz.*) Oh, my love, my darling, hold me, take – take – aah! –

CLAIRE: (*As Zabulon.*) Grandier! Grandier!

JEANNE: (*As Beherit.*) Grandier! Grandier!

LOUISE: (*As Eazaz.*) Grandier! Grandier!

JEANNE: (*As Leviathan.*) Grandier! Grandier!
(*Pandemonium.*)

BARRÉ: Let one speak for all!
(*RANGIER and MIGNON move in among the Sisters scattering holy water. The screams and shouts gradually die away.*)

DE CONDÉ: Father, may I question these things?

BARRÉ: By all means, sir.
(*RANGIER, MIGNON and the Carmelites hustle the wretched Sisters forward until they are ranged in front of DE CONDÉ, who stares down at them.*)

DE CONDÉ: (*Addressing the Sisters.*) Gentlemen. You have given us your views on the character and worth of our blessed Saviour. (*Hissing from the devils.*) Which of you will answer me on a matter of merely national importance?

JEANNE: (*As Beherit.*) I'll try.

DE CONDÉ: You will? Good. What's your name?

JEANNE: (*As Beherit.*) Beherit.

DE CONDÉ: Well, Beherit, tell me this. What's your opinion of His Majesty, the King of France, and his adviser, the great Cardinal?
(*Silence.*)

311

Come now, as a political devil you must have some
views. Or do you find yourself in the quandary of most
Oppositions? Having to speak with more than one voice.

JEANNE: (*As Beherit: muttering.*) Don't understand.

DE CONDÉ: You understand very well. If you, Beherit,
praise the King and his minister you condone, and imply
that their policy is hellish. If you, Sister Jane, dispraise
them, you run the risk of treason against powerful men.
I sympathize with your difficulty. Father Barré –
(*BARRÉ comes forward, as DE CONDÉ takes a small box
from one of the boys.*)
I have here a relic of the most holy worth. It has been
lent to me by a great cathedral of the north. I feel the
bits and pieces which you've assembled from local
sources may not be powerful enough to dispel these
impudent demons. So why not try this?

BARRÉ: What is in the box, sir?

DE CONDÉ: A phial of the blood of our Lord Jesus Christ.
(*BARRÉ reverently takes the box in his hands: kisses it.*)
Tell me, Father, what effect would the close proximity of
this relic have on devils such as these?

BARRÉ: It would put them to flight.

DE CONDÉ: At once?

BARRÉ: Immediately. I couldn't guarantee, of course, that
when the relic was removed they wouldn't return.

DE CONDÉ: Of course not. That would be asking too
much. Would you like to try?
(*BARRÉ goes towards JEANNE.*)

BARRÉ: In the name of our Heavenly Father, I conjure thee,
most frightful beings, by this most sacred substance, to
depart!
(*BARRÉ applies the box to JEANNE's forehead. At once, in
a number of horrible screams, the devils leave her body by
way of her distorted mouth. Silence. Then JEANNE rises to
her full height. She speaks calmly, with the voice of a young
girl, in her own person.*)

JEANNE: I am free. I am free.
(*She goes to DE CONDÉ, kneels, and kisses his hands.*)

DE CONDÉ: I'm very pleased to have been of some service, madam.

BARRÉ: (*Triumphantly.*) You see!

(*DE CONDÉ takes the box from BARRÉ, opens it, and holds it upside down: it is empty.*)

DE CONDÉ: You see, Father?

BARRÉ: (*After a moment.*) Ah, sir, what sort of trick have you played on us?

DE CONDÉ: Reverend Sir, what sort of trick are you playing on *us*?

(*Silence between the two men, DE CONDÉ smiling: hushed crowd: terrified women.*

The moment is broken by MIGNON. He starts to run in tiny circles, holding his little head in his hands.)

MIGNON: (*As Leviathan.*) Fooled again!

(*As Beherit.*) Make way!

(*MIGNON cries out, as Beherit forces an entry.*

RANGIER suddenly begins to neigh like a horse, and high stepping in fine style, proceeds to exhibit. The Sisters begin to grunt and groan in sympathy, one of them offering herself obscenely to RANGIER, who mounts. Only JEANNE stands alone and still. A boy by DE CONDÉ begins to laugh in a ringing, hysterical way. There is a disturbance in the crowd. Two women have become possessed.

BARRÉ stares about him in horror. Then, wielding the crucifix like a club, he plunges among the devils, laying about him.)

BARRÉ: We are besieged! Clear the place at once!

(*The Carmelites hurry away the Sisters, and the dancing MIGNON and RANGIER. The guards disperse the crowd. BARRÉ is passing among the people, laying the cross on possessed and unpossessed alike, and shouting.*)

…per factorem mundi, per eum qui habet potestatem mittendi te in gehennam, ut ab hoc famulo Dei, qui ad sinum Ecclesiae recurrit, cum metu et exercitu furoris tui festinus discedas.

(*RANGIER, MIGNON and the Sisters go into the distance, followed by BARRÉ. The crowd go yawning home.*

The boy standing beside DE CONDÉ still laughs himself to tears.)

DE CONDÉ: (*Smiling.*) Be quiet, child.

(*DE CONDÉ stares across at JEANNE, who stands alone, some way off.*)

Mother, I am often accused of libertinage. Very well. Being born so high I have to stoop lower than other men. Soiled, dabbling myself, I know what I am doing and what I must give. I'd say you'll have your wish about this man Grandier, seeing the way the world goes. But do you know what you must give? (*Casually.*) Your immortal soul to damnation in an infinite desert of eternal bestiality.

(*DE CONDÉ and the boys go.*

CLAIRE and LOUISE enter apart from JEANNE. Gay voices.)

CLAIRE: I was never any good at prayer.

LOUISE: Neither was I.

CLAIRE: We could have spent our lives on our knees.

LOUISE: And no one would have heard of us.

CLAIRE: They're selling my picture in the town.

LOUISE: We're famous all over France.

CLAIRE: Are you still worried about being damned?

LOUISE: Not any more.

CLAIRE: Not since your beautiful legs have been so admired.

LOUISE: Sweetheart, what do you think of in chapel now?

CLAIRE: This and that. New ways.

LOUISE: To amuse?

CLAIRE: Yes. (*A bell.*) Come on.

(*Laughing, they go. JEANNE stands silent for a moment. Then:*)

JEANNE: (*As Leviathan.*) Clear your mind of cant, you absurd little monster.

(*As herself.*) I'm afraid.

(*As Leviathan.*) Nonsense. We'll support you in anything you do.

(*As herself.*) I wish to be pure.

(*As Leviathan.*) There is no such thing.

(*As herself.*) O God: God, yes, there is.

(*Women's voices are raised from the nearby chapel.*)
(*As Leviathan.*) No, there isn't. Now think, my dear.
Remember the night-time visions. He and – (*Obscene
giggles.*) – oh, that thing – and you, agape – no, no, my
darling, not purity, not even dignity. What are you
thinking of? Not only all impure, but all absurd.
Remember?
(*JEANNE starts to laugh: Leviathan joins her.
Darkness.*)

A Council of State. Night.

*LOUIS XIII, RICHELIEU, FATHER JOSEPH and LA
VRILLIÈRE, Secretary of State.*

DE CONDÉ is apart.

*DE LAUBARDEMONT comes forward and speaks to the Council.
A clerk stands beside him, handing over relevant papers from time to
time.*

DE LAUBARDEMONT: Your Majesty. Your Eminence. You
    have asked me to report on the case of possession at
    Loudun. The man's name is Urbain Grandier.
DE CONDÉ: He is innocent.
    (*Both men speak to the Council.*)
DE LAUBARDEMONT: I have been advised by priests of
    the district and by reputable medical men that the
    possession is genuine.
DE CONDÉ: I have also been there. The man is innocent.
DE LAUBARDEMONT: Grandier's house has been
    searched. Various manuscripts have been found. There
    was a pamphlet written some years ago and directed
    against Your Eminence. Other papers confirmed
    Grandier's support of D'Armagnac in his defiant attitude
    about the fortifications of the town, which has distressed
    you so much, Your Majesty. There were letters and
    notebooks of a more personal kind. A treatise on
    Sacerdotal Celibacy was found. The man seems to have
    been in love when this was written. It is reported that a

mock marriage took place with a daughter of the Public Prosecutor. There were letters from other women, one of which appears to suggest that he has committed the veneric act in church.

DE CONDÉ: For the love of Jesus Christ, if you wish to destroy the man, then destroy him. I'm not here to plead for his life. But your methods are shameful. He deserves better. Any man does. Kill him with power, but don't pilfer his house, and hold evidence of this sort against him. What man could face arraignment on the idiocy of youth, old love letters, and the pathetic objects stuffed in drawers or at the bottom of cupboards, kept for the fear that one day he would need to be reminded that he was once loved? No. Destroy a man for his opposition, his strength or his majesty. But not for this!
(*Silence.*)

DE LAUBARDEMONT: (*To the Council.*) I should now give you any evidence in the man's favour...
(*He is interrupted by a sign from RICHELIEU.*)

RICHELIEU: The Devil must never be believed, even when he tells the truth.

DE LAUBARDEMONT: I shall act on your instructions at once.
(*DE LAUBARDEMONT comes forward. Guards gather about him. They move off.*)

A brilliant morning.

GRANDIER comes to the SEWERMAN, carrying flowers.

SEWERMAN: Why, whatever's this?

GRANDIER: I must have picked them somewhere. I can't remember. You have them.

SEWERMAN: Thank you. They smell sweet. Very suitable.

GRANDIER: Can I sit with you?

SEWERMAN: Of course. I've no sins this morning, though. Sorry.

GRANDIER: Let me look at you.

SEWERMAN: Do you like what you see?

GRANDIER: Very much.

SEWERMAN: What's happened? You're drunk with mystery.

GRANDIER: I've been out of the town. An old man was
  dying. I sat with him for two nights and a day. I was
  seeing death for the hundredth time. It was an obscene
  struggle. It always is. Once again a senile, foolish and
  sinful old man had left it rather late to come to terms.
  He held my hand so tightly that I could not move. His
  grimy face stared up at me in blank surprise at what was
  happening to him. So I sat there in the rancid smell of
  the kitchen, while in the darkness the family argued in
  whispers, between weeping, about how much money
  there would be under the bed.
  He was dirty and old and not very bright. And I loved
  him so much. I envied him so much, for he was standing
  on the threshold of everlasting life. I wanted him to turn
  his face to God, and not peer back through the smoky
  light, and stare longingly at this mere preliminary. I said
  to him: Be glad, be glad. But he did not understand.
  His spirit weakened at dawn. It could not mount
  another day. There were cries of alarm from the family.
  I took out the necessary properties which I travel in
  this bag. The vulgar little sins were confessed, absolved,
  and the man could die. He did so. Brutally, holding on
  to the last. I spoke my usual words to the family, with
  my priest's face. My duty was done.
  But I could not forget my love for the man.
  I came out of the house. I thought I'd walk back, air
  myself after the death cell. I was very tired. I could hear
  Saint Peter's bell.
  The road was dusty. I remembered the day I came here.
  I was wearing new shoes. They were white with dust. Do
  you know, I flicked them over with my stole before
  being received by the bishop. I was vain and foolish,
  then. Ambitious, too.
  I walked on. They were working in the fields and called
  to me. I remembered how I loved to work with my
  hands when I was a boy. But my father said it was
  unsuitable for one of my birth.

I could see my church in the distance. I was very proud,
in a humble way. I thought of my love for the beauty of
this not very beautiful place. And I remembered night in
the building, with the gold, lit by candlelight, against the
darkness.
I thought of you. I remembered you as a friend.
I rested. The country was stretched out. Do you know
where the rivers join? I once made love there.
Children came past me. Yes, of course, that's where
I got the flowers. I didn't pick them. They were given
to me.
I watched the children go. Yes, I was very tired. I could
see far beyond the point my eyes could see. Castles, cities,
mountains, oceans, plains, forests – and –
And then – oh, my son, my son – and then – I want to
tell you –

SEWERMAN: Do so. Be calm.

GRANDIER: My son, I – Am I mad?

SEWERMAN: No. Quite sane. Tell me. What did you do?

GRANDIER: I created God!

(*Silence.*)

I created Him from the light and the air, from the dust
of the road, from the sweat of my hands, from gold,
from filth, from the memory of women's faces, from
great rivers, from children, from the works of man,
from the past, the present, the future and the unknown.
I caused Him to be from fear and despair. I gathered in
everything from this mighty act, all I have known, seen
and experienced. My sin, my presumption, my vanity,
my love, my hate, my lust. And last I gave myself and
so made God. And He was magnificent. For He is all
these things.
I was utterly in His presence. I knelt by the road. I took
out the bread and the wine. Panem vinum in salutis
consecramus hostiam. And in this understanding He
gave Himself humbly and faithfully to me, as I had
given myself to Him.

(*Silence.*)

SEWERMAN: You've found peace.

GRANDIER: More. I've found meaning.

SEWERMAN: That makes me happy.

GRANDIER: And, my son, I have found reason.

SEWERMAN: And that is sanity.

GRANDIER: I must go now. I must go to worship Him in His house, adore Him in His shrine. I must go to church.
(*GRANDIER moves forward and enters the church.*
Soldiers lounge against the altar. DE LAUBARDEMONT
comes forward.)

DE LAUBARDEMONT: You are forbidden this place.

GRANDIER: Forbidden?

DE LAUBARDEMONT: You are an impious and libertine priest. You must not enter.

GRANDIER: It is my church! My beloved church!

DE LAUBARDEMONT: No longer. You're under arrest. Charges will be read. Come with me. Bring him.
(*GRANDIER, between soldiers, is brought from the church*
into the sunlight, DE LAUBARDEMONT leading the way.
They pass through the street.
ADAM, MANNOURY and TRINCANT lean from an upper
window, jeering.
PHILIPPE, with a silent old man beside her, watches.
RANGIER and MIGNON move in the church with a censer,
intoning, exorcising.
BARRÉ is on his knees in the street as GRANDIER passes.
The SEWERMAN watches. A crowd of townspeople gather
round him, noisy and enquiring.
And as GRANDIER moves on the street and the church are
filled with the clamour and laughter of devils, issuing from
every mouth.
Laughter. Laughter.)

CURTAIN

ACT THREE

Night.

A cell. Another room above. GRANDIER alone.

Distant shouts and laughter from an unseen crowd.

BONTEMPS, a gaoler, comes to GRANDIER.

BONTEMPS: Have you slept?

GRANDIER: No. No, the noise. The crowd. Have they
    slept?

BONTEMPS: Thirty thousand people have come into the
    town. Where do you expect them to find beds?

GRANDIER: Why should they want to sleep, anyway? Did
    I, as a child, the night before the treat?

BONTEMPS: They're certainly looking forward to it.

GRANDIER: What? Say it.

BONTEMPS: The execution.

GRANDIER: I haven't been tried yet.

BONTEMPS: All right. Have it your own way. The trial,
    then.

GRANDIER: Are you a merciful man?

BONTEMPS: Look, this is your system. Just be thankful
    that you can get men to do the job. Don't ask that they
    should be humane as well. I came to tell you that you're
    to be called early. So try and get some sleep.

GRANDIER: Thank you.

BONTEMPS: Is there anything you want? There's not
    much I can offer.

GRANDIER: Nothing. Nothing.

JEANNE and MIGNON.

JEANNE: Don't go!

MIGNON: It's three o'clock in the morning. I'm an old
    man. Need sleep.

JEANNE: I don't want to be left alone with him.

MIGNON: With your persecutor? Grandier?

JEANNE: Yes.

MIGNON: He's under close guard.

JEANNE: No. He's here. Within me. Like a child. He never revealed to me what sort of man he was. I knew him to be beautiful. Many said he was clever, and many said he was wicked. But for all his violence to my soul and body he never came to me in anything but love. No, let me speak. He's within me, I say. I'm possessed. But he is still, lying beneath my heart, living through my breath and my blood. And he makes me afraid. Afraid that I may have fallen into the gravest error in this matter.

MIGNON: What do you mean?

JEANNE: Have I been mistaken? Did Satan take on the person of my love, my darling, so as to delude me?

MIGNON: Never. The man is his agent.

JEANNE: I have such a little body. It is a small battleground in which to decide this terrible struggle between good and evil, between love and hate. Was I wrong to allow it?

MIGNON: No, no. Don't you understand? These very thoughts are put in your mind by the forces of dread. It's wrong to believe that Hell always fights with the clamour of arms. It is now, in the small hours, that Satan sends his secret agents, whispering, with their messages of doubt.

JEANNE: I don't know. I don't know. You all speak with so many voices. And I am very tired. (*She cries out.*) Father! Father!

GRANDIER alone in his cell.

GRANDIER: There will be pain. It will kill God. My fear is driving Him out already.
Yes. Yes. We are flies upon the wall. Buzzing in the heat. That's so. That's so. No, no. We're monsters made up in a day. Clay in a baby's hands. Horrible, we should be bottled and hung in the pharmacy. Curiosities, for amusement only.
So. Nothing.

Shall I withstand the pain? Mother, mother, remember my fear!

Oh, nothing. This morning on the road. What was that? It was a little delusion of meaning. A trick of the sun, some fatigue of the body, and a man starts to believe that he's immortal. Look at me now. Wringing my hands, trying to convince myself that this flesh and bone is meaningful.

Sad, sad, though, very sad. To make a man see in the morning what the glory might be, and by night to snatch it from him.

Most Heavenly Father, though I struggle in Your arms like a fretful child –

This need to create a meaning. What arrogance it is! Expendable, that's what we are. Nothing proceeding to nothing.

Let me look into this void. Let me look into myself. Is there one thing, past or present, which makes for a purpose? (*Silence.*) Nothing. Nothing.

Who's there?

(*FATHER AMBROSE, an old man, has come in.*)

AMBROSE: My name is Ambrose.

GRANDIER: I know you, Father.

AMBROSE: I was told of your trouble, my son. The night can be very long.

GRANDIER: Yes. Stay with me.

AMBROSE: I thought I might read to you. Or, if you'd like it better, we can pray together.

GRANDIER: No. Help me.

AMBROSE: Let me try.

GRANDIER: They are destroying my faith. By fear and loneliness now. Later, by pain.

AMBROSE: Go to God, my son.

GRANDIER: Nothing going to nothing.

AMBROSE: God is here, and Christ is now.

GRANDIER: Yes. That is my faith. But how can I defend it?

AMBROSE: By remembering the will of God.

GRANDIER: Yes. Yes.

AMBROSE: By remembering that nothing must be asked of him, and nothing refused.

GRANDIER: Yes. But this is all in the books. I've read them, and understood them. And it is not enough. Not enough. Not now.

AMBROSE: God is here, and Christ is here.

GRANDIER: You're an old man. Have you gathered no more than this fustian in all your years? I'm sorry. You came in pure charity. The only one who has done so. I'm sorry.

(*AMBROSE opens a book.*)

AMBROSE: Suffering must be willed, affliction must be willed, humiliation must be willed, and in the act of willing –

GRANDIER: They'll be understood. I know. I know.

AMBROSE: Then you know everything.

GRANDIER: I know nothing. Speak to me as a man, Father. Talk about simple things.

AMBROSE: I came to help you, my son.

GRANDIER: You can help me. By speaking as a man. So shut your books. Forget other men's words. Speak to me.

AMBROSE: Ah, you believe there is some secret in simplicity. I am a simple man, it's true. I've never had any great doubt. Plain and shy, I have been less tempted than others, of course. The devil likes more magnificence than I've ever been able to offer. A peasant boy who clung to the love of God because he was too awkward to ask for the love of man. I'm not a good example, my son. That's why I brought the books.

GRANDIER: You think too little of yourself. What must we give God?

AMBROSE: Ourselves.

GRANDIER: But I am unworthy.

AMBROSE: Have you greatly sinned?

GRANDIER: Greatly.

AMBROSE: Even young girls come to me nowadays and confess things I don't know about. So it's hardly likely that I'll understand the sins of a young man of the world such as you. But let me try.

GRANDIER: There have been women and lust: power and ambition: worldliness and mockery.

AMBROSE: Remember. God is here. You speak before Him. Christ is now. You suffer with Him.

GRANDIER: I dread the pain to come. The humiliation.

AMBROSE: Did you dread the ecstasy of love?

GRANDIER: No.

AMBROSE: Or its humiliation?

GRANDIER: I gloried in it. I have lived by the senses.

AMBROSE: Then die by them.

GRANDIER: What did you say?

AMBROSE: Offer God pain, convulsion and disgust.

GRANDIER: Yes. Give Him myself.

AMBROSE: Let Him reveal Himself in the only way you can understand.

GRANDIER: Yes! Yes!

AMBROSE: It is all any of us can do. We live a little while, and in that little while we sin. We go to Him as we can. All is forgiven.

GRANDIER: Yes. I am His child. It is true. Let Him take me as I am. So there is meaning. There is meaning, after all. I am a sinful man and I can be accepted. It is not nothing going to nothing. It is sin going to forgiveness. It is a human creature going to love.

(*BONTEMPS has come in.*)

BONTEMPS: He's got to leave. If you want a priest they say you can ask for Father Barré or Father Rangier.

GRANDIER: They say?

BONTEMPS: Out there.

GRANDIER: De Laubardemont?

BONTEMPS: That's right.

AMBROSE: Must I go? Does he say I must go?

GRANDIER: Yes, Father. You are dangerous in your innocence. But they are too late.

AMBROSE: I don't understand.

GRANDIER: It is better that way. Let me kiss you.

(*BONTEMPS and AMBROSE go.*
GRANDIER alone.)

What? Tears? When was the last time this happened?
What are they for? They must be for what is lost, not for
what has been found.
For God is here.

Sudden daylight. Laughter.

CLAIRE, GABRIELLE and LOUISE come into the open air.

GABRIELLE: The town's like a fairground.

CLAIRE: They were singing not far from my window all
night.

GABRIELLE: There are acrobats. I wish we could see them.
I loved acrobats.

CLAIRE: Haven't we entertained each other enough in that
way?

(*They laugh.*)

LOUISE: We don't seem to amuse other people any more.
None of the Fathers or the great Parisians have been near
us for days.

(*JEANNE has come up to them, unobserved.*)

JEANNE: You must understand, Louise, that the darlings of
the public have their day, which ends, like any other.

LOUISE: Is it all over, Mother?

JEANNE: Soon. He's appearing before his judges this
morning to make his last statement.

LOUISE: I didn't mean Father Grandier. I meant us. What
shall we –

JEANNE: Then they'll speak the sentence. And at last there
will be the Question.

LOUISE: But what will become of us, Mother?

JEANNE: We shall live. You've a lifetime before you, pretty
Louise. Think of that.

A cell: MANNOURY alone.

ADAM is let in.

ADAM: Hullo.
MANNOURY: Hullo.

ADAM: Were you sent for?

MANNOURY: Yes.

ADAM: So was I. By De Laubardemont?

MANNOURY: That's it.

ADAM: I've brought my things. Have you?

MANNOURY: Yes.

ADAM: What I thought would be necessary.

MANNOURY: Difficult to say, isn't it?

ADAM: Have you done this before?

MANNOURY: No.

ADAM: Neither have I. Hm. Cold in here.

MANNOURY: Yes.

ADAM: Cold out.

MANNOURY: 'Tis.

ADAM: For a summer day.

MANNOURY: August. Yes.

(*DE LAUBARDEMONT comes in.*)

DE LAUBARDEMONT: Good morning, gentlemen. Glad to find you here. He's being brought back from the court. Should be on his way now.

MANNOURY: What exactly do you want us to do?

DE LAUBARDEMONT: Prepare the man. A decision has been reached. Unanimously. He is condemned.

ADAM: Well, well.

MANNOURY: Not surprising.

ADAM: There it is.

DE LAUBARDEMONT: I want you to be as quick as you can. There was an extraordinary amount of sympathy for the creature when he made his statement. There were even some unhealthy tears. So I want him ready and back there to hear the sentence as soon as possible.

MANNOURY: We'll do our best.

DE LAUBARDEMONT: Adam, would you be good enough to go and see the gaoler? He's getting all the necessary stuff together. Bring it in when he's done.

ADAM: All right.

(*ADAM goes.*)

DE LAUBARDEMONT: The man made something of an impression. Father Barré explained that it was the devil's doing. He said the calm was the brazen insolence of hell, and the dignity nothing but unrepentant pride. Still, the man made quite an impression.

(*GRANDIER is brought in by a captain of the guard. GRANDIER is dressed in full canonicals, looking his finest.*)

GRANDIER: Good morning, Mister Surgeon.

MANNOURY: And good morning to you.

GRANDIER: De Laubardemont I've already seen.

DE LAUBARDEMONT: You must return to the court at once.

GRANDIER: Very well.

DE LAUBARDEMONT: For the sentence.

GRANDIER: I understand.

DE LAUBARDEMONT: So now I must ask you to undress.

GRANDIER: Undress?

DE LAUBARDEMONT: You can't go like that.

GRANDIER: I suppose not.

(*GRANDIER takes off his biretta, and then begins to remove his cape. ADAM comes in with BONTEMPS. ADAM carries a tray, on which there is a bowl of water, some oil and a razor.*)
Good morning, Mister Chemist. What have you got there?

ADAM: (*Stammering.*) It's a razor.

GRANDIER: (*After a moment: to DE LAUBARDEMONT.*) Must it be this way?

DE LAUBARDEMONT: Yes. Order of the court.

(*MANNOURY has taken the razor: tests it on his thumb.*)

GRANDIER: Well, Mister Surgeon, all your study and training have brought you only to this. Those late nights spent discussing the existence of existence have brought you only here. To be a barber.

DE LAUBARDEMONT: Get on with it.

GRANDIER: Just a moment.

(*GRANDIER touches his black curls, and then fingers his moustaches.*)
Have you a glass?

DE LAUBARDEMONT: No, no. Of course not.

BONTEMPS: There's this.

(BONTEMPS takes an empty metal cup from the tray. He polishes the base of the cup on his sleeve and gives it to GRANDIER.
GRANDIER stands looking long and deeply at his reflection.)

A public place.

A large crowd. Town and country people. Yawning, at ease, calling to each other. Apart: an enclosure holding some well-dressed women of the bourgeoisie. Chatter from them. There is a CLERK within a mountain of books.

Sudden silence. All heads turn towards us.

The CLERK rises. He reads.

CLERK: Urbain Grandier, you have been found guilty of commerce with the devil. And that you used this unholy alliance to possess, seduce and debauch certain Sisters of the holy order of Saint Ursula (they are fully named in this document). You have also been found guilty of obscenity, blasphemy and sacrilege.

It is ordered that you proceed and kneel at the doors of Saint Peter's and Saint Ursula's and there, with a rope round your neck and a two-pound taper in your hand, ask pardon of God, the King and Justice. Next, it is ordered that you be taken to the Place Sainte-Croix, tied to a stake and burned alive: after which your ashes will be scattered to the four winds.

It has been decided that a commemorative plaque shall be set up in the Ursulines' chapel. The cost of this, yet to be ascertained, will be chargeable to your confiscated estate.

Lastly, before sentence is carried out, you will be subjected to the Question, both ordinary and extraordinary.

Pronounced at Loudun, 18 August 1634, and executed the same day.

(GRANDIER slowly comes into sight. His hands are tied behind his back. He is dressed in a nightgown and slippers, but with a skull cap and biretta on his head. DE

LAUBARDEMONT, MANNOURY and ADAM accompany
him. Also BARRÉ, RANGIER and MIGNON, who are
scattering holy water with consecrated whisks and intoning
formulas of exorcism.

DE LAUBARDEMONT steps forward. He snatches the hat
and cap from GRANDIER's head, and flings them to the
ground. GRANDIER is revealed. He is completely shaven.
Gone are the magnificent curls, the moustaches, even the
eyebrows. He stands, a bald fool.

There is a sudden, hysterical giggle from the women in the
enclosure.

Silence.

GRANDIER speaks to us.)

GRANDIER: My lords, I call God the Father, God the Son
and God the Holy Ghost, together with the Virgin, to
witness that I have never been a sorcerer. The only
magic I have practised is that of the Holy Scripture.
I am innocent.

(*Silence. Then murmurs from the women: a silly laugh.*)
I am innocent, and I am afraid. I fear for my salvation.
I am prepared to go and meet God, but the horrible
torment you have ordered for me on the way may drive
my wretched soul to despair.

Despair, my lords. It is the gravest of sins. It is the short
way to eternal damnation. Surely in your wisdom you do
not mean to kill a soul. So may I ask you, in your
mercy, to mitigate, if only a little, my punishment.

(*GRANDIER looks from face to face: silence.*)
Very well. When I was a child I was told about the
martyrs. I loved the men and women who died for the
honour of Jesus Christ. In a time of loneliness I have
often wished to be of their company. Now, foolish and
obscure priest that I am, I cannot presume to place
myself among these great and holy men. But may I say
that I have the hope in my heart that as this day ends
Almighty God, my beloved Father in Heaven, will
glance aside and let my suffering atone for my vain and
disordered life. Amen.

(Silence. Then somewhere in the crowd a man's voice clearly echoes GRANDIER's amen. Then another. Silence again. Only the sound of a woman bitterly weeping.)

DE LAUBARDEMONT: *(To the captain of the guard.)* Get them all out of here!

(At once the guards begin to clear the place. The public go away along corridors and down steps, complaining, some protesting.

GRANDIER is left with DE LAUBARDEMONT, the CLERK, BARRÉ, RANGIER and MIGNON. He has not moved, as he stands facing his judges.

DE CERISAY and D'ARMAGNAC can be seen. They are apart, overlooking the scene.

DE LAUBARDEMONT faces GRANDIER: speaks to him.) Confess your guilt. Tell us the names of your accomplices. Then perhaps my lords, the judges, will consider your appeal.

GRANDIER: I cannot name accomplices I've never had, nor confess to crimes I've not done.

DE LAUBARDEMONT: This attitude will do you no good. You will suffer for it.

GRANDIER: I know that. And I am proud.

DE LAUBARDEMONT: Proud, sir? That word does not become your situation. Now look here, my dear fellow – untie his hands – this document is a simple confession. Here is a pen. Just put your name to this paper and we can forget the next stage of the proceedings.

GRANDIER: You must excuse me. No.

DE LAUBARDEMONT: I just want your signature. Here. That's all.

GRANDIER: My conscience forbids me to put my name to something which is untrue.

DE LAUBARDEMONT: You'll save us all a lot of trouble if you'll sign. The document being true, of course. *(He shouts.)* True! You've been found guilty.

GRANDIER: I'm sorry.

DE LAUBARDEMONT: I fear for you, Grandier. I fear for you very much. I have seen men before you take

this brave standing in the shadow of the Question.
It was unwise, Grandier. Think again.

GRANDIER: No.

DE LAUBARDEMONT: You will go into the darkness
before your death. Let me talk to you for a moment
about pain. It is very difficult for us standing here, both
healthy men, to imagine the shattering effect of agony.
The sun's warm on your face at the moment, isn't it?
And you can curl your toes if you want in your slippers.
You are alive, and you know it. But when you are
stretched out in that little room, with the pain screaming
through you like a voice, let me tell you what you will
think. First: how can man do this to man? Then: how can
God allow it? Then: there can be no God. Then: there is
no God. The voice of pain will grow stronger, and your
resolution weaker. Despair, Grandier. You used the word
yourself. You called it the gravest sin. Don't reject God at
this moment. Reconcile yourself. For you have bitterly
offended Him. Confess.

GRANDIER: No.

D'ARMAGNAC: Are those tears on De Laubardemont's
face?

DE CERISAY: I'm afraid so.

D'ARMAGNAC: Does he believe what he's saying?

DE CERISAY: Yes. Touching, isn't it?

DE LAUBARDEMONT: (*To GRANDIER.*) Very well. I ask
you once more. Once more! Will you sign?
(*GRANDIER shakes his head.*)
Take him away.
(*The guards surround GRANDIER.*)

GRANDIER: I would like to ask something.

DE LAUBARDEMONT: What?

GRANDIER: May I have Father Ambrose with me?

DE LAUBARDEMONT: No.

GRANDIER: He's a harmless old man. He won't impede
you.

DE LAUBARDEMONT: He's no longer in the town. He's
been sent away. If you want spiritual consolation address
yourself to one of these gentlemen.

(*GRANDIER stares at BARRÉ, RANGIER and MIGNON for a moment before turning away between the guards and going. DE LAUBARDEMONT and the CLERK follow.*)

MIGNON: I found the Commissioner's last appeal very moving.

RANGIER: Very.

BARRÉ: I suppose you understand that Grandier's refusal to sign was the final proof of guilt.

MIGNON: Yes. Yes, I suppose so.

BARRÉ: Lucifer has sealed his mouth: hardened his heart against repentance.

MIGNON: Of course. That's the reason.

BARRÉ: Shall we go?

(*BARRÉ, RANGIER and MIGNON go.*)

D'ARMAGNAC: Come to my house with me, De Cerisay.

DE CERISAY: All right, sir.

D'ARMAGNAC: I don't want you to talk to me.

DE CERISAY: Very well.

D'ARMAGNAC: We'll just sit together. And think over the day. Two – I hope – reasonable men. We'll sit and – we'll drink. Yes, that's it, we'll get drunk. Drunk enough to see visions. Come on.

(*D'ARMAGNAC and DE CERISAY go.*)

A garden. JEANNE enters. She is bare-headed, and dressed only in a simple white undergarment. Her little, deformed person looks childlike. She has a rope round her neck, and carries a candle in her hand. She stands quite still.

CLAIRE, GABRIELLE and LOUISE gather some little way from JEANNE, frightened, watching her. Then CLAIRE comes forward to her.

CLAIRE: Come in, dear Mother.

JEANNE: No, child.

CLAIRE: But the sun is very hot after the rain. It will do you no good.

JEANNE: Find me a place – it needn't be so high – where I can tie this rope. I have been looking.

CLAIRE: No, Mother. It is the most terrible sin.

JEANNE: Sin?

CLAIRE: Yes.

(CLAIRE unknots the rope and takes it away. LOUISE comes forward with a cloak, which she puts about JEANNE.)

LOUISE: Don't frighten us, Mother.

JEANNE: I have been woken night after night by the sound of weeping. I've gone about trying to find out who it is. I have a heart like anyone else. It can be broken by such a sound.

LOUISE: It's no one here.

JEANNE: I'd never have thought it was possible for anyone to suffer such despair, such desolation.

LOUISE: But it's no one.

JEANNE: No one?

CLAIRE: It is the devil. He can snivel to order. Yes, Mother, think. Father Grandier would have you go to hell with him. So he gets the devil to cry at night and break your heart, makes you put a rope round your neck, and hang yourself. Don't be deceived.

JEANNE: Is there no way? And is that Claire speaking? Claire, who used to talk to me of the innocence of Christ? What's the time?

LOUISE: Just past noon.

JEANNE: Let me sit here. I promise not to harm myself. Leave me.

(CLAIRE, LOUISE and GABRIELLE go, leaving JEANNE alone. The silence is broken by a hideous sound of hammering. A scream.)

The upper room. GRANDIER is stretched on the floor, bound. His legs, from the knees to the feet, are enclosed in a kind of box. Movable boards within the box, driven inward by huge wedges, crush his legs. BONTEMPS is hammering the wedges home.

MANNOURY, ADAM and MIGNON are crouched in the lower room.

BARRÉ, who is sitting by GRANDIER's head, leans forward.

BARRÉ: Will you confess?

(*Slowly, GRANDIER shakes his head. BARRÉ glances at DE LAUBARDEMONT, who stands against the wall.*)

DE LAUBARDEMONT: (*To BONTEMPS.*) Another.

(*BONTEMPS picks up another wedge, but it is at once snatched out of his hand by RANGIER.*)

RANGIER: Just a moment! (*He sprinkles the wedge with holy water, and makes signs over it.*) Very necessary. The devil has the power, you see, to make the pain less than it should be.

BONTEMPS: Finished?

RANGIER: Yes.

(*He gives the wedge to BONTEMPS, who inserts it.*)

BARRÉ: Hit! Hit!

(*BONTEMPS strikes with the mallet. A scream. In the lower room.*)

MANNOURY: What's the cubic capacity of a man's breath?

ADAM: Don't know.

MANNOURY: Just wondered.

ADAM: It doesn't occur to you when you start something, that – Hm.

MANNOURY: What did you say?

ADAM: Nothing. Just thinking aloud.

(*A blow with the mallet. BARRÉ leans forward.*)

BARRÉ: Confess.

GRANDIER: I'm only too ready to confess my real sins. I have been a man, I have loved women. I have been proud. I have longed for power.

BARRÉ: That's not what we want. You've been a magician. You've had commerce with devils.

GRANDIER: No. No.

BARRÉ: Another. Oh, give it to me!

(*BARRÉ snatches the wedge and the mallet from BONTEMPS and, with the wedge unexorcised, drives it home with two mighty blows.*

GRANDIER's scream echoes in the garden where JEANNE sits alone.)

JEANNE: Is it only in the very depths that one finds God? Look at me. First I wanted to come to Him in innocence.

It was not enough. Then there was the lying and
play-acting. The guilt, the humiliation. It was not enough.
There were the antics done for the dirty eyes of priests.
The squalor. It was not enough. Down, down further.
(*The sound of hammering. GRANDIER's voice:*)

GRANDIER: God. God. God. Don't abandon me. Don't let
this pain make me forget You.

JEANNE: Down. Down. Into idiot oblivion. No thought. No
feeling. Nothing. Is God here?
(*The upper room. DE LAUBARDEMONT comes forward.*)

DE LAUBARDEMONT: Take him out. It's no good.
(*BARRÉ, RANGIER and BONTEMPS lift GRANDIER
from the box and seat him on a stool. BONTEMPS covers
GRANDIER's shattered legs with a rug. GRANDIER stares
down at himself.*)

GRANDIER: Attendite et videte si est dolor sicut dolor meus.
(*JEANNE gets up.*)

JEANNE: Where are You? Where are You?
(*JEANNE goes from the garden.
BARRÉ and RANGIER have come down into the lower room.*)

ADAM: Any good?

BARRÉ: No.

MANNOURY: No confession?

BARRÉ: No.

ADAM: I say!

BARRÉ: Perfectly good reason.

MANNOURY: What?

BARRÉ: He called on God to give him strength. His god is
the devil and did so. Made him insensible to pain. We'll
get nowhere like this.

ADAM: Insensible to pain? What were all those screams?

BARRÉ: A mockery.
(*BARRÉ, MIGNON and RANGIER go down into the street.*)

The upper room.

GRANDIER: Take no notice of these tears. They're only
weakness.

DE LAUBARDEMONT: Remorse?

GRANDIER: No.

DE LAUBARDEMONT: Confess.

GRANDIER: No. There are two things a man should never be asked to do in front of other men. Perform with a woman, and suffer pain. You people know how to bring hell on earth for someone like me. Make it all public.

DE LAUBARDEMONT: That is vanity, Father.

GRANDIER: Is it? I don't think so. A man is a private thing. He belongs to himself. Those two most intimate experiences, love and pain, have nothing to do with the mob. How can they concern it? For the mob can feel neither.

DE LAUBARDEMONT: The mob is made up of Christian souls. Six thousand of them are waiting for you in the market place. Tell me, do you love the Church?

GRANDIER: With all my heart.

DE LAUBARDEMONT: Do you want to see it grow more powerful, more benevolent, until it embraces every human soul on this earth?

GRANDIER: That would be my wish.

DE LAUBARDEMONT: Then help us to achieve this great purpose. Go to the market place a penitent man. Confess, and by confessing, proclaim to these thousands that you have returned to the Church's arms. By going to the stake unrepentant you do God a disservice. You give hope to the sceptics and unbelievers. You make them glad. Such an act can mine the very foundations of the Church. Think. You are no longer important. Are you any longer important?

GRANDIER: No.

DE LAUBARDEMONT: Then make a last supreme gesture for the Catholic faith.

(*Silence. DE LAUBARDEMONT eagerly leans forward. Then GRANDIER looks up. His face is drawn in an agonized smile.*)

GRANDIER: This is sophistry, Laubardemont, and you're too intelligent not to know it. Pay me the same compliment.

DE LAUBARDEMONT: You can laugh? Now?

GRANDIER: Yes. Because I know more about it than you.

DE LAUBARDEMONT: When I tell you, Grandier –

GRANDIER: Don't persist. I can destroy you. At least in argument. Keep your illusions, Mister Commissioner. You'll need them all to deal with the men who will come after me.

DE LAUBARDEMONT: Confess.

GRANDIER: No.

DE LAUBARDEMONT: Confess.

GRANDIER: No.

DE LAUBARDEMONT: Sign.

GRANDIER: No.

(*DE LAUBARDEMONT goes to the door. He calls down the stairs.*)

DE LAUBARDEMONT: Let me have the guard here!

A street.

A crowd is staring into the distance. The people are quiet, shifting, uneasy, withheld. BARRÉ, RANGIER and MIGNON come towards them. RANGIER and MIGNON are scattering holy water and intoning exorcisms. BARRÉ moves along the crowd, taking men and women by the arm, speaking to them individually.

BARRÉ: My dear children, you are about to witness the passage of a wicked and unrepentant man to hell. I beg of you – you, sir – take the sight to your heart. Let it be a lesson that will stay with you – my good woman – all your life. Watch this infamous magician who has trafficked with devils and ask yourself – my child – is this what a man comes to when he scorns God?

(*A drum. GRANDIER comes into sight. He is seated on a chair which has been lashed to a kind of litter, and is carried by four soldiers. He wears a shirt impregnated with sulphur, a vivid yellow, and there is a rope round his neck. His broken legs dangle. He is a ridiculous, hairless, shattered doll. The CLERK walks beside him. DE LAUBARDEMONT and soldiers follow.*)

Saint Ursula's Convent.

The procession comes to the convent door and stops. The CLERK puts a two-pound taper into GRANDIER's hand.

DE LAUBARDEMONT: You must get down here.

GRANDIER: What is this place?

DE LAUBARDEMONT: It is the Convent of Saint Ursula. A place you have defiled.

(*A soldier lifts GRANDIER from the litter like a child, and puts him on the ground.*)

Do what must be done.

GRANDIER: In this strange and unknown place I ask pardon of God, the King and Justice. I beg that I may – (*He falls forward on his face: cries out.*) Deus meus, miserere mei Deus!

(*The convent door opens and from the dark entrance come JEANNE, GABRIELLE, CLAIRE and LOUISE.*)

DE LAUBARDEMONT: Ask pardon of this Prioress, and these good Sisters.

GRANDIER: Who are these women?

DE LAUBARDEMONT: They are the people you have wronged. Ask their forgiveness.

GRANDIER: I have done no such thing. I can only ask that God will forgive them.

(*Utter silence as GRANDIER and JEANNE stare at each other.*)

JEANNE: They always spoke of your beauty. Now I see it with my own eyes and I know it to be true.

GRANDIER: Look at this thing which I am, and learn the meaning of love.

(*The drum. GRANDIER is lifted back on to the litter. The procession moves on into the distance.*

A great bell. Voices:)

Dies irae, dies illa, solvet saeclum in favilla, teste David cum Sybilla.

Quantus tremor est futurus, quando judex est venturus, cuncta stricte discussurus!

(*JEANNE, alone, comes forward. Darkness.*)

The streets of Loudun. Night.

The town seems to be on fire. Distant buildings are silhouetted against a harsh red sky. A church door gapes like a sulphurous mouth. Armed men with banners cross a bridge. A man is climbing a ladder, waving into the distance in hopeless distress.

The crowd (which watched GRANDIER into the distance) has broken up and is rushing, hysterical, screaming, laughing, through the streets.

JEANNE wanders on alone.

MANNOURY and ADAM.

MANNOURY: Very odd, you know.

ADAM: What?

MANNOURY: That business of human fat being rendered down by heat to the consistency of candle wax and then igniting with a flame of such exquisite colour.

ADAM: Rum business, altogether.

MANNOURY: Interesting, though. I'd say, Adam, if there's any aesthetic appeal in your work as a chemist it lies in that direction. Wouldn't you?

ADAM: Maybe.

(*They go.*
BARRÉ, MIGNON and RANGIER.)

BARRÉ: He's in hell. Be sure of it.

MIGNON: Tonight he roasts.

BARRÉ: Unrepentant, frightful man!

RANGIER: You know, I saw his women sitting there, watching. One was in tears, it's true. But she was watching. Never turned away.

BARRÉ: Devils. All devils. What's the matter with you?

MIGNON: I don't feel very well.

BARRÉ: (*Hitting him on the back.*) Smoke got down you, I expect.

MIGNON: I think I'll go to bed now, if you don't mind.

BARRÉ: We're all going to get to our beds, Mignon. How long we shall be allowed to lie there depends on friend Satan. We vanquished him and brought peace to his place today. But you can be sure that even now he is creeping back. Ah, my dear friends, men of our kind will never lack employment.

(*They go.*

PHILIPPE. She is monstrously pregnant, and lumbers forward leading the old man by the hand.)

PHILIPPE: Come along home, dear husband. You must try to walk a little quicker. What?

(*The old man whispers to her.*)

Watching all this today has made you quite excited.

(*He whispers again.*)

Yes, you shall do whatever you like. And I'll do all I can for you. Wipe your mouth. We've many happy years ahead together. What? Yes, of course there's a way. I'll turn and turn about for you. Jesus, I will. I'll show you tricks. So come home, darling.

(*PHILIPPE and the old man go.*

D'ARMAGNAC and DE CERISAY. They are drunk.)

D'ARMAGNAC: We shouldn't be doing this, De Cerisay. We are the rational, forward-looking men of our age. We should be taking a stand.

DE CERISAY: Quite right.

D'ARMAGNAC: About something or other. I'm not quite sure what. Why is the air full of insects tonight? What was I saying?

DE CERISAY: We should take a stand.

D'ARMAGNAC: And assert ourselves.

DE CERISAY: What about?

D'ARMAGNAC: What we believe.

DE CERISAY: And what do we believe?

D'ARMAGNAC: Ask me tomorrow. Am I mad? Were they fornicating in the street up there? And what did that old woman have in the basket? Human remains? Why was that animal leading a man on a rope. What is the strange, sweet smell that hangs over the place? And that musician crucified upon the harp. What does it all mean, De Cerisay? As rational men we should be able to explain it.

DE CERISAY: I can't.

D'ARMAGNAC: Neither can I. So take me home.

(They go.

JEANNE's wandering through the streets has brought her to the SEWERMAN.)

SEWERMAN: When it was done they shovelled him to the north, the south, the east and the west.

JEANNE: Do you know who I am?

SEWERMAN: Yes, madam, I know.

(Some of the crowd are passing. They are fighting among themselves for some objects which are passed from hand to hand.)

JEANNE: What are they doing?

SEWERMAN: It's bits of the body they're after.

JEANNE: As relics?

SEWERMAN: Don't try to comfort yourself. No, they want them as charms. There's a difference, you know. *(He snatches a charred bone from one of the men.)* They don't want to adore this. They want it to cure their constipation or their headache, to have it bring back their virility or their wife. They want it for love or hate. *(He holds out the bone.)* Do you want it for anything?

(JEANNE shakes her head. The crowd has gone. The SEWERMAN goes. JEANNE alone. She cries out in her own voice.)

JEANNE: Grandier! Grandier!

(Silence.)

CURTAIN

The End.

Introduction to

NOMAN
and
THE NOMADS

In 1939, after registering as a conscientious objector at the beginning of the war, John Whiting changed his mind and joined the anti-aircraft section of the Royal Artillery. He was commissioned in 1942 as a second lieutenant, and in 1944, while still in the army, he began a novel, calling it *Not a Foot of Land*. He completed it after being discharged in 1944 on grounds of poor health.

Together with three men and a girl, the central character, Timothy Crashaw, plans to destroy the shrine of "the holy Master", who is venerated by the whole of society. Like much else in the novel, Timothy's motives remain unexplained, but he wants to make a negative gesture signalling his rejection of life. In one episode he recalls traumatic panic after a childhood fall. "I looked up at the sky and was overcome with unreasoning terror... All acts of violence were inexplicable to me... Revenge, premeditated revenge of the bloodiest kind was the answer!"

Another character describes his attitude as "falling in love with death". We also find a reference to "old Paul", a celebrated pamphleteer who was hanged for his writings. If *Saint's Day* was the first play in which Whiting recycled real and imagined experiences, *Not a Foot of Land* was his first fiction to bridge in this way between his past life and his future drama.

Themes from the novel are reprised in the unfinished play *Noman*. During a 1961 interview which is included in *At Ease in a Bright Red Tie* (pp 37-56) Whiting was asked about his six years of working on filmscripts after he finished *The Gates of Summer*.

> I did begin two plays. I wrote half of one. It was hopeless, it wouldn't work at all. I put it away, and I started another one, of which again I wrote half. A very fascinating subject, couldn't ever work, boring beyond words, so I put that away. It was only recently that I realised that the first play

I started is perfectly all right. I've just changed the place and I've changed the basic idea. It was simply that I was writing the wrong play, that's all.

In 1958 he worked on *Noman,* which was to have consisted of two acts. Some preliminary notes are dated 18 August, and the first act exists in a complete manuscript draft dated 21 August. He rewrote about two thirds of this in a manuscript dated 20 October. What follows is the notes, followed by the second draft as far as it goes, and the end of the first draft. The continuity is only approximate, because he was changing a great deal as he revised, and there is some repetition.

Absentmindedly, he made the characters take the plaster hands out of the glass case twice, and in the first draft he ends the act with it. It therefore figures three times in this duplex version of the play's first half.

In 1961, when he started rewriting the play as *The Nomads,* he changed more than the place and the basic idea. He may have thought of it as the same play – in the same way he thought of *A Walk in the Desert* as being the same play as *Conditions of Agreement* – but for the reader, the similarities do not add up to identity.

Noman and *The Nomads* help to explain why *The Devils* is so different in style and approach from his previous plays. Writing for the screen was encouraging him to break the rule of the three unities – confining the action to one place, one theme and a period of 24 hours. But since all we have of *Noman* and *The Nomads* is fragments, and since he has left no indications of how he might have developed them, we should not read them in the same way as the rest of his work. We know we do not know what changes he would have made.

It was a good idea to make Lang survive the attempted murder and become curator of a museum devoted to his own memory. (A playwright is always the first curator of the museum devoted to his memory.) But Whiting was unsatisfied with the way he was developing this idea theatrically. By keeping the audience in ignorance of the deception Lang is practising, Whiting was building towards a moments of revelation, but until this comes, the irony makes no impact, and in the draft there is too little action to sustain the discussion.

We shall never know whether Whiting would have been able to correct the imbalance, or whether he would have persevered in 1958 had he been less depressed by the commercial failure of his plays. Nor can we know whether he would have resumed work on *The Nomads* in 1963, had he survived the cancer that was diagnosed in the winter of 1962.

He made four abortive attempts at the play – the first in September 1961, the last in January 1963. He died five months later, not yet forty-six.

NOMAN

NOTES – 18th August 1958

TWO ACTS

PLACE

Set town (by plan).

A museum on a street.

Front door: stairs to: two main rooms of relics (define these): 3 or 4 stairs to: small living room (confusion) bed. stove: ladder to: attic: rubbish: small window looking over town: other rooms, other windows:

House above the Taurian Steps (40 of them?) The place of assassination (a plaque?): The steps go down to the town. A lamp-post.

Town church clocks.
Draw all this from actual place. (Perhaps composite.)

TIME:

Between late evening (nightfall) summer and morning of the following day.
Actual year?

PEOPLE

Visitors to the museum: schoolchildren: schoolmaster (woman?) back to bus: a man with camera: old woman:
People in the street:
workers: general activity: lamp-lighter.

Man – woman (a child) on steps through night. Tramps on the move.

Reality – to these, the common people, is what comes within the immediate experience.

The Caretaker.
The Leader: Meyer – Mayer.
1st Man.
2nd Man.
3rd Man
Girl.

LANG. Brendel.
(Let us look at these people.)
NAMES.
Mayer. Meyer.
Ganze.
Helm.

Walter.
Elisabeth.
Lucie.
Jakob.
Jake.
Peter.

1st Man. too old for this sort of thing. 45-50? – trying to be young – pathetic – contempt from others – and from Caretaker. Background? (Walter?)

Stresses within the group.

Group's title: Union for?

2nd Man. 22: young working man: cool foul-mouth: (Peter?) brothers.

Group action – revolutionary action – opposed to that of the individual.

3rd Man. 24. Intellectual: with girl. (Jakob. Jake)

Meyer keeps to himself the need to kill the Caretaker in last resort. *All resolves itself to two men.*

Girl:

Why bring her? Women's place Balls!

Meyer: [no doubt here].
The Caretaker [NAME?] Lang.

The Power of Revolt.

SCHEME

In two parts:
Part I ending with destruction of museum.
Part II ending with murder on the steps. (By Walter?)

1. Open with schoolchildren on steps.
Schoolmaster.
Old woman in house.
Man (with camera) and wife [tourists] in house.
Brendel

Tell story of Lang through these people.

(Arrival of Meyer, Elisabeth, Peter, Walter and Jakob through this action. They come separately – Jake and Elisabeth together – and go into house.)

2. Closing of museum, Brendel and handbell.
Distraction by children. (To cover concealment of the 5.)

3. Visitors go: dying movement in the street: cyclist: lamplighter. Brendel to his room: pot on stove: he prepares supper while –

4. Arrival of night people – man, woman and child – preparing to spend night on the steps. They settle.

5. Emergence from shadows of the 5.

6. Confrontation of Brendel.

7. Statement of aims.

Progression: Brendel: from lonely, frightened old man to full stature: to revelation as Lang.
[Do you ever have people come here? No. Do you ever go out? No.]

8. The 5's attitude to Lang – examination of the relics.

[I heard that was all faked. B: it's not true!]

9. The actual time for action.

Cut in to all this the night people. Carry through this relations between 5.
Brendel observes.

10. Leading to moment of destruction.

Plaster mask: broken: Brendel's cry: coming of the night people.

END OF PART ONE

11. open with night people.

12. To: scene of absolute destruction in museum.

13. Question of Brendel's murder: put by Walter. The others' disgust and horror. Walter's insistence – contempt for Meyer. He believes he will fail to carry it through.

Brendel in his room with Peter and Elisabeth. Walter and Meyer in 1st Room: Jakob alone. Can only be done by one man.
Walter: otherwise, this will just

look like the work of hooligans.
Danger to ourselves.
Meyer insists that he must carry
it out.

14. The breakup of the group.   Growing power of Brendel.

15. They go.

16. Meyer and Brendel alone.   Core of argument here.

17. Revelation of Brendel as   Story (Ironic – savage) 'within
Lang.   two days of my death they saw
me as a different man. They saw
me as *that*!'
(the portrait).

Full stature of Brendel-Lang
here. – matched by Meyer.

18. Departure of the night   (on way to harvesting in south?
people.   'should have avoided town').

19. Brendel-Lang and Meyer
come from the house into early
light of summer morning.
Conversation at top of steps.

20.Walter on steps. Murder of
Brendel.

END OF PART TWO

Characters

SCHOOLMASTER

BOYS

GIRLS

OLD WOMAN

BRENDEL

PRIEST

MAN

WOMAN

MEYER

PETER

JACOB

WALTER

LEONIE/ELIZABETH

ACT ONE

The action of the play takes place in and near a museum; and on the Taurian Steps.

The Taurian Steps are in the foreground. This public way goes down from sight and leads to the town. The wide stone steps are old and forbidding. They are marked by the weather.

A narrow street crosses the top of the steps, like a terrace. It is paved. There are some railings which lean, splay out. Among the iron bars there is faded gilt on an imperial shield. And there is a lamp-post.

Two houses stand on the street. The first, of which only part can be seen, is a derelict shell. All but one of its windows are boarded over. It is divided from the second house by an alley.

The second house is a museum. The interior can be seen.

From the front door on the street there is a way by a few steps through a passage to the first room. A second and smaller room adjoins this. The division is made by curtains. Both rooms form the museum and are dedicated to the memory of a man called LANG, and they contain the relics of his life. Steps go down from the second room to a door at the back of the house. This opens on to the alley.

There are glass cases in the museum rooms. They hold small personal belongings. The kind of things a man carries about his person at one time or another: perhaps accumulates on his desk. A tailor's dummy has a greatcoat round the shoulders and a cap on the faceless wooden head. There are several shelves of books. In the small room there is an old gramophone with a pile of records. A violin. Some walking sticks.

The walls of the rooms are covered with pictures, mostly photographs. There are some frames of letters and documents. The big room is dominated by one picture: a life-size portrait of LANG. It is a realistic painting in the revolutionary style of the 1920s. A greatcoat flung over his shoulder, LANG stands against a winter landscape with an arm stretched out in an embracing gesture of reconciliation. His proud bitter Jewish face stares beyond horizons. The artist in his love has overreached himself. No man ever looked like this.

There is a stairway beyond the door of the larger room. It goes steeply up to a narrow landing and a third room. This is the curator's living room. It has the desolate, makeshift qualities of a solitary man. There is a bed with a table beside it. Clothes hang behind the door. There is a cooking pot on a stove. The walls are bare and discoloured. A ladder goes up from a corner of the room through an open trap to an attic. This can be seen. Rubbish lies about. A man could not stand upright in the place for rafters slope steeply across it. A small unclean window looks out over the town.

It is summer: late in the evening.

There are people in the museum. An OLD WOMAN moves slowly from one object to another in the first room. Unseeing eyes: great weariness. In the second room a PRIEST is bending over a glass case. A man of energy and decision. He carries pamphlets in his hand and a camera hangs from his neck.

The curator of the museum, BRENDEL, stands by the door of the first room. He wears a blue jacket with brass buttons and a cap.

The door to the street is open, propped back with a stone.

A group of schoolchildren stand at the top of the Taurian Steps. There are four BOYS and two GIRLS. They have a SCHOOLMASTER with them. He uses his walking stick like a rod of office.

SCHOOLMASTER: What is the name of these steps?

FIRST BOY: The Taurian Steps.

SCHOOLMASTER: They have many historical associations, but are notable for one thing. What is that?

SECOND BOY: The murder –

SCHOOLMASTER: The word is assassination.

SECOND BOY: The assassination of Lang.

SCHOOLMASTER: When did it happen?
   (*Silence: the children look at each other; the SCHOOLMASTER points his stick at FIRST GIRL.*)

FIRST GIRL: (*A whisper.*) Fourteen years ago.

SECOND GIRL: Sixteen years ago.

SCHOOLMASTER: Guesses! It was twenty-three years ago.
   (*WALTER comes up the steps. He is reading a tightly folded newspaper.*

He sits on the top step smoking a cigarette and continuing to read.)

Twenty-three years. Remember that. Who killed Lang?

SECOND BOY: His brother.

SCHOOLMASTER: Have you a brother?

SECOND BOY: Yes, sir.

SCHOOLMASTER: Then you will understand this terrible thing. (*He points to a plaque set into the stones of the steps: the children gather round.*) Take your hats off. (*The boys do so.*) Read.

THIRD BOY: (*Reading the inscription.*) 'Lang died here. He loved mankind. Lang died here.'

SCHOOLMASTER: He died on that bitter winter morning. He was horribly murdered. They found him lying here on the steps. He was carried into the house...

(*The SCHOOLMASTER begins to shepherd the group of children to the door of the house. WALTER, pushing the newspaper into his pocket, gets up and moves with them. Inside the house: the OLD WOMAN stands staring down at an armchair in the first room.*)

OLD WOMAN: And is this where they put him?

BRENDEL: Yes. What was left of him.

OLD WOMAN: When did he breathe his last?

BRENDEL: He died at five twenty-three exactly.

OLD WOMAN: God rest him.

BRENDEL: Why, yes, indeed.

(*The children are clattering up the stairs into the room, followed by the SCHOOLMASTER. WALTER comes after them. He goes straight to the second room, and from sight. The children crowd round one of the museum cases.*)

OLD WOMAN: Is there a picture of the corpse?

(*She turns the rack of postcards and pamphlets which is in the room.*)

BRENDEL: No, there are some postcards of the tomb. Would that do?

(*LEONIE and JACOB come along the street. The girl carries a shopping basket. Inside the house: the PRIEST pushes his way through the crowd of children to BRENDEL.*)

PRIEST: He had a great feeling, I believe, for minorities.

BRENDEL: Do you mean the less happy people?

PRIEST: Yes, I suppose I do. The less fortunate.

BRENDEL: He put it all in books. You can look at them, if you like.

(*He nods towards the shelves.*)

PRIEST: Thank you. Am I allowed to take photographs?

BRENDEL: Yes.

PRIEST: I'm from another country, you know. I'm on a visit.

BRENDEL: There's not much of interest to photograph here, I'm afraid. Have you seen the tomb? That's very fine.

PRIEST: Yes, I've seen that. Look at that child's face. (*He means the FIRST BOY who, alone, is staring up at LANG's portrait.*) That's the meaning of this place. (*The PRIEST begins to unfasten his camera.*)

(*BRENDEL goes across the room towards the stairs. He will go up the stairs and into his room. When he is there he will take a look into the cooking pot on the stove, straighten the covers of the unmade bed, and push some clothes which are lying on the floor under the bed with his foot.*

LEONIE and JACOB have come into the house from the street and gone from sight through into the second room.

The FIRST BOY who stands in front of the portrait speaks to the SCHOOLMASTER.)

FIRST BOY: Please, sir, is there a picture of the murderer?

SCHOOLMASTER: This house is a shrine, boy. And your question is disgusting.

(*The PRIEST has approached the SCHOOLMASTER.*)

PRIEST: I'd like to photograph the children.

SCHOOLMASTER: Why?

PRIEST: Well, I come from another country. I've been watching the children's faces in this house. Although their faith is secular I find it moving. This boy was looking at the portrait. I would like some record.

SCHOOLMASTER: All right.

(*The PRIEST begins to arrange several of the children in front of the portrait. They are docile, tired, bored, with vacant faces.*

358

PETER comes along the street. He turns into the house without hesitation and goes up into the first room. He glances at the PRIEST and the group of children and then at the OLD WOMAN who has sat in the armchair. She speaks to PETER.)

OLD WOMAN: This place isn't as comfortable as the Art Gallery. And it's not as interesting as the Railway Station. They ought to provide better amusements for old people.

(PETER smiles and after a moment will go through into the second room. The children have been arranged and a flashlight photograph is taken. The PRIEST steps back and speaks to the SCHOOLMASTER.)

PRIEST: Thank you.

SCHOOLMASTER: Don't use it for propaganda.

PRIEST: What do you mean?

SCHOOLMASTER: I know your sort in other countries. The things you make children believe. It's disgraceful. This man Lang lived. He didn't claim to be anything very much. His life isn't surrounded by mystery and superstition...

PRIEST: Surely his death is.

SCHOOLMASTER: Perhaps. But his life was simple and good. A model for these children. Because we bring them up to believe in him is no reason for you to go back and show that photograph and say: See, this is the way they worship.

PRIEST: I don't mean to do that.

(The children are wandering about the room looking at various objects. The SCHOOLMASTER catches hold of one of the boys and holds him almost passionately to his side.)

SCHOOLMASTER: These children need a human being to love. Not someone divine masquerading as a man. They want to be able to touch his belongings and look upon his true face. Not a sentimental invention by besotted artists. They have to live and so they want truth. Lang gives them that.

(MEYER comes up the Taurian Steps. He hesitates at the top, looking back the way he has come. Then he goes quickly towards the door of the house. As MEYER enters the house...

...BRENDEL, in his room, has picked up a handbell and is sitting on his bed holding the bell and watching an alarm clock which is on the table.

MEYER comes up into the first room. The PRIEST has turned away from the SCHOOLMASTER and gone to the bookshelves. He takes down a book. Reads.

The bell sounds through the house. BRENDEL is coming from his room and down the stairs. He swings the bell as he walks. The people in the room shift and turn at the sound, and as MEYER passes them on his way to the second room. BRENDEL is approaching.)

Form up in the street, please. We march to the station. (*To the FIRST BOY.*) Take charge.

(*The children go down the stairs and into the street, where they begin to get into line. BRENDEL has come down into the first room. He has stopped ringing the bell.*)

BRENDEL: If you please, the museum is closing.

(*The clocks of the town are sounding the hour: ten o'clock. BRENDEL speaks to the SCHOOLMASTER.*)

Have the children got a long journey?

SCHOOLMASTER: Half an hour.

BRENDEL: I hope they've enjoyed themselves.

SCHOOLMASTER: Enjoyed? I don't know. It's part of their education.

(*The SCHOOLMASTER goes towards the street door. The PRIEST looks up from the book at BRENDEL.*)

PRIEST: You're an old man. Too old to have grown up under Lang's influence. What do you think?

BRENDEL: He was good.

PRIEST: No one doubts that. But was he...

BRENDEL: It's all in the books.

(*The PRIEST smiles and puts the book back on the shelf. He gives some money to BRENDEL.*)

PRIEST: Take this. It's not given with pride. I may come back.

BRENDEL: Everyone is welcome.

(*The PRIEST goes out of the room. The children, directed by the FIRST BOY, are formed in two lines in the street. The*

SCHOOLMASTER has come down to them and now marches them away. The PRIEST comes into the street and walks slowly away, enjoying the evening.

Inside the house: the OLD WOMAN is still sunk in the armchair. BRENDEL speaks to her.)

Time to go home, dear.

OLD WOMAN: Who keeps the place clean?

BRENDEL: I do.

OLD WOMAN: All the brushing and dusting –

BRENDEL: And scrubbing. I do it all.

OLD WOMAN: Not much else to do.

BRENDEL: No.

(A moment: the OLD WOMAN is staring at the portrait.)

OLD WOMAN: I suppose he was a great man.

BRENDEL: Yes.

OLD WOMAN: I suppose we do owe him a lot.

BRENDEL: That's right.

OLD WOMAN: Did he give anything for old people?

BRENDEL: They say he loved everybody.

OLD WOMAN: Well, that's silly. Just talk. Like the dead always being good. Hoo!

(BRENDEL has been picking up rubbish from the floor. Now he stands looking at the OLD WOMAN. She pulls herself up from the chair.)

All right. I'm going.

(She is on her feet and going to the door. BRENDEL follows her down the few steps to the street. The OLD WOMAN comes out, and stands for a moment looking at the sky.)

(Murmurs.) I'll get a bus.

BRENDEL: Good night.

(The OLD WOMAN goes away down the street. She passes a man wheeling a bicycle. He puts on the gas street lamp and when he has done this he will lift his bicycle on to his shoulder and carry it down the steps.

BRENDEL has kicked away the stone and is locking and bolting the front door of the house. When he has done this he goes up through the first room and by way of the passage to the second room. There, out of sight, he locks and bolts the other outer door. This done, he comes back to the first room. He glances round, switches off the lights, and goes towards the stairs leading to his room. He is fumbling with and undoing the buttons of his coat.

A MAN and a WOMAN come up the steps. They are wretchedly dressed and drag bundles with them. They might be any age: shapeless clothes hide the years and almost the sex. The MAN throws down his bundle and sits on the steps.)

MAN: Not going any more tonight. No.

(*Voice: thin and hoarse. The WOMAN stares down at him: her lips move.*)

What you say? (*Shouts.*) What you say?

WOMAN: We should've kept away from the town. Here. This –

MAN: You would come!

WOMAN: We should've kept to the country. Out there.

MAN: You would do it!

WOMAN: I know. I wanted to see the shops.

MAN: Oh dear, well that's not much to ask. (*He finds it funny.*) To see the shops. They're full of things to make you happy. Food, clothes, fur, jewels, cars, food, drugs, gramophone records, flowers, hats, coats, food, furniture, silk, satin, tobacco… (*Suddenly.*) I'm not going any more tonight!

WOMAN: You can't be expected to. You're a sick man.

MAN: I know. I'm very sorry for myself. I grieve.

(*The WOMAN is sitting on the steps below the MAN, her bundle beside her.*

Inside the house: BRENDEL has gone up to his room. He has taken off his buttoned jacket and his cap and hung them behind the door. He has taken down a woollen coat which he now puts on. In a moment he will go over to the stove and will stand stirring the cooking pot.

The MAN on the steps suddenly reaches forward and shakes the WOMAN by the shoulder.)

Wake up!

WOMAN: Yes!

MAN: You can't sleep like that. Who do you think you are? An animal? Lie down.

WOMAN: Here?

MAN: Yes. They never move you if you're near a river. Or on steps. You would come through the town. Had to see the shops.

WOMAN: It's not much to ask, you said.

MAN: No. Whenever have I denied you the smallest luxury?

(*The MAN has pulled a blanket from his bundle. The WOMAN does the same. They roughly cover themselves, leaning back against the bundles.*)

WOMAN: Warm, isn't it?

MAN: Might be worse. (*In a friendly way.*) Take your boots off, you dirty old lady.

(*The WOMAN begins to do so: silence.*)

WOMAN: The lights look pretty.

MAN: What lights?

WOMAN: Down there.

MAN: Ah! I expect they're shops.

(*Inside the house: BRENDEL has ladled some stew from the pot and taken it to the table beside the bed. He breaks a piece from a loaf of bread and puts it on the plate. He sits on the bed. He takes a book from under the pillow and props it up in front of him. He begins to eat, reading.*

The MAN has been running his fingers over the plaque which is set into the steps beside him. He reads.)

'Lang died here. He lov – ed man – kind. Lang died here.'

WOMAN: Lov – ed what?

MAN: Mankind. You. Me.

WOMAN: Well, that's nice, then.

(*After putting her boots on the step beside her the WOMAN has been wrapping her feet in newspaper. Now she leans back against the bundle, pulling the blanket over her legs. The MAN is covered up to the neck: he stares down the steps. It is darker now. The street lamp throws little more than shadows. BRENDEL's room: harsh white light from an unshaded lamp.*)

MAN: Yes. If someone came this way…yes, and looked… and saw us…

WOMAN: Whatever would he think?

MAN: Rubbish. We must look as if we've been thrown down here…left…forgotten and unwanted. Yet, wait. Cheer up. Do you remember that old armchair which got the bugs in it? Remember how we tried to get rid of it. They wouldn't take it away. It wouldn't burn. Whatever I did to it nothing could make it stop being an armchair. Even when I dragged it from the house, down the road and across the fields in the middle of the night and threw it into a ditch, leaving it there, what did it look like? It looked like an armchair which had been left in a ditch. So I expect we still look like people.

WOMAN: I expect so.

MAN: Mind, armchairs have no right to be in ditches. And we have no right to be here.

WOMAN: It's wrong.

(*Inside the house: BRENDEL has finished eating and pushed the plate aside. He sits, his head in his hands, reading.*
Now figures can be seen emerging from the darkness of the passage which leads from the second room. Five people. They come silently forward and will soon be gathered together in the first room.
The words of the MAN and WOMAN on the steps are broken, hesitant, until at last the voices pass into sleep.)

I keep thinking. We should've afforded the railway fare.

MAN: No. I wanted to walk home. It wasn't the money. I wanted to see the country. For the last time. When they say you're going to die you've got to believe them, you know. You can't go on in the old way.

WOMAN: There's not much you can do.

MAN: Not much more than we're doing. Pack up and go home.

WOMAN: It'll all be changed. They say it's quite different now.

MAN: Doesn't matter. I don't know why you ever leave a place. You're born there and it's all right.

WOMAN: What took you away? You've never said.

MAN: When I was a boy there was no work so I moved ten miles to find it. Then I moved another fifty miles to better myself. Then there was the war and they moved me three hundred miles. That's the way it goes. Nothing ever seems to take you back. So you have to wait until the day when they say, You've had it, you're no use, you'll be dead... then you can pack up and go home. Like we're doing.

(*Silence.*)

'Lang died here. He lov – ed mankind.'

WOMAN: If he'd lived, I expect he'd have loved us.

MAN: Small change we'd have got from it.

(*Silence.*

In the house: BRENDEL is turning the pages of the book. The five figures in the darkness have come forward into the first room. They are, MEYER, WALTER, JACOB, PETER and the girl, LEONIE.

Let us look at these people.

MEYER is twenty-six years old. The bone structure of his head is good, but there seems to be an overdevelopment of the brow. This clouds an otherwise handsome face. His pale eyes – perhaps he needs glasses – sometimes become hooded as if with tiredness. This is not likely to be affectation. His teeth are bad. His clothes show that he looks after himself, and his body is well exercised.

The girl, LEONIE is twenty. Her body is a little too fat to be pretty, but it is a matter of taste. The warm curves might suit a man very well, as they do JACOB. Her wide unpainted mouth is innocent. Her ears are too small. There is no effect in her clothes. She wears them as a covering, nothing more. When she speaks she does so like a provincial who can make a native language sound like a foreign tongue.

WALTER is forty-six, much older than the other four. His face and body seem to have fallen forward into a permanent attitude for the study of boring and abstruse documents. In fact, he is a librarian of no importance. His clothes have the shabby friendliness of a present day ecclesiastic. He sometimes picks at his face.

JACOB is a beautiful creature. Seen closely it is difficult to find any blemish of head or body, although in certain levels of society he might be faulted for an almost imperceptible animal smell. He is twenty-two.

PETER, JACOB's brother, is a year older. He is greedy, and the effects are beginning to show in his face. Women like him, for his square tobacco-stained hands are expert, capable of rousing great expectation. But a lack of fulfilment, of decision, gives him a tension which quickly leads to anger. He wears thin cotton trousers which cling to his fat legs, and a leather jacket: like a mechanic.

And BRENDEL is apart in his room. He is sixty-three years old. His face is closely shaven and his hair cropped very short. His reading glasses sit squarely on his large nose. He has been seen preparing and eating his supper and his behaviour has all the small absurdities of an unobserved man: the close scrutiny of well-known objects, the exaggerated method in preparation for the meal, the audible self-reproach at some minor mishap. Now, however, he is still, quite concentrated on his reading of the book.

The MAN and WOMAN on the steps are asleep.

In the first room: LEONIE is with JACOB. PETER is sitting in the armchair, watching them. WALTER is running his hands over the surface of one of the glass cases: slightest of sound. MEYER is at the front of the stairs. He looks round. WALTER nods his head. MEYER turns and goes up the stairs. He comes to the door of BRENDEL's room. He hesitates. Then he puts out his hand and the movement of the latch is startlingly loud as the door is opened. MEYER goes into the room. BRENDEL stares at him: gets up.)

BRENDEL: The museum is shut.

MEYER: I know.

(He is looking about the room: hardly even at BRENDEL.)

BRENDEL: Who are you?

MEYER: Where does that go?

BRENDEL: To an attic.

MEYER: Come downstairs.

BRENDEL: There's nothing to steal here.

MEYER: Come with me, please.

(BRENDEL, with MEYER, comes out of the room and on to the stairs. He hesitates, looking down at the four people in the room below.)

BRENDEL: What do you want?

WALTER: Come down here.

(*BRENDEL comes down into the first room. MEYER follows.*)

BRENDEL: This is wrong. No one is allowed in…

MEYER: What's your name?

BRENDEL: Brendel. Arthur Brendel.

MEYER: Do you live here alone?

BRENDEL: Oh yes, quite alone.

WALTER: Do you ever have visitors?

BRENDEL: Well, this is a museum. People come all the time.

WALTER: I didn't mean that.

MEYER: He means, do your friends come here?

BRENDEL: I don't know anybody like that.

MEYER: So no one's likely to come tonight.

BRENDEL: No.

MEYER: What do you usually do with yourself now?

BRENDEL: After I've locked up?

MEYER: Yes.

BRENDEL: I go up to my room, have my supper, and read. Just as you found me.

MEYER: And then?

BRENDEL: Then I go to sleep.

MEYER: And in the morning?

BRENDEL: I get up…

MEYER: At what time?

BRENDEL: About six. And I clean the house.

MEYER: How do you manage about food?

BRENDEL: When I've done the house I go shopping.

MEYER: Just round about here?

BRENDEL: Oh, yes. Never very far away.

MEYER: And then you come back and open the museum?

BRENDEL: At ten o'clock. Yes.

MEYER: And do you do this every day?

BRENDEL: Every day.

(*BRENDEL is standing in the middle of the group. He has been looking from face to face as he answers the questions. Each person has stared back at him.*)

MEYER: You've had a good look at us all. Now I want you
to tell me something. What do you see?

BRENDEL: You're all young. Much the same age. Except him.
(*He means WALTER, who laughs.*)

MEYER: His tragedy is no less because it came later in life.

WALTER: More touching, I think. I am a pathetic figure.
Spit on me.

MEYER: (*To BRENDEL.*) You lied.

BRENDEL: No.

MEYER: You lied.

BRENDEL: I'm an old man. And I didn't tell a lie.

MEYER: You said you lived here alone.

BRENDEL: I do. Quite alone.

MEYER: No, you live here with Lang. Look around.

WALTER: He's right.

MEYER: Why did you tell me you're an old man?

BRENDEL: I don't want to be hurt.

MEYER: Why should being an old man stop you from
getting hurt? Where do you think you're living? And
when? Before we know where we are we shall start
getting petitions for money from children and pregnant
women, from the sick and insane.

BRENDEL: What do you want?

MEYER: You live here with Lang. Admit it.

BRENDEL: Lang's dead.
(*Silence. It is dark in the street now. Some light from the
moon. Very deep shadows.*
The MAN and WOMAN lie like sacks on the steps.
Inside the house MEYER confronts BRENDEL.)

MEYER: Lang never died.

BRENDEL: He did. He did.

MEYER: Oh, the murder happened out there on the steps,
that's certain. And Lang's body lies in that bloody great
tomb. But the man is not dead. We've grown up with him
in our head and our heart. You're young. That's what you
said. And you smiled as if it was something pleasing and
you could forgive us anything. Well, forgive us this. We
were young. We could be young…

WALTER: Good morning, children.

PETER/JACOB/LEONIE: Good morning, sir.

(PETER, JACOB and LEONIE turn to WALTER and the group makes a little class before him. MEYER will join the group in a moment. WALTER, standing, looks down on them and speaks.)

WALTER: The subject, boys and girls, kiddies, you hope of the future, young citizens for whom nothing is good enough, the subject, my darlings, is history. A question. When did history begin?

PETER: Sir, history began with the emancipation of man.

WALTER: I hope you're using words you understand.

PETER: I hope so too, sir.

WALTER: Go on.

PETER: Man was set free, sir, by Mr Lang, sir.

WALTER: How?

PETER: For hundreds of years...

JACOB: Thousands of years...

LEONIE: Millions of years...

PETER: Well, anyway, for a very long time, they had believed in one way or another that they owed their existence to a superior being.

WALTER: You baffle me, boy. Explain.

PETER: It's not easy, sir. In the years since history began about 1923 much has been made clear and much has been obscured. I'm trying to answer your question, sir.

WALTER: Thank you.

PETER: I want to do so in simple terms.

WALTER: Thank you again.

PETER: So let me say this. In the years of pre-history men thought there might be a time before the womb and a time after the grave. Lang's great achievement is that he snapped off these useless tag ends and revealed by its practical length life's true purpose.

WALTER: Were people grateful to him for showing them this?

PETER: Very grateful, sir. It did away with one of the most tiresome aspects of life. Silence and meditation.

WALTER: Thank you, Peter. Your homework has been well done.

(MEYER has now joined the group. He will sometimes turn to speak to BRENDEL outside the mockery of the proceedings of the classroom.)

You're late, Meyer. Why?

MEYER: It was such a fine morning, sir. I stopped in the park. The band of the Tramway Workers' Guild was practising. The flowers were bursting like bombs. A breeze swept off the boating lake and carried the idiotic language of children. Birds were shitting on the public statues. Four park-keepers were hanging by their necks from the historic oaks. I stopped, sir, just for a moment to be happy. I'm ready for my punishment.

WALTER: Very well. The subject is history. Tell us all you know.

MEYER: He was born of humble parents, the lucky man. His mother was a cripple and his father was a fool. And he was called Lang. He had a brother. All of them lived in poverty. They had nothing but love. And it was love which made mother kick little Lang down the stairs with her twisted leg and hit his brother on the head with her crutch. It was love which made father get drunk a Friday night and fall forward on to the stove. When he rushed into the street blazing the children danced around him like a festival. It was from these simple good people that Lang began to understand the real meaning of his existence. *(Pause.)* Please, sir, I'm finding it hard to concentrate. Jacob and Leonie are doing funny things. They were doing funny things behind the bicycle shed yesterday, too.

WALTER: *(Gently.)* Jacob and Leonie are in love, Meyer. People in love do funny things. Just don't look.

MEYER: Very well, sir.

WALTER: Go on with the lesson. What was the true meaning of Lang's life?

MEYER: The meaning of all our lives, sir. That we're all in the same boat. And adrift. There's nothing for it but to trust each other. And love each other. And believe.

WALTER: But that's an absurd proposition. Are you drunk
   boy?

MEYER: No, sir.

WALTER: Then I can't understand you. Do you mean that
   I am to trust – *you*?

MEYER: And I must trust and love you, sir.

WALTER: (*He begins to laugh: MEYER is smiling.*) And these
   others. They're all to love and trust?

MEYER: (*Now he is laughing with WALTER.*) Yes, sir.

WALTER: And this old man...and out there...everyone...
   everyone...

MEYER: I'm only speaking my lesson, sir. That is what
   you've taught us to believe.

WALTER: (*Suddenly silent.*) Yes, of course. And quite right.
   What are you grinning at, Meyer? What's funny about so
   noble an ideal?

MEYER: Everything, sir. Nothing, sir, I don't know, sir.

WALTER: You worthless boy! Sit down.
   (*MEYER does so: WALTER turns to the girl.*)
   Leonie, take your hands out of Jacob's pockets and pay
   attention.

LEONIE: All right.

WALTER: Would you agree with the following? It was
   Lang's appeal to the rational man which began history.
   Do you agree with that?

LEONIE: If you want me to.

WALTER: I do.

LEONIE: All right, I will.

WALTER: Listen, my dear child, you stand there clothed in
   Lang's teaching. You are free. Nothing you do is touched
   with superstition as it was once. You are free to live and
   to love. You are the true individual at liberty to act
   entirely within your own instinct. Doesn't that make you
   feel good?

LEONIE: Fine.

WALTER: For hundreds of years the immortal soul of your
   kind of slut was threatened by your dirty sinful little
   ways. Not any more. All of you, my darlings, can live

your beautiful free lives. Because of Lang. You can
live your unconstrained span of years of pleasure and
goodness and love and then you can rot in the earth for
ever and ever and ever and ever…

MEYER: (*Shouting.*) Shut up! Shut up!

(*He turns to BRENDEL and lifts his lowered face.*)

That's how we were taught. That's what we were taught.
And the children today. Who was this man?

BRENDEL: He suffered for his ideas. He was persecuted.

MEYER: Persecuted! He should have been crucified. Who
was he?

(*He snatches down one of the photographs from the wall and
holds it out before him, staring down at it.*)

Look at this. Just an ugly little boy in a badly fitting suit
and a hand on Papa's knee. Was it this that destroyed
God? (*He throws the picture aside: takes down another.*) And
this. A spotty student gripping a diploma. And this. A
private soldier grinning like an imbecile against a canvas
battlefield. How do we reach that ending – (*He means the
big portrait.*) – from these beginnings?

WALTER: Shall we go on with the lesson?

MEYER: The lesson is done! Shut up your books. We'll live
all we've been taught. (*To BRENDEL.*) Open this.

(*He raps his fist on one of the glass cases.*)

BRENDEL: No! You mustn't touch…

MEYER: Open!

(*Mute, BRENDEL shakes his head. MEYER takes a wrench
from his hip pocket and with the palm of his hand strikes
down with it. The glass of the case is shattered. BRENDEL
gives a cry and starts forward. PETER grips his arm and
holds him back. MEYER has reached into the case and taken
out a pair of plaster hands. MEYER holds them before him.*)

How did this come about?

BRENDEL: They took a cast of his hands after his death.
Let me have them.

MEYER: You're going to lose your occupation.

BRENDEL: What do you mean?

MEYER: He was taken prisoner in 1915.

BRENDEL: Yes. In France.

MEYER: They let him out in 1920 and he came home.

BRENDEL: Yes.

MEYER: (*Suddenly: to JACOB.*) How long since you've seen that girl? A week, isn't it?

JACOB: Yes. Why?

MEYER: Give it another twelve hours, will you?

JACOB: All right.

(*He wanders across the room away from LEONIE.*)

MEYER: (*To BRENDEL.*) So he came home. 1920. Look, we just want to get it straight, that's all. We don't want to do…what we're going to do without having it straight.

BRENDEL: What do you want to know?

MEYER: What did he find? You were here then. What was it like?

BRENDEL: I can't remember. It's so long ago. I was a young man.

MEYER: Think. Forty years ago. Nothing to an old man.

BRENDEL: They came back by the trainload, stinking in their rotting uniforms. It was a beautiful springtime. The flowers covered the land in such a profusion that they might have been hiding a corpse. The strange feeling at that time was that there was nothing to do. Don't misunderstand. Not that there was nothing to be done in the idealistic sense. Just that there was nothing to do. We looked into each other's faces and hated what we saw. Men would go from house to house, begging. Not for want, but as if searching. I did it myself. It was to this kind of life that Lang came back.

MEYER: And what was the first thing he said? And where did he say it?

BRENDEL: I can't remember. It's all in the books.

MEYER: Forget the books. They always lie.

BRENDEL: How does a man spread an idea? I don't know. If it's something that is wanted then I suppose it gets about. If it's not wanted then it dies on the lips.

MEYER: And Lang's hateful ideas were wanted?

BRENDEL: Of course. For they were a message of comfort. You have been forsaken, he said. There has been

373

treachery in high places. In the highest place a man can imagine. Everyone has been betrayed. The common people, the governors, the priests and the kings and queens. The gates have been shut for ever. There is no way out of the world.

MEYER: Jesus Christ!

BRENDEL: That is all *he* said, my dear boy. Others who came after him and loved him developed from this simple idea a way of life.

MEYER: Our way of life.

BRENDEL: I'm an old man. I've lived here for nearly twenty years. I don't know the way of the world. This world from which there is no escape.

MEYER: You should be happy to meet us. We are the people of that world. Look around you. Look at those two.

(*JACOB has now rejoined LEONIE.*)

That's what is known as love. A state of mind and body highly praised by Lang, I believe.

LEONIE: Yes, he went on about it, didn't he? In the books. But why didn't he ever have a woman? That worries me. (*Laughter.*)

WALTER: It's the word, Leonie. It can mean man's highest duty to man or it can mean the beastly little act you're itching for with Jacob. It's the word, darling.

LEONIE: But Lang didn't want anything. A man's inclination seems to lie towards boys, beasts or bitches...

PETER: In your experience.

LEONIE: In my experience. But Lang... what did he have?

JACOB: (*To BRENDEL.*) Well, satisfy the lady. What did he have?

MEYER: The man who is speaking to you now...you must have known his kind in the old days. He's with us because he loves me. He'll follow me as men followed Lang. They never really know why, these silent holy fools. Unfortunately he's also a natural animal and has to have that – (*The girl.*) – every so often. And Peter. He's the youngest. And he's Jacob's brother. You think that's a

good reason for him to be with us? You're wrong. He hangs round Jacob and Leonie for the day when they break up, or the one day too long that Jacob has to be away. It may already have happened. Has it, Leonie?
(*LEONIE calmly and silently mouths an obscenity at MEYER, who laughs.*)
Never mind.

WALTER: You're forgetting me.

MEYER: No, I was coming to you, Walter.
(*MEYER puts an arm round WALTER's shoulders.*)
How could I forget you? Our theorist. The man who guides our principles. (*To BRENDEL.*) So, you see, we all have each other, as is taught. Each man a brother. What have you got?

BRENDEL: Nothing. Why are you here?

WALTER: Because one day I was sitting at my desk in the public library giving and getting the books as usual. I settled for the job ten years ago. People come to me and ask for books which will tell them how to paint the walls, make a table or a model railway train. I give out these books. A thousand and one ways to waste time, or How to Do for Yourself. That's all they want. Some guidance as to how to pass the time Lang gave us. He set an end and a beginning to it all: he never fitted in the middle. And so this dirty procession of men, women and children pass in front of my desk. Not one believes that he'll find anything more in the mass of print than a way of living. How to Bath the Baby, How to Make Love, How to Grow Roses. And stories about themselves. Stories of people bathing babies, making love and growing roses. All unquestioned. This is it. They've been told so. Lang said so and now the books say so. Therefore no questions. This is it.
(*Silence.*)
Then, one day, Meyer put down a pile of books in front of me. He said:

MEYER: Isn't there anything better?

WALTER: I didn't answer. I was checking the books. Lang's *The Task Ahead, Letters from Geneva* and *The New Gospels.*

A symposium called *The Happy Humanist* and two
volumes of American poetry. Meyer spoke again:

MEYER: I asked you a question. Isn't there anything better?

WALTER: It was a question I'd waited a long time to hear.

MEYER: You sat back in your chair, pushed up your glasses
and looked at me. Finally you answered:

WALTER: No, there's nothing better. In the circumstances.

MEYER: Nothing?

WALTER: Nothing. Meyer walked away across the room.
The fog had got into the place that morning. I could
hardly see him at the door.

MEYER: I was outside on the steps. Walter came out putting
on his coat. He sort of ran up to me. Stared at me.

WALTER: Why did you ask that question?

MEYER: I didn't know what he was talking about. He
looked like a lunatic. Collar turned in, glasses crooked,
steamed up. Stammering:

WALTER: Why did you ask that question?

MEYER: You're the librarian. I wanted to know.

WALTER: And now you do know?

MEYER: I can't remember what I did then. I must have
turned away...

WALTER: Yes, you went on down the steps. I followed you.

MEYER: I wanted to get away. I jumped on a tram. I'd
asked an innocent question. I wouldn't do it again. But
did I get away?

WALTER: No. I had his address on the card at the library.

MEYER: Next morning. Sunday. The windows wanted
cleaning and the bedclothes were dirty. My clothes were
in a heap where I'd stepped out of them. But it was
home. I was half awake and lay playing about. Pastime.

WALTER: They said go up. Two floors. I waited. Then
knocked on the door.

MEYER: No answer.

WALTER: So I went in. The room smelled like a cage.
Meyer was naked in bed.

MEYER: He didn't give me a moment, but began to talk.
I was still asleep and whatever was in my mind wasn't
this sort of thing.

WALTER: Why should you think there's something better?
Why should you want something better? You're young.
You can enjoy food and women. Have you ever heard of
what they call the beauty of nature? There are the arts.
There is science. Both hold some of man's highest
achievements. Both offer a kind of faith badly needed by
your sort.

MEYER: He went on talking while I got up and washed,
picked up my clothes and dressed. He must have spoken
of everything a man can do – decent or not – between
being born and dying. It sounded very good. I was
shown all I could be. At one moment I was sitting at my
fireside with my beautiful satisfying wife: children,
legally got, laughed with me: there were flowers in the
garden: a radio played daylong music of an optimistic
kind: all my possessions about me announced that they
were earned by honest work.

WALTER: Meyer's face rose from the dirty water of the
wash basin. It rejected this picture.

MEYER: And I rejected the next. Lonely, solitary, friendless,
impossibly dedicated to some nonsense. It was one of
Walter's poorer efforts, shamelessly borrowed from
nineteenth-century fiction. I laughed that one out of
existence.

WALTER: I insisted. There must be some known pattern of
life which could apply. Meyer pulled his shirt over his
head and answered:

MEYER: None.

WALTER: Out into the streets.

MEYER: Sunday morning. People enjoying themselves.
Happiness. Leisure. Desolation.

WALTER: The river steamers were pulling away from the
banks. Shouts and music from across the water. Buses
were setting off for the countryside. Comic hats and
packed food.

MEYER: We sat at a safe table. Everything was laid on to
impress us with the urgent need to accept ourselves as
we are. Lovers went past. Nothing much can be given to

the old and the ugly but at least they had dignity that day. Children's voices were silver, uncorrupted. It was a beautiful morning. And the horror and the emptiness of that beauty, the forsaken sorrow of that free human activity has brought us here tonight.

BRENDEL: Why? How do you see yourself?

MEYER: As you see this place. There is everything here to make a man. His image and his work. His clothes – (*He is running his hands over the glass case.*) – his watch, rings, gloves, spectacles, pocket book, pen and cigarette machine. Yes, everything is here. You would say this is a man. False. This is no man. He is dead. And in my filthy room at the other end of the town you'll find the same sort of thing. You'd look around and think...an animal smell, boots under the bed, best suit hanging from the picture rail, a gramophone, some dead flowers and fruit. Yes. And many small and useless things kept for a reason. An attempt to build a past of some substance. Reminders. There was a day. And from this you would say, Yes, here is a man. A man called Meyer. Wrong. This is no man. He is dead.

BRENDEL: (*After silence: speaking to JACOB.*) Do you believe this?

MEYER: It's not important.

BRENDEL: Surely.

MEYER: I believe it.

BRENDEL: But do they? Of themselves.

MEYER: Leave it!

BRENDEL: Why?

MEYER: They are with me. Now. That counts.

BRENDEL: I must do everything I can to stop you.

MEYER: Stop me?

BRENDEL: From doing this.

MEYER: Go on.

BRENDEL: You can't accept yourself. That's very sad. But what is the point of destroying something you don't believe in? That's what you mean to do.

MEYER: Yes.

(*MEYER is standing over the glass case. With a sudden movement he strikes down with his fists. The wood and glass of the case splinter and shatter. MEYER reaches into the case and takes out the plaster cast of a pair of hands. They are startlingly white. Blood runs on MEYER's hands. BRENDEL has started forward. PETER grips his arms and holds him back.*)

BRENDEL: But all this is nothing! You've said so. Why destroy it?

MEYER: The world sees a man in these things. This junk heap: they see Lang. My dirty little room: they see me. (*MEYER is standing with the plaster hands extended. The MAN on the steps suddenly starts up from his sleep. He gives a shout of despair. It is heard in the house.*)

MAN: (*Then a whisper.*) Oh my dear God! (*The MAN covers his face with his hands. The WOMAN crawls up the steps to him.*)

WOMAN: There, there. It's the middle of the night. (*The people in the house are silent: BRENDEL speaks.*)

BRENDEL: Don't do it.

MEYER: Quiet. (*To WALTER.*) What was it?

WALTER: Somebody shouted in the street.

MEYER: Take him to his room. Keep him quiet. (*MEYER goes from the room and along the passage to the door at the back of the house. He will unchain and unbolt this door and then go out. WALTER and PETER take BRENDEL by the arms. He does not resist as they push him up the stairs and into his room. LEONIE and JACOB are left alone. The WOMAN has her arms round the MAN. He looks up at her.*)

MAN: Nothing to hold to. That's the trouble. I was falling back. Nothing to hold to.

WOMAN: Now we've had this all before. And we made up our minds.

MAN: What did we decide? Tell me over again.

WOMAN: We weren't going to worry any more about what we were once. Used to be.

MAN: That's right, we weren't. I was an important man with my job in the bank.

WOMAN: Well, you had to give it up because of your illness. And we had our pretty little house…

MAN: Oh it was a pretty little house. You kept it beautiful.

WOMAN: You did the garden. That was a picture.

MAN: All gone. How dirty it got. You remember. We had to start throwing things away. And the garden overgrown. Take care of yourself, they said. Lift nothing. Rot. So we had to start throwing things away. And the garden…

WOMAN: So you see there's nothing to worry about. Nothing to be sad about. It had all gone before we set out.

MAN: But didn't it mean anything? All those years of work. The position I reached. They used to call me sir. The house. The garden. The fact that I paid my way. Did it all mean nothing at all?

WOMAN: Nothing at all. We decided. Remember? Now sleep.

(Inside the house: WALTER and PETER have taken BRENDEL to his room. He sits on the bed. PETER is looking up into the attic. WALTER has picked up the book from the table.

In the first room: JACOB and LEONIE have come together.)

LEONIE: Why do you go with Meyer?

JACOB: He doesn't care.

LEONIE: About other people? He's simple. He could find what he's looking for in a bed. It's all there, all, yes! Jacob, all there. The destruction and the shame. All in this little centre. You know. Come on, you know I know. It means something. Admit it.

JACOB: All right.

LEONIE: Look, we live now. Yes? All right? All this waiting till you're dead. What's all that about? It's now or never. You've got to take what you're given. You've got to say well Jesus Christ you haven't done such a good job with me. I'm not a very good example of Lang's mankindliness. There are mistakes in everything. Make the best of it. And the best can be very good. Let's go now.

JACOB: No.

LEONIE: Why not? What will you find here?

JACOB: I can't leave Meyer.

LEONIE: But what will you find here that we can't find down by the river, or back at your place? Why break up this old man's house? I don't want the taste of blood and dust in my mouth, I want the taste of your sex. Let Meyer get rid of his energy this way, but you come to me.

JACOB: I can't leave him.

(*JACOB turns away: LEONIE stares after him.*)

LEONIE: All right.

JACOB: You can go.

LEONIE: No. You love him.

JACOB: I hate Lang. That's enough.

(*MEYER has come down the alley beside the house into the street. He sees the MAN and WOMAN.*)

MAN: It was a dream. But what is a dream?

WOMAN: Don't speak of it. Forget. It's the best we can do. To forget.

MAN: Who is it?

WOMAN: I don't know.

(*MEYER has approached them.*)

MEYER: What are you doing here?

WOMAN: We're staying the night. We're on our way somewhere. How dare you? Who are you? He's a sick man. He must sleep.

MEYER: Did you shout just now? Did you cry out?

WOMAN: He had a dream.

MAN: Young man, will you tell me something?

MEYER: Yes.

MAN: Standing where you are now...look at me. What do you see?

(*Silence.*)

What do you see?

MEYER: A man. And a woman.

MAN: (*He turns to the WOMAN.*) There you are! It's all right. We can still be seen for what we are. It's all right. I can sleep now. Sleep till morning. (*To MEYER.*) Thank you.

MEYER: It's nothing.

MAN: How did you recognise us? Tell me. Why didn't you just see us as rubbish?

MEYER: By one thing. You're afraid. It shows in your face. Fear. You're a man all right.

(*MEYER stares at them for a moment and then moves away down the street going from sight. Soon he will return, cross the street, go up the alley and come back into the house.*)

MAN: He might have said he recognised me because I've a kind face. Because I've got a sort of twinkle in my eye. Or because my voice showed I was once a man of authority. He didn't say anything like that. He said: Because you're afraid. You get comfort. And it's taken away. By a word.

(*Inside the house.*)

LEONIE: (*To JACOB.*) What's the matter with you? Are you trying to prove yourself superior to something?

(*No answer. In the upper room: WALTER, PETER and BRENDEL. WALTER has picked up the book from the bed and has been looking at it.*)

PETER: Walter, when you were a little boy did you smash up your toys?

WALTER: Can't remember. I expect so.

PETER: I did. Remember very well. I deliberately broke them up.

WALTER: What are you talking about?

PETER: I used to get punishment every time. This made me think of it. I used to get so scared. If I don't do it, I thought, things will go on as they are. I shan't get hurt. But in the end I'd want to finish it. Be done with it. That was a long time ago. You can take toys away from children. But you can't take all this away from grown men. Let's get on with it! Where's Meyer?

This is where the second draft of the act ends. What follows is the first draft, from the point where MEYER rejoins the others inside the room.

MEYER has come back down the street and after a glance at the MAN and WOMAN, who are now settled again, has gone into the house and bolted the main door behind him. Now he comes up into the first room.

WALTER: What was it?

MEYER: There are some tramps sleeping on the steps out there.

WALTER: Did you move them?

MEYER: No. They're cattle. If I move them they'll set up complaints which'll wake the town. Better leave them. Where are the others?

WALTER: (*He nods towards the stairs.*) Up there.

MEYER: (*He smiles.*) I hope they've found a bed. It's painful to watch Jacob and the girl.

WALTER: Why did you bring them?

(*The tone of WALTER's voice turns MEYER to him. They stare at each other for a moment.*)

MEYER: Because they're part of our –

WALTER: Go on.

MEYER: Well, call it what you like. Group, movement, idea... I don't know.

WALTER: They're no part of it.

MEYER: What do you mean?

WALTER: You and I could have done this job alone.

MEYER: Yes.

WALTER: Yet you had to bring the others. Why?

MEYER: You seem to know. Tell me.

WALTER: Because you can't see yourself as a leader unless you've got someone to lead. I'm no good to you because I gave you the ideas. You decided to put them into action, certainly. Something that was beyond me. But you can't lead me because I'm a step ahead. I know what should be done. You know how to do it.

MEYER: (*He laughs.*) Don't make excuses for yourself.

WALTER: I'm not. Don't be misled, that's all.

MEYER: How?

WALTER: Into thinking that Jacob, Peter and the girl can help in any way except to provide a group on which you can base your self-esteem. You believe that they follow you. Very well. That belief isolates you. Which means that you must finally decide.

MEYER: Decide what?

WALTER: Really, Meyer. Do you think that when you've destroyed this house that will be the end? There'll be more to come.

MEYER: You're wrong. We act as a group. It is the only way. You say there'll be more to come. I don't quite see what you mean, but whatever has to be done will be discussed and decided by all of us. You despise the others.

WALTER: Not really. I let them exist in this because from the first I saw that it was necessary for you. You must have someone to explain to why you do certain things. You're a leader, Meyer. You must have followers.

MEYER: I don't see myself in that way at all.

WALTER: I'm sorry. Then how do you see yourself?

MEYER: This will shock you.

WALTER: I doubt it.

MEYER: I believe I am a representative. It's not possible any more for a man to lead, for one person to make absolute decisions. The gamble's too great, The stakes too high. A man in my position is not a leader. That's out of date. It's –

WALTER: Archaic.

MEYER: Yes. I must act on the opinion of others. In this case, our group. If you had all been unable to reach a conclusion about tonight I could have done nothing. We shouldn't have come here.

WALTER: Wouldn't you have come here alone?

MEYER: No.

WALTER: Yes, I'm very shocked. This isn't what I looked for in you, Meyer. Not at all.

(*Silence.*)

A chairman. A committee member. Dear me.

(*WALTER suddenly reaches over and pulls BRENDEL upright.*)

That's the way Lang thought, isn't it?

BRENDEL: What?

WALTER: Don't pretend you haven't been listening.

BRENDEL: Well, yes, I'd say Lang thought much the way Meyer – is that his name? – does. Much the same way.

WALTER: And he died. He was murdered because of that.

BRENDEL: Quite true.

MEYER: Because of it? What do you mean?

BRENDEL: I've always had the feeling that his death was a voluntary act. A way out. Think of the circumstances.

(*JACOB has come down into the first room.*)

JACOB: Meyer...

(*MEYER motions him to be quiet: speaks to BRENDEL.*)

MEYER: Go on.

BRENDEL: Well, you know, there was this man Lang, and it was the seventeenth day of March. He'd spent the morning at his desk. From nine to two. There's nothing in the records to show any out of the way happening. He was working on a report about the proposed reform of the national theatre companies. It was not a subject of importance, but he was interested. He drank coffee and ate some fruit at midday. He sent out for some cigars. At two o'clock he shut the files on the theatre organisation and went down into the street where a delegation of schoolchildren waited for him. As usual when he was in a public place a crowd gathered. Lang was without a hat or coat. It was a cold day. He was seen to rub his hands together for warmth. He looked well. He was laughing. He stayed with the children for half an hour. Their cheers and a patriotic song followed him back to the office. He was seen at the window for a moment. He waved. And then he went from sight.

(*PETER has come down from the attic into BRENDEL's room. ELIZABETH*, who still sits on the bed, has picked up the book from the table. PETER sits beside her on the bed, takes the book from her, and shuts it. He whispers to her: some kind of obscenity. ELIZABETH laughs. The laugh is heard by the men below in the first room. For a moment they turn towards the sound, but BRENDEL goes on.*)

Lang saw four people that afternoon. They were minor officials from various ministries. The last was a woman. Lang questioned her closely on the conduct of her

* She becomes Leonie in the next draft.

department. He was not critical and not unkind. The woman couldn't answer his questions. Lang joked with her and suggested that she go back to her office and bring him the files under discussion. She did this. Her office was across the square and she was back within ten minutes. She found Lang's room empty. She sat down and waited for half an hour. Lang didn't return. The woman went down and spoke to the guard at the door. No one had seen Lang leave the building.

(*Again ELIZABETH laughs. MEYER does not look in the direction of the sound, but speaks to JACOB.*)

MEYER: Tell that bitch of yours to shut up.

(*JACOB goes.*)

BRENDEL: Lang was next seen at half past nine that night. He was sitting at a table outside Grossmann's Café. He was not alone. The man with him was known later to be his brother, Oscar. They were seen together at this place by a senior police officer who was off duty, and with his wife and two children. It is probable that this policeman was the only person to recognise Lang. It was unknown for Lang to appear unaccompanied in a public place. Even the policeman might have doubted whether it was really the prime minister sitting there had Lang not looked up and smiled in recognition. So the man introduced his wife. And Lang gave the children some biscuits and nuts from the table. He made no reference at all to his brother, or to the unusual circumstance that he should be sitting in a public café. The policeman and his family took their leave after some small talk. They were the last people to see Lang alive.

(*JACOB has come up into BRENDEL's room. PETER and ELIZABETH are still sitting on the bed.*)

JACOB: Meyer says be quiet.

(*In the first room MEYER turns BRENDEL's face to him: a moment.*)

MEYER: So they were the last people to see Lang alive.

BRENDEL: The rest…well, everybody's got their own ideas. Nobody knows. Lang and his brother must have come back there that night. The brother lived here. When they went through the house it was squalid and filthy. Lang spent his last night here. Christ knows what went on. But he came here of his own free will, that's certain. He needn't have come. So he needn't have been found dying on the steps.

MEYER: He was still alive.

BRENDEL: Yes. They were cleaning the streets. One of the hoses washed his cap…there it is… (*The cap with the hat on the stand.*) …along a gutter. They came back and found the body.

MEYER: Why was the murder so brutal?

BRENDEL: Savage? Yes, it was. The spade was at the bottom of the steps. Lang's left arm had almost been severed by one blow. An eye hung on his cheek. It was like a big tear, they say. He never spoke. They carried him in here and put him where I'm sitting now. Then he died.

(*In the room above PETER, JACOB and ELIZABETH speak in whispers.*)

PETER: Let's go down.

JACOB: Can't we get on?

PETER: Does Meyer know what he's doing?

ELIZABETH: Do any of us?

JACOB: Does it matter?

PETER: No.

JACOB: Then let's get on with it.

(*They begin to come down towards the first room where BRENDEL has got up from the chair and now stands facing MEYER and WALTER.*)

BRENDEL: He died. He died. Whatever you may say…he died! He left what any man might leave. Look around you. Forget that he was a famous man. And what does all this become? A junk shop.

WALTER: Then why are you so concerned?

BRENDEL: Leave it. Let it alone. You can destroy this place. You can, I know. All right. But you won't touch the man. Lang. He doesn't exist here. So leave this place as it is…

WALTER: Why are you so concerned?

MEYER: Because it will be his place we break up. He lives here. He looks after it. He's responsible. Like a priest in a church. He's responsible.

WALTER: He doesn't care about Lang. Do you mean that?

MEYER: Why should he? (*To BRENDEL.*) Why should you?

BRENDEL: I do care. I care very much.

(*JACOB, PETER and the ELIZABETH have come down into the room.*)

PETER: Meyer, when do we start? It's late. I'm tired. I want to...

(*PETER beats his fist down on the glass case.*)

MEYER: Shut up!

BRENDEL: I care very much!

PETER: Let's get on.

BRENDEL: It seems such a senseless thing to do.

MEYER: That's it!

WALTER: For Christ's sake...!

MEYER: That's it! It's pure. All, beautiful...

PETER: What is he...?

MEYER: I'd read the books. But I'd forgotten. A senseless thing. It seems such a senseless thing. A senseless thing to do. Walter, you read books and you get ideas and you get a feeling in your head or where? ...Here? ...I don't know. But you feel. And you, Peter, you want a girl and you get a feeling in your...my God, we know...and you, darling... (*ELIZABETH.*) ...you know...and when it's over there's something left...even then, there's something left, Jacob. And Jacob, come here...you love me...and it's a feeling in your guts...because what I do seems right... and when I speak and act...when I do anything... it's good...because it's Meyer doing it...and it makes you feel all right yes all right...satisfied...good hell good... here.

(*He lightly punches JACOB in the stomach. Then he stands back, his arms outstretched: an attitude to reveal.*)

But this...it's a senseless thing...there's no feeling...even a motiveless, gratuitous act gives you something. But this. Nothing. Nothing.

(*He takes a deep breath: then very quietly:*)
So that's why we're here. That's why we're here. That's what it's all about.
(*Silence: stillness: then, with love and care, MEYER reaches into the glass case and takes out a pair of white plaster hands. He holds them before him for a moment, and they make by their structure an impressive gesture. Then MEYER smashes them together and they fall in pieces.*
A bitter night wind is sweeping the steps. It stirs the MAN and WOMAN as if they were paper.)

CURTAIN

THE NOMADS

a play in two acts

1963

January 1963: definitive draft

De tous les plaisirs, le voyage est le plus triste.

Montherlant

The utmost degree of coherence, of mutual relatedness of
the single elements, being one of the chief artistic aims of
Schoenberg and his followers, there was only one step
from bringing the independently invented motives of a
composition into close relationship to creating first a
melodic prototype which would comprise the whole
available material in a characteristic pattern, allowing the
deviation of the individual motives from that pattern, in
which their relatedness would be ascertained by their
originating in a common matrix.

Ernst Krenek

General Notes

1. An absolute scheme *must* be made before beginning the play. Remember writing 'The Devils'.
2. Total narrative. The necessity of 'the happening'.
3. Define the *poised* position of each person early. *What will they do?*
4. What is the matter of life and death (apart from the boy) which concerns me here. It must be found. *Story.*
5. The Nazi period. Caught in as inexorable a passion as that of sex. The excesses of destruction: impossibility of release from sex.
6. Political history of Robert, Frederic and Elisabeth (1st decade).
   Jessica and Bill   (2nd decade).
   Anderson's son   (3rd decade).
   Define with historical data.
   1st.   Have lived violent lives.
   2nd.   Have partly engaged.
   3rd.   Refused to engage. Totally withdrawn.
7. An atmosphere of wealth: arrogance.
8. Use of music. (Young Anderson sees *Tristan and Isolde* at Regententheater (steps of).)
9. Style. Harsh: direct, idiomatic: cut the plush.
10. Shifting society ('The Nomads'). Passion for technical objects. (Frederic's engineering), etc.
11. Rage. Conflict. Hate.
12. M: Sex. Sticking yourself into another person.

Notes for *The Nomads*: 4 June 1961

1. The idea of the city. Munich. A known and identifiable place. Use it.
2. The play is basically about the destruction of our ideal. Or at least, Western Europe's inability to come up to the ideal.
3. The idealist: young Anderson.
4. The pattern of society is formed by the others.
5. Their attitude: defined by their despair, their false values, impotence, sex, homosexuality, incest, money.
6. Particulars: Jessica and Bill: brother and sister.
   Jews.
   Rich.
   Once incestuous.
   Bill now homosexual (Frederic).
   Jessica – Robert.

Robert – photographer   The old woman's love
Father of   affairs–no marriage.

Married to Englishwoman
  (not divorced)

Love affair with Jessica

Past love affair (before war) with
Elisabeth

Friend of Frederic

Robert to (Hanna) in Paris.
There's a girl. She's 20. They say
she's pretty. She cooks my meals
and shares my bed. Father French:
Mother American. After Jess I
don't think of the word love any
more. But I wasn't going to be a
fucking monk

Jessica's magpie attitude
about the past – the
mixed-up letters, diaries,
etc.

Jessica – scene with young
novice priest. Later – Mark
scene in wandering with
him.

State funeral–famous
soldier? Watched by
Jessica, Robert, Frederic
and Mark. R. and F. go.
Beginning of J. and M.?

Characters

ROBERT ANDERSON

Born 1917. England. Father: professional soldier, wounded 1918:
  invalid.

Mother: countrywoman: alive.

Robert's childhood in country. Shadow of war (as late as 1924 my
  father slept with a loaded pistol by his bed). Solitary life (his
  few childhood friends were all to be killed in 1939-45 war).

Nature: read Richard Jefferies (Does anyone read him now?) and
  Edward Thomas.

Loneliness: (I remember as a small boy staring at myself in a mirror
  and thinking: Well, you're ugly. Nobody's going to love you.
  So you'd better make your way by fame.) Childhood despair.
  (This is a terrible thing. People forget. Mercifully.)

Preparatory school in the country. Happiness.

A public school. Misery. Bullying. 1920 to early 30's. Unrest
  communicated?

Left school. (A failure. I was happy about it. No strings.)

Money left by grandfather (old radical, he was, in a hard black
  hat).

1934 (age 17). Robert took money and went to Europe. First France
  (historical facts) then Germany (I bought my first camera).

Germany 1934-38. (Historical fact.) Robert poor, made living by various means.

Meeting with Elisabeth and Frederic. Elisabeth two years older than Robert. Their love affair. Robert's uneasy friendship with Frederic. German society near Munich, and in Berlin, in middle and late 1930's.

Robert and Elisabeth (up to 21 and 23), their life together in France and Germany. The break (partly ideological) at the outbreak of war 1939. Robert's return to England (good offices of Frederic and his father).

Robert in army 1939-45. Undistinguished career. Boredom.

Meeting with wife: London 1940. Marriage. (Legalized weekends.)

Wife: Englishwoman. Same age.

End of war. (The great hiatus.)

1946. Birth of child.

Happiness with wife. Job. Settled. Dead.

Then revelation through violence.

Bedrooms: looking out on a floodlit abbey, a chestnut tree, across a lake, the roofs of Arles, many squares, a railway, the sea (thunderstorms), mountains.

Jess is one of those people who can't be happy (happily) in love.

Jessica and Mark's mockery of Tristan leading to love scene.

The mulish look on her face when she takes off her clothes for love.

Petit bourgeois! passionate regard for *people* – not for the person. (Tragedy is not that we die, but that we survive. So obsessed with death we have become that we make no plans to live.)

You can't do such violence to life, and not expect it to retaliate. The sort of woman to whom one-night stands often mean more than prolonged affairs with their dwindling entanglements.

All over Europe these film gentlemen with wives who were once 'beauties'.

Toutes les bonnes choses finissent pour recommencer.

Mon mari est un écrivain très connu.

She plays at life instead of living it. [strange, urgent little body]

Here we are, two sad little Jews out on a limb. Pity us.

(That's what you're always asking for)

What have you left to give, Jess?

J: Initiation?

M: Not really. There was a girl about six months ago. She smelt of soap.

J: Tell me.

M: I'm left on my own a lot, you know etc.

Terrible incapability of *showing* love: meeting at Geneva.

LACK OF FAITH. The tragedy of Jessica at 28: nothing left to give.

The impression presented to the world (our gay (little J) –

My father was very shocked by a social lapse. But he never seemed to mind if I behaved like a whore.

With no care for the past, and no love or hope for the future: living in the present becomes an obsessional intensity.

Such things wouldn't matter (would be unimportant) if you loved me.

'I *dare* not imagine.'

J: Do you always wear glasses?

M: No. I don't like to see too clearly. But my father shouts at me when I take them off.

J: I should wear them. I'm as blind as a bat.

M: Why don't you?

J: Same reason as you.

M: They think we're vain.

J: I know. Idiots (*She kisses him.*) Take those things off.

There have been those hopeless attempts to explain me in a rational way. By my family. My friends have tried. And my lovers. She's lonely, they said. She treats sex like a man. She's frustrated in the work she tries. All wrong. All hopelessly off the mark.

What is the truth!

Hanna: scene with Mark – he opts out.

Hanna and Robert: last scene.

MARK born 1946. Mother an English girl. She was drowned swimming off the South coast of England. The pram alone on the shore. (Mark's description of inquest evidence to Jessica.) The birds around the pram. I was laughing. The sea lapped the wheels. Her clothes blown away. (His own death.)

Bring Hanna into the action of the play.

Use of music?

HANNA: Frederic's in love. It's disturbing for all of us.

ROBERT: Who is he?

HANNA: An Englishman. A very plain boy indeed.

FREDERIC: He's a Jew.

ROBERT: What's his name?

FREDERIC: Gorski.

ROBERT: Bill?

FREDERIC: That's right.

ROBERT: He's got a sister.

FREDERIC: Jessica. Yes. I met them at an actor's party…

Hanna's praise of romantic love (1 speech), Schumann – morning – car radio.

You're a wonderful woman! And an impossible person.

JESSICA throws the book into the water. They stare at it.

JESSICA: Down it goes.

BILL: Another?

JESSICA: Why not? (*She throws two more books into the water.*)

BILL: There's one more.

JESSICA: Have a go?

Places

1. Steps leading up from a river: a bridge nearby.
2. The railway yards.
3. Entrance to a theatre.
4. Bill and Jessica's rooms.
5. Frederic's house.
6. Streets.
7. Hotel rooms.
8. The airport.
9. An unrestored bombed building.
10. A museum: art gallery.
11. A library.

Scenario

1. Jessica and Bill	River	
2. Robert and Mark to	Street	
3. Hanna and Frederic /Robert and Mark	Room	Frederic comes to Hanna
Mark to factory with Frederic		Robert and Mark in street. They come to H. and F. Frederic: I've been with Gorski. The usual tall arguments as to why we should, or should not, love each other.
4. Bill to	Street	
5. Frederic and Bill/ Mark and Frederic	Railway	
to		
6. Elisabeth, Frederic and Bill		

7. Jessica
    to
8. Robert and Jessica   Erotic element in meeting
9. Robert, Jessica and Mark
10. Jessica and Mark
11. Robert and photographs
    Pistiorski. Mark assisting

Characters

JESSICA GORSKI

BILL GORSKI

ROBERT ANDERSON

MARK ANDERSON

HANNA FORSTER

FREDERIC FORSTER

The action of the play takes place in the city of Munich.
The time is the present day.

ACT ONE

Munich. Morning.

Steps lead up from a river. There is a bridge nearby.

JESSICA GORSKI comes this way. She carries some books. She wanders: hesitates: sits on the steps. After looking around, she opens a book. She reads.

Some little time.

BILL GORSKI comes to JESSICA by a different way.

BILL: I got lost.
JESSICA: There now.
BILL: Have you been here long?
JESSICA: No.
BILL: You were late too.
JESSICA: Yes.
BILL: Good. (*He sits by JESSICA.*) What have you got?
JESSICA: Reading matter.
BILL: Will these help?
JESSICA: They might. They might –
BILL: What?
JESSICA: – have a secret.
BILL: No, they'll just muddle you, darling. Muddle you until your head hurts. What are they, after all? Each man's view of a private mess. But not your mess.
JESSICA: All right. Throw them away.
BILL: Have you paid for them?
JESSICA: Not yet. Does it matter?
BILL: Not a bit. Poems. Verlaine.
JESSICA: (*She takes the book: hesitates.*) Will it float?
BILL: I don't know. Try.
    (*JESSICA throws the book into the water. She stares at it.*)
JESSICA: Down it goes.
BILL: Have another.
JESSICA: Why not?

BILL: *A History of Modern Israel.* Another?

JESSICA: Yes, please.

BILL: Notebooks. Montherlant.

JESSICA: Thank you.

BILL: Such reading.

(*JESSICA throws two more books into the water.*)

BILL: There's one more.

JESSICA: I know.

BILL: *The Face of Europe*: photographs by Robert Anderson. And no paperback.

JESSICA: I'm in it.

BILL: Show me.

JESSICA: There.

BILL: It was marked. You cheat.

JESSICA: Always.

BILL: So there you are. Naked on a bed.

JESSICA: It was in London. June, would it be? I remember. Four o'clock in the afternoon.

BILL: Dirty pictures. Hm.

JESSICA: The sun was shining.

BILL: You were just going to sleep.

JESSICA: Yes. I remember.

BILL: Do you want it?

JESSICA: (*A moment.*) No. Your turn.

(*BILL kisses the book, and then throws it into the water.*)

BILL: Now let's go home and burn that painting you bought yesterday.

JESSICA: All right. Then we'll sit at the opera tonight and whistle all the tunes.

(*They do not move. Silence.*)

BILL: What shall we do?

JESSICA: I thought of buying some biscuits and going into the country.

BILL: It's miles.

JESSICA: Miles. Where have you been?

BILL: This morning?

JESSICA: Yes. What have you been doing?

BILL: I've been with Frederic.

JESSICA: Making love?

BILL: No.

JESSICA: Go on. Have you?

BILL: No. Not this morning. (*He takes a leaf from JESSICA's coat, and crushes it in his hands.*)

JESSICA: Yes. It's late.

BILL: It'll be later up north.

JESSICA: It's cold, whenever it is.

BILL: Huddle up, little sister.

JESSICA: Billy, Billy. Why did you stay out all night? That place we have is not nice on my own. I couldn't sleep.

BILL: What was wrong?

JESSICA: There's nothing right, Billy. Not when a woman of nearly thirty, a good Jewish girl with money in the bank, has to wander in the kitchen at four in the morning, making tea, taking pills, five of them, and wanting her brother home. Her brother, Billy. Are you listening?

BILL: This town's got cemeteries all round it. No, I'm not listening to you.

JESSICA: Most towns have nowadays.

BILL: There's one to the north, south, east and west. It says so, on the map for the buses.

JESSICA: Shall we go back to London?

BILL: Let's not.

JESSICA: Then we'll go on. We'll go south.

BILL: No. I want to stay here.

JESSICA: Because of Frederic?

BILL: And other things.

JESSICA: Why does he love you? Turn round. You look like a bull. You're ugly.

BILL: Don't you love me?

JESSICA: Yes, Billy.

BILL: Why have you grown to look this way?

JESSICA: How do I look?

BILL: Beautiful. I think.

JESSICA: It's the light.

BILL: Don't laugh.

JESSICA: What, then? Cry?

BILL: No. Just hold my hand. Look, there it is.

JESSICA: Thank you very much.

(*ROBERT ANDERSON, and his son, MARK.*)

ROBERT: What's the matter with you? Look at me. You've hardly said a word since we left the airport. Look at me. Oh, put your glasses on. You know you can't see a bloody thing without them. Better?

MARK: I suppose so.

ROBERT: Well? What can you see?

MARK: You. My father. And it looks as if it's going to rain. That car's a Porsche. That's a Thunderbird. That building over there's been burnt out –

ROBERT: Shut up. Wear them all the time. What stops you? Vanity? At sixteen? It's disgusting. Anybody would think you're a woman. Come on.

MARK: Where are we going?

ROBERT: To friends of mine.

MARK: Why not to the hotel?

ROBERT: Later.

MARK: I don't like this town.

ROBERT: What are you talking about?

MARK: This place. I don't like it.

ROBERT: It's the same as any city.

MARK: You've been here before.

ROBERT: I've been here a lot.

MARK: You've been everywhere.

ROBERT: I once lived here. What's that got to do with it?

MARK: I don't care for your past. I don't like going over the rotten ground again. It stinks. Why make me?

ROBERT: (*After a moment.*) Carry the bag.

MARK: All right. Is it far?

ROBERT: Ten minutes walk. Less.

(*They go.*)

JESSICA and BILL.

JESSICA: We should have been poor. You know: no money.

BILL: What difference would that have made?

JESSICA: You could have worked your fingers to the bone for some good woman.

BILL: I don't like women.

JESSICA: Except me. And I could have slaved for some good man. On my feet all day, and on my back all night. Ah, darling, think how happy we could have been.

BILL: Why didn't you marry him?

JESSICA: All we needed was less time to spend money. That's all.

BILL: Are we going to sit here all day?

JESSICA: I want to go and buy some clothes. Why didn't I marry him?

BILL: I asked. Don't dress like a tart. We're cursed with bad taste.

JESSICA: I dress, if you'll forgive me, with what must be described as perfect taste. Come and choose.

BILL: Anderson wanted to marry you. What went wrong?

JESSICA: I couldn't leave you, love. Perhaps you're right. About the clothes. Yes, I was picked up by a waiter yesterday. A baby-faced Aryan. Your type.

BILL: Did you go with him?

JESSICA: Not all the way. He lay on his bed, picking sausage from his very good teeth, and suggested doing something so odd, I laughed. I thought about it afterwards, and wondered if I could play such games.

BILL: Could you?

JESSICA: Yes. I'm innocent.

BILL: No. You just won't learn.

(*They go.*)

HANNA FORSTER, an old woman, alone.

HANNA: I went walking the other day. Not such a usual thing now. This is an old city, but not so old that it can't still breed the young. There were girls in the streets with hands like claws. There were young boys with bird faces lying in the gardens, and the sunlight made them transparent, green. Do they wear black glasses so that I shan't know their eyes have been torn out? There's no war, no gunfire now. But they're still at it, I saw that. They're looking for hatred, and crying when they can't find it. Crying naked in their enemy's arms.

I've no courage to take a step forward. The continent is sinking under our feet.

I was sixteen years old in the summer of 1898, and I was beautiful. Were my hands like talons then? The steps down from the house seemed long. A long way to go for such a young and unprepared girl. It was to meet a king. He kissed me disgustingly, passed me to my father, and went in to his dinner. This was Bavaria. The little man had come to talk about war. The horses of the cavalry escort were fouling the yard. I imagined the lances entering my body. I wanted to live. I have lived. Too long. But something has died. What is it? That's a question.

(*FREDERIC FORSTER, her son, comes to her.*)

Freddy darling, are there still kings in the world? Do they reign?

FREDERIC: As best they can. Mother, why don't you go back to the house in the country?

HANNA: The way up to the house is too long for me now.

FREDERIC: What's happened to the woman who cleans for you?

HANNA: She's ill. Dying, they say.

FREDERIC: Can't you get another?

HANNA: I've not tried. Aren't you working today?

FREDERIC: I thought I'd stay in the city.

HANNA: To be near him?

FREDERIC: Yes.

HANNA: Are you afraid he'll leave?

FREDERIC: His sister is always wanting him to go.

HANNA: Where to?

FREDERIC: Some other place than where he is.

HANNA: Don't love him so much.

FREDERIC: You shouldn't live alone. He makes me happy.

HANNA: He's an ugly boy.

FREDERIC: I know. It touches me very much.

HANNA: Leave him.

FREDERIC: No.

End of fragment.

Bibliography

PLAYS

The Plays of John Whiting, (London, 1957), contains *Saint's Day, A Penny for a Song* and *Marching Song*.
The Devils, (London, 1961).
The Collected Plays of John Whiting, ed. Ronald Hayman, (London, 1969), contains *Volume One* (*Conditions of Agreement, Saint's Day, A Penny for a Song, Marching Song*) *Volume Two* (*The Gates of Summer, No Why, A Walk in the Desert, The Devils, Noman, The Nomads*)
No More A-Roving, (London, 1975)
John Whiting: Plays One, ed. Ronald Hayman, (Oberon Books, London, 1999), contains *No More A-Roving, Conditions of Agreement, Saint's Day, A Penny for a Song*)

CRITICISM etc.

John Whiting on Theatre, (London, 1966).
The Art of the Dramatist, ed. Ronald Hayman. (London, 1970), contains fragments of creative writing, lectures, play reviews, book reviews, essays and articles on drama and the theatre.
At Ease in a Bright Red Tie, ed. Ronald Hayman, (Oberon Books, London, 1999), contains lectures, play reviews, book reviews, essays and articles on drama and the theatre.

TRANSLATIONS

Jean Anouilh, *Traveller without Luggage*, (London, 1959).
Jean Anouilh, *Madame de...*, (London, 1959).
André Obey, *Sacrifice to the Wind* in *Three Dramatic Legends*, ed. Elizabeth Haddon, (London, 1964).

BOOKS ON WRITING

Ronald Hayman, *John Whiting*, (London, 1969).
Simon Trussler, *The Plays of John Whiting: An Assessment*, (London, 1972).
Eric Salmon, *The Dark Journey: John Whiting as Dramatist*, (London, 1979).